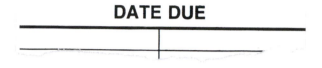

DATE DUE

Voices of Unbelief

Voices of Unbelief

Documents from Atheists and Agnostics

Dale McGowan, Editor

 GREENWOOD

AN IMPRINT OF ABC-CLIO, LLC
Santa Barbara, California • Denver, Colorado • Oxford, England

Copyright 2012 by ABC-CLIO, LLC

Library of Congress Cataloging-in-Publication Data

   Voices of unbelief : documents from atheists and agnostics / Dale McGowan, editor.
     p. cm.
   Includes bibliographical references (p.) and index.
   ISBN 978–1–59884–978–3 (hardcopy : alk. paper) — ISBN 978–1–59884–979–0 (ebook)
1. Atheism—History—Sources. 2. Agnosticism—History—Sources. 3. Faith. I. McGowan, Dale.
BL2747.3.V59   2012
211′.8—dc23   2012018238

ISBN: 978–1–59884–978–3
EISBN: 978–1–59884–979–0

16 15 14 13 12   1 2 3 4 5

This book is also available on the World Wide Web as an eBook.
Visit www.abc-clio.com for details.

Greenwood
An Imprint of ABC-CLIO, LLC

ABC-CLIO, LLC
130 Cremona Drive, P.O. Box 1911
Santa Barbara, California 93116-1911

This book is printed on acid-free paper ∞

Manufactured in the United States of America   93.00

CONTENTS

DOCUMENTS

Contents

Contents

ACKNOWLEDGMENTS

My sincere thanks must begin with Hemant Mehta and Amanda Metskas, each of whom played a part in sending this engaging project my way.

The staff at ABC-CLIO have been a pleasure and privilege to work with, including Michael Wilt, George Butler, and Erin Ryan. Thanks as well to Magendra Varman at PreMediaGlobal and to Deborah Bader for brilliant proofing—including the single best catch I've ever seen.

Cliff Walker at Positive Atheism and Emmett Fields at the Bank of Wisdom are among the unsung heroes of freethought. Their patient efforts to make key writings by atheists and agnostics publicly available and searchable have been invaluable to me in this and other projects. Other important resources include the Investigating Atheism project of the University of Cambridge and Oxford Bibliographies Online.

I am grateful to Thomas Lawson, whose book *Letters from an Atheist Nation* brought to my attention Charles Chilton Moore of the *Blue Grass Blade* and his extraordinary "Why I Am an Atheist" project of 1903; also to the "Chronicling America" project of the National Endowment for the Humanities and the Library of Congress, which is preserving American history through the digitizing of daily newspapers. This is just one of countless cultural and historical contributions by the NEH.

I am indebted to David Joyce and Charles Blinderman of Clark University in Vancouver, Washington, whose Huxley Project online was the first to bring T. H. Huxley's correspondence to my attention, as well as Vipan Chandra of Wheaton College (Massachusetts) for helping me locate the source of a crucial Jain text.

The work of several scholars has been especially important in the production of this book, including Alan Charles Kors for research into French atheism in the 17th and 18th centuries; Tullio Gregory for work on the pre-Enlightenment clandestine manuscripts; Emmanuel Le Roy Ladurie for his seminal microhistory of 14th-century *Montaillou*; Sarah Stroumsa for her unique contribution to our understanding of freethought in medieval Islam; and Annie Laurie Gaylor for *Women Without Superstition*, the definition study of the intersection of feminism and freethought.

The influence of Jennifer Michael Hecht's brilliant book *Doubt: A History* on this project and on many other freethought works in recent years is inestimable.

Thank you as well to Brian Keith Dalton, Alice Walker, Richard Dawkins, Alan Tacca, and Sikivu Hutchinson for their personal assistance in bringing their works into this collection, and to Beth Lamont, a bright light in humanism, for permission to use her late husband's work.

Only a few sections of the 14th-century Fournier Register, a uniquely fascinating historical document, have ever been translated into English. I had the good fortune to work with translator Dareth Pray, who under the supervision of Professor Nancy Stork at San Jose State University had translated the precise Fournier interrogations I needed. I am indebted to both of them, as well as Anastasia Makeeva and Tony Patricolo for help in translating the Occitan prayers.

Thanks to the staff at the Georgia State University Library and Kennesaw State University Library for assistance in locating key research materials.

Finally, all thanks and love to my wife, Becca, and my children, Connor, Erin, and Delaney, for support and encouragement during this long and complex project.

INTRODUCTION

BELIEF AND UNBELIEF

Belief in the existence of a supernatural deity is found in every human culture, time, and place. Archaeological evidence over 130,000 years old testifies to the presence of the compelling idea that an unseen force—usually in the form of a god or gods—is responsible for the creation, operation, and ultimate fate of the world around us.

Over the course of 10,000 human generations, this hypothesis has fractured into countless distinct religious traditions. Any attempt to map these diverse beliefs geographically—labeling this country "Christian," another "Islamic," and yet another "Hindu," for example—gives the false impression that all individuals in a given place and time answer the big questions in the same way, something that is never fully accurate.

If instead we listen carefully to the disparate voices in any culture, a much more interesting picture emerges. In addition to orthodox believers in the majority religion, there will always be dissenting voices within that religion (sometimes called heretics), adherents of minority religions, religious doubters, those who say the answers are simply unknowable (agnostics), and some who reject belief in gods entirely (atheists).

Though atheism and agnosticism are most evident in modern times, every religious hypothesis advanced in history and prehistory, back to the earliest evidence of religious observance in Neanderthal sites over 130,000 years old, was almost certainly met with doubt or outright unbelief in at least some listeners. Whether these dissenting opinions were then voiced aloud, recorded in some form, and passed down to subsequent generations is a question that will recur throughout this book. Fortunately, there are enough whispers, even from corners of history dominated by religious perspectives, to allow us to hear voices of unbelief in every era for which written records are available. It is the purpose of this book to draw out those voices, presenting as full as possible a picture of this fascinating thread of human thought—the rejection of supernatural explanations for the world around us.

WHAT IS ATHEISM?

In the broadest terms, *atheism* (from the Greek *atheos*, "without god") is the lack of belief in the existence of a supernatural deity or deities. As will become evident throughout this book, it is difficult to make further generalizations beyond this single characteristic. Some atheists are strictly secular, for example, avoiding not only belief in the supernatural but all spiritual or religious practice as well. Others, including Jains, Wiccans, and many Buddhists, observe religious and spiritual practices nontheistically—without the framing concept of a supernatural being.

"Atheist" in ancient Greek was an epithet used by one's opponents or accusers, especially in cases of perceived impiety or lack of proper reverence toward the divine. Socrates, whose impertinent questions challenged the religious and political norms of his day, was called *atheos*, even though he stated clearly that he believed in gods—just not those recognized in his time and place.

By the fifth century BCE, the term "atheist" occasionally reflected the more specific accusation that a person actively denied or rejected the gods. But just as often, the word would be hurled by one group of religious believers (e.g., believers in the Olympic pantheon) at believers in another god or gods (e.g., early Christians)—a usage that often serves to confuse the definition.

It was not until the 16th century in France that "atheist" (Fr. *athée*) began to more reliably indicate an individual who disbelieved in the existence of any supernatural gods, though even at this late date it was used only as an insult or accusation by others. The 17th century saw the circulation of anonymous documents known as "clandestina," the first published books written from an explicitly atheistic point of view, and the first reliable usage of "atheist" for self-identification was in the European Enlightenment of the late 18th century. And no sooner had the American Revolution secured the independence of the United States than several writers and thinkers in that new country began adding their voices to the chorus of articulated unbelief.

WHERE IS ATHEISM?

A critical reader will note that the description above seems to imply that atheism is essentially a European phenomenon—that its development can be fully understood by tracing the well-worn path of European ideas from ancient Greece to the salons of revolutionary Paris to the printing presses of the United States. This path is fascinating and important, but it is just one of many human stories of the rejection of religious assumptions. Because all cultures develop religious expressions, and each religious expression is met with at least some doubt and unbelief, any collection of atheist and agnostic voices must include non-Western voices as well. So in addition to voices of unbelief from England, France, and the United States, this book includes atheist and agnostic documents from the cultures of China, Persia, India, and Uganda.

WHAT IS AGNOSTICISM?

In addition to atheist voices, the current anthology includes documents from agnostics. Though agnostic positions had been asserted for centuries, it was the British biologist Thomas Henry Huxley who first coined the useful term in 1869, joining the "a" prefix ("without") to the Greek word "gnosis" ("knowledge") to mean "without knowledge." When applied to religion, its original and most common use, an agnostic is someone who says, "I do not know whether gods exist." In actual usage, the term generally indicates that a given concept is not only unknown but unknowable.

In "Am I an Atheist or an Agnostic?," included in this collection, British philosopher Bertrand Russell spoke of the common misconception that agnostics occupy a kind of shrugging gray area halfway between belief and unbelief. He noted that he was unable to say with certainty that God does not exist in the same way he could not say with certainty that the Homeric gods of ancient Greece do not exist, or that far out in space, between the orbits of Mars and Jupiter, a tiny bone china teapot is not in orbit around the Sun. "I have no evidence for the existence of these things," he said, "but neither can I say with certainty that they do not exist. It seems highly unlikely that they do, or that the Christian God does, so barring further evidence to the contrary, it seems reasonable to live and act as if they do not." That, not a shrugging middle ground, is an excellent description of the position of most agnostics, including those represented in this anthology. Though they have chosen to emphasize the limits of knowledge, most agnostics, in a practical sense, can also be called atheists. Russell called himself one or the other, depending on the audience's likely understanding of what "agnostic" really means.

Approached from the other direction, few atheists claim to know with certainty that God does not exist. Atheism is a statement of what one believes, based on the evidence at hand: "I don't believe gods exist." Even Richard Dawkins, perhaps the most famous atheist of the early 21st century, put his own unbelief at "6" on a scale of "7," noting that scientific inquiry never deals in certainties. The "6" then expresses a high degree of confidence that God does not exist without lapsing into the delusion of certainty. In this respect, then, most atheists can also be called agnostics.

HERETICS

There are countless other voices of dissent against the dominant religions of their times who were not unbelievers. Many Greek philosophers, including Socrates and Epicurus, expressed deep skepticism regarding the gods of the Greek pantheon but were not strictly atheists or even agnostics. Though the early Christian leader Arius (ca. 250–336) created one of the first major theological crises of the early Christian church, he believed fully in the Christian God, Jesus, and the Holy Spirit, but disagreed with the church over their relationship to each other.

Desiderius Erasmus (1466–1536) penned a blazing satire against the church but was himself an Augustinian monk. The 17th-century Dutch philosopher Baruch Spinoza, though sometimes called an atheist, was a believer in a concept of God that differed deeply from the Judeo-Christian deity, but he was neither an atheist nor an agnostic. And several of the founders of the United States of America, including Thomas Jefferson, James Madison, and Thomas Paine, were adherents of deism, the belief that a god exists but is indifferent to—possibly even unaware of—humanity and the rest of creation.

These fascinating thinkers, usually labeled "heretics" by the churches with whom they differed, are well worth getting to know and are often included in anthologies similar to this one. But this anthology is more strictly focused on documents that challenge not just a single religious perspective, but the very idea that any god or gods exist.

WHICH VOICES SURVIVE?

Much of our knowledge of the past, especially in the realm of ideas, depends on written records passed down through the centuries. Our picture of a given place and time is deeply influenced by this subjective and unreliable process.

In order for an idea conceived in ancient times to reach the 21st century, it must have first been written down. This is no small step in itself. Even as influential a figure as Socrates, for example, wrote nothing of his own. Had others such as Plato not recorded his thoughts, one of the foundational figures of Western philosophy would have been entirely lost to history.

The game is hardly begun once ideas are written down. The written document must then avoid destruction, accidental or intentional, not only in its own time but in every subsequent era as well.

Ideas recorded on such perishable media as parchment, papyrus, paper, bamboo, or bark would need frequent recopying as the original succumbed to moisture, fire, or dry rot. Each generation naturally tends to invest time primarily in the preservation, recopying, and transmission of those ideas it values most. Approximately 100 generations stand between the current era and classical Greece, each with the ability and incentives to preserve, edit, ignore, or destroy the documents received from its predecessors.

Because of this highly selective process, orthodox ideas—those that conform to mainstream values in each generation—are the most likely by far to survive, leaving an impression that past eras were less ideologically diverse than was probably the case. Because atheist and agnostic ideas have always been well outside of orthodox opinion, these have been among the least likely voices to survive.

Interesting and useful exceptions are works found so troubling in their own time that they provoked written counterarguments. In the process of quoting the ideas they reviled, often verbatim and at length, these critics have frequently been the unintended means of preserving unorthodox ideas for the consideration of posterity.

MAKING ROOM FOR SELDOM-HEARD VOICES

Most anthologies of nontheistic writings consist primarily of published texts written by those prominent individuals—philosophers, scientists, academics, polemicists, and orators—whose work constitutes the better-known "canon" of freethought. The current book has attempted to broaden and deepen the representation of religious disbelief, demonstrating that doubt is not the sole purview of the privileged classes, of Europeans, or of men. In addition to a strong sampling of the usual high-profile spokespersons of atheism, you will hear the voices of French villagers in a medieval interrogation, an atheist activist in 20th-century India, atheists and agnostics in small-town America over a century ago, bloggers, humorists, courageous women at the dawn of modern feminism, and humanists living in a newly evangelical Africa—many of them speaking not through published books but through journals, diaries, blogs, letters to the editor, scripts, and personal correspondence.

To make room for this broader presence, some difficult choices have been necessary. Many of the canonic writers whose place in freethought anthologies is usually guaranteed may be missing here or represented only by a short excerpt. It is my hope that readers whose favorite voice has been omitted or given short shrift will understand the reasoning, even if they do not agree with it.

HOW TO USE THIS BOOK

This book is a collection of excerpts from existing documents by atheists and agnostics written with a high school and early college readership in mind. In order to facilitate engagement, study, and activities related to the text, each document is presented as follows:

> ❧ A topical **Introduction** provides general information about the author, period, and significance of the piece.

- ⮞ A brief section titled **Keep in Mind as You Read** provides additional context that may be helpful in assessing and understanding the document.
- ⮞ The document itself follows.
- ⮞ A section titled **Afterward** describes events following the original publication of the document, with special attention to the subsequent life of the author and the impact of the document itself.
- ⮞ **Ask Yourself** offers follow-up questions to assess readers' comprehension of the piece and to suggest productive directions for further exploration of the issues raised.
- ⮞ **Topics and Activities to Consider** provides ideas for engaging the ideas raised in the document more fully through additional research or individual/group activity.
- ⮞ Finally, two sections marked **Further Information** and **Web Site(s)** give direction to readers interested in deeper exploration of a given author or subtopic.

Regarding dating conventions: This book will make use of the religiously neutral notations BCE/CE (Before Common Era/Common Era) in lieu of BC/AD (Before Christ/Anno Domini). Years without a specific designation are in the Common Era.

CAVEAT LECTOR! (READER BEWARE!)

Though every effort has been made to present an accurate and objective review of the history and key works in atheism and agnosticism, the critical reader must always keep in mind the many hands through which any given text has passed. In addition to the sieve of history mentioned earlier (see "Which Voices Survive?"), most of these documents have passed through the hands of many scholars, editors, and laypeople. At each step, the potential exists to clarify meaning and correct past errors, but also to distort meaning (intentionally or otherwise) and introduce new errors and biases. The best editors will make their own interventions as transparent as possible so that readers can retrace his or her steps and make an independent judgment.

Because most anthologies of this kind necessarily include excerpts of some works rather than the entire original text, readers should also recognize that the editor has made choices about what to include and what to omit. Such a process is inevitably subjective, and readers with additional interest in a given subject are urged to follow the provided references to view the complete text in a form as close to the original as possible.

SELECTIVE CHRONOLOGY OF THE HISTORY OF RELIGIOUS UNBELIEF

11th–5th c. BCE	Book of Psalms written by various authors. Psalm 14 ("The fool says in his heart 'There is no God' ") acknowledges existence of atheism in ancient Judaic culture
Ninth c. BCE	Life of Parshva (India). Earliest historical figure of Jainism, among the oldest nontheistic religions
Sixth c. BCE	Life of Gautama Buddha (India). Founding of Buddhism, including rejection of the idea of a creator god
	Life of Confucius (K'ung-fu-tzu), founder of Confucianism, a nontheistic ethical and philosophic system
	Pre-Socratic philosophers of Greece, including Xenophanes of Colophon, lay foundations for later religious skepticism
Fifth c. BCE	Period of Sophists in Greek philosophy, including Diagoras of Melos, often called the "first atheist"
Fourth c. BCE	Greek philosopher Epicurus promotes materialistic philosophy and disinterested gods
Third–First c. BCE	First historical writings of Samkhya and Mimāṃsā, two atheistic branches of Hinduism
First c. BCE	Bārhaspatya-sūtras written, a founding text of Cārvāka, an Indian philosophic system with specifically atheistic and naturalistic beliefs, named for the author of the sūtras
First c. BCE	Roman poet/philosopher Lucretius writes *De Rerum Natura* for the stated purpose of freeing men's minds from superstitious beliefs; Roman philosopher Cicero names famous atheists of past eras
Second c. CE	Greek/Roman philosopher Sextus Empiricus names and quotes atheists of Greek Hellenistic and Classical periods
Seventh c. CE	Dharmakirti (India) writes *Nyāyabinduprakaraṇa* (Drop of Reasoning)

Ninth c.	Indian Acharya (religious teacher) Jinasena authors *Mahapurana,* a foundational text of the Jain religion, including an articulate refutation of belief in gods
10th c.	Muhammad ibn Zakariyā Rāzī (Persia) writes *On the Refutation of Revealed Religions*
11th c.	Confucian moral philosopher Chang Tsai (China) writes *Correcting the Unenlightened*
1184	Pope Lucius III issues papal bull *Ad abolendam,* setting in motion 400 years of inquisitions and purges
13th c.	Icelandic saga of Hrafnkell, a warrior chieftain whose renunciation of belief in gods leads him to a more peaceful life
1318–1325	Inquisitional interrogations by Jacques Fournier, Bishop of Pamiers (later Pope Benedict XII)
1546	First known modern use of "atheism" (in French, as *athéisme*)
1659	*Theophrastus Redivivus,* published anonymously in France, considered oldest specifically atheistic document still existing. Recaps classical arguments against religious belief, claims that all great philosophers have been atheists, touches off a century of discussion of atheism
1678	*Symbolum sapientiae,* published anonymously in Germany, further challenges religious belief
1680s	*Treatise of the Three Impostors,* rumored to have existed for four centuries, written anonymously and disseminated
1697	Last execution for blasphemy in Britain (Thomas Aikenhead)
1729	Death of atheist priest Jean Meslier (France) and discovery of his Testament completely renouncing theistic belief
1770	Baron d'Holbach (France) pseudonymously publishes *The System of Nature,* a detailed avowal of naturalistic atheism
1789	"Dechristianization of France" during French Revolution results in confiscation of church lands, removal of special rights for clergy, and revocation of Catholic Church's taxing authority
1793	Establishment of the Cult of Reason, an atheistic alternative to Christianity, during the French Revolution. First state-sponsored atheism
1794	French dictator Robespierre denounces the Cult of Reason, executes leaders, establishes Cult of the Supreme Being in its place
1811	Poet Percy Bysshe Shelley (England) expelled from Oxford for authoring "The Necessity of Atheism"—first written exposition of atheism in English

1841	Philosopher Ludwig Feuerbach (Germany) publishes *The Essence of Christianity*, suggesting that God is only a projection of humankind's inner nature
1844	Karl Marx refers to religion as "the opium of the people" in *Contribution to Critique of Hegel's Philosophy of Right*
1851	"Secularism" coined by George Jacob Holyoake, meaning "a form of opinion that concerns itself only with questions, the issues of which can be tested by the experience of this life"
1876	English biologist Thomas Henry Huxley coins term "agnostic"
1880	Atheist Charles Bradlaugh elected to British Parliament but barred from taking office for six years after claiming the right to affirm rather than swear a religious oath
1882	Friedrich Nietzsche first uses the phrase "God is dead" in *The Gay Science*
1887	First edition of *Autobiography of Charles Darwin*, edited by his son Francis, with Charles's agnostic views expunged
1888	New Oaths Act, championed by Charles Bradlaugh, establishes right of British MPs to solemnly affirm allegiance to the Sovereign rather than take religious oath
1911	Last blasphemy prosecution in England (John William Gott)
1922–1926	After a period of relative tolerance, policy of *gosateizm* (state atheism) in Soviet Union results in persecution, destruction of church property, and executions of clergy
1926	Strict anticlerical and separationist reforms introduced by Mexican President Plutarco Elias Calles, an atheist, precipitate the Cristeros War, a Catholic rebellion
1927	Philosopher Bertrand Russell (England) publishes *Why I Am Not a Christian*
1933	First *Humanist Manifesto* lays out basic tenets of god-optional humanism
1947	Jawaharlal Nehru, an atheist, becomes first prime minister of India
1949	Establishment of official state atheism in People's Republic of China
1952	First Amsterdam Declaration at inaugural World Humanist Congress
1958	New edition of Darwin's *Autobiography*, edited by his granddaughter Nora Barlow, with agnostic passages restored
1973	*Humanist Manifesto II* explicitly rejects religion, updates basic principles and values of humanism

1990	American Religious Identification Survey (ARIS) puts U.S. nonreligious self-identification at 8.0 percent of population
2001	Second ARIS survey estimates 14.1 percent of U.S. population is nonreligious
2003	*Doubt: A History* by historian Jennifer Michael Hecht lays the foundation for a renaissance in freethought literature
	Publication of *Humanism and Its Aspirations*, aka Humanist Manifesto III
2004–2007	Several authors referred to collectively as "The New Atheists" publish best-selling titles directly critical of religious belief, including Sam Harris (*The End of Faith*, 2004), Richard Dawkins (*The God Delusion*, 2006), Daniel Dennett (*Breaking the Spell*, 2006), and Christopher Hitchens (*God Is Not Great*, 2007)
2009	In his inaugural address, U.S. President Barack Obama includes "nonbelievers" among worldviews of which the nation consists—the first such public reference by a sitting president
2010	Pew Research Center releases finding that 26 percent of Americans born after 1981 are religiously unaffiliated—double the percentage of baby boomers at the same age

UNBELIEF IN THE ANCIENT WORLD

1. Atheism in Ancient Judea—Psalm 14:1

INTRODUCTION

The presence of religious unbelief cannot always be ascertained by direct evidence. If atheism is persecuted in a given place and time, atheists of that culture are unlikely to record their opinions in writing at all, much less publish widely. Even if the culture in question permitted open unbelief, later generations are unlikely to carefully recopy and preserve thoughts that contradict their own values. As a result, the presence of religious unbelief must frequently be deduced from secondary sources, many of them critical of unbelief.

As strange as it may seem to include a Bible verse in a collection of documents of atheists and agnostics, Psalm 14:1 of the Old Testament of the Bible provides precisely this kind of indirect evidence. By railing against unbelief, the psalmist acknowledges that unbelievers were in fact present in ancient Judea.

KEEP IN MIND AS YOU READ

Psalm 14 continues with several claims about unbelievers: that they "devour . . . people as men eat bread" and "frustrate the plans of the poor." This is the first of several documents in this collection that will reflect the common concern, present in every era, that the absence of belief in a god or gods equates with the absence of a reliable code of ethics.

Document: Psalm 14:1, Book of Psalms, from Tanakh (Jewish)/Old Testament (Christian)

The fool says in his heart, "There is no God." They are corrupt, their deeds are vile; there is no one who does good.

Source: *Holy Bible*, New International Version. Grand Rapids, MI: Zondervan, 1984.

AFTERWARD

A secular humanistic Judaism has increasingly asserted its presence in modern Jewish culture. But historian Jennifer Michael Hecht describes a strong presence of secular Judaism in ancient times as well. "In the Hellenistic Period," she writes in *Doubt: A History*, "a great number of Jews grew secular in their habits, doubting the God and laws of Moses so strongly that they rededicated the Temple—*the* Temple, in Jerusalem—to Zeus, and did so in a mood of cosmopolitan universalism, in appreciation of Greek philosophy and culture"—a culture of which they were then the tangible eastern flank.

Humanistic Jewish identity, including entirely secular expressions, was to remain alive in some form throughout the millennia, flowering at last into one of the five recognized branches of Judaism in the 20th century.

ASK YOURSELF

Was it reasonable 2,500 years ago to see theistic belief as the obviously correct view of the universe and atheism as foolish? Is that any different today?

TOPICS AND ACTIVITIES TO CONSIDER

Name three things that are common knowledge today that were unknown, thought false, or considered foolish in previous eras.

Further Information

Hecht, Jennifer Michael. *Doubt: A History: The Great Doubters and Their Legacy of Innovation from Socrates and Jesus to Thomas Jefferson and Emily Dickinson*. New York: HarperCollins, 2003.

2. Unbelief in Ancient China—Xun Zi (Third Century BCE)

INTRODUCTION

Xun Zi (ca. 312–230 BCE) is considered the last great advocate of Confucian philosophy in the era before the unification of China under the Qin dynasty (221–207 BCE). He was one of several nontheistic Chinese philosophers active during China's Warring States Period, an era noted for both political unrest and an extraordinary flourishing of different schools of philosophical thought in China.

Xun Zi was of the opinion that human nature tended toward disorder and immorality, tendencies that could be tamed and corrected through education and ritual tradition. His view is often placed opposite his contemporary Mencius (Meng-Tse), who believed human nature tends toward the good.

In "A Discussion of Heaven," Xun Zi opposes superstition and supernatural beliefs, suggesting instead that what we see as the actions or will of heaven is simply the predictable result of natural law and circumstance.

KEEP IN MIND AS YOU READ

The concept of *t'ien* (heaven) is one of the central themes of Chinese philosophy and differs fundamentally from the Western conception of a destination for human souls after death. Chinese philosophers use "heaven" to mean "that which causes the world to be as it is." Theistic philosophers therefore use heaven to denote a deity, while naturalistic philosophers like Xun Zi see no consciousness and no will at work in the world, only predictable and comprehensible natural laws.

Xun Zi's essay "A Discussion of Heaven" was written to promote and encourage this interpretation of *t'ien* and to urge the rejection of the idea that heaven includes a caring mind to which we can appeal to change the conditions in which we live. Good things, he said, are achieved only through the "deliberate effort" of human beings on their own behalf.

Document: Xun Zi, "A Discussion of Heaven"

Heaven's ways are constant. It does not prevail because of a sage like **Yao**; it does not cease to prevail because of a tyrant like **Chieh**. Respond to it with good

Chieh (or Jie, 1728–1675 BCE): an oppressive king of the Xia Dynasty. Chinese legends describe massive natural disasters resulting from his excesses and cruelty

Yao (traditionally ca. 2356–2206 BCE): a legendarily wise and benevolent Chinese emperor

Yü the Great (traditionally ca. 2200–2100 BCE): an ancient Chinese ruler extolled for his high moral character

government, and good fortune will result; respond to it with disorder, and misfortune will result. If you encourage agriculture and are frugal in expenditures, then Heaven cannot make you poor. . . . But if you neglect agriculture and spend lavishly, then Heaven cannot make you rich. If you are careless in your provisions and slow to act, then Heaven cannot make you whole. If you turn your back on the Way and act rashly, then Heaven cannot give you good fortune. Your people will starve even when there are no floods or droughts; they will fall ill even before heat or cold come to oppress them; they will suffer harm even when no strange or uncanny happenings occur. The seasons will visit you as they do a well-ordered age, but you will suffer misfortunes a well-ordered age does not know. Yet you must not curse Heaven, for it is merely the natural result of your own actions. . . .

Are order and disorder due to the heavens? I reply, the sun and moon, the stars and constellations revolved in the same way in the time of **Yü** as in the time of Chieh. Yü achieved order; Chieh brought disorder. Hence order and disorder are not due to the heavens. . . .

Heaven does not suspend the winter because men dislike cold; earth does not cease being wide because men dislike great distances; the gentleman does not stop acting because petty men carp and clamor. Heaven has its constant way; earth has its constant dimensions; the gentleman has his constant demeanor.

The king of Chu has a retinue of a thousand chariots, but not because he is wise. The gentleman must eat boiled greens and drink water, but not because he is stupid. These are accidents of circumstance. To be refined in purpose, rich in virtuous action, and clear in understanding; to live in the present and remember the past—these are things that are within your own power. . . .

You pray for rain and it rains. Why? For no particular reason, I say. It is just as though you had not prayed for rain and it rained anyway. The sun and moon undergo an eclipse and you try to save them; a drought occurs and you pray for rain; you consult the arts of divination before making a decision on some important matter. But it is not as though you could hope to accomplish anything by such ceremonies. They are done merely for ornament. Hence the gentleman regards them as ornaments, but the common people regard them as supernatural. He who considers them ornaments is fortunate; he who considers them supernatural is unfortunate.

Source: Xun Zi. *Xunzi: Basic Writings.* Translated by Burton Watson. New York: Columbia University Press, 2003, 85–89.

AFTERWARD

The work of Mencius, Xun Zi, and Xun Zi's student Han Feizi refined and codified Confucian philosophy, creating a secular philosophical underpinning of Chinese life and law that has endured for over two millennia.

ASK YOURSELF

Throughout recorded history, Chinese philosophy has accepted the presence of strong non-theistic voices along with theistic points of view. Why do you think Chinese culture differs from Western culture in this way?

TOPICS AND ACTIVITIES TO CONSIDER

Write a rebuttal to Xun Zi's essay from the perspective of a theistic philosopher in the Warring States Period, making the case that the evidence of the world supports the idea of a conscious, responsive deity acting in the world.

Further Information

Ivanhoe, Philip. *Readings in Classical Chinese Philosophy*. Indianapolis, IN: Hackett, 2006.

Lai, Karyn. *Introduction to Chinese Philosophy*. Cambridge: Cambridge University Press, 2008.

Xun Zi. *Xunzi: Basic Writings*. Translated by Burton Watson. New York: Columbia University Press, 2003.

3. Unbelief in Ancient India—the *Bārhaspatya-sūtras* (Third Century BCE)

INTRODUCTION

The *Bārhaspatya-sūtras* are the central text of Cārvāka, a system of philosophy originating in the Mauryan period in ancient India (321–185 BCE) and continuing for over 1,500 years. Like Jainism and many forms of Buddhism, Cārvāka is entirely nontheistic. The *Bārhaspatya-sūtras* spell out a fully naturalistic worldview, including the belief that religion is a human invention, that there is nothing wrong with indulging in sensual pleasure, and that death is the end of existence.

Even in cultures with a long history of worldview pluralism, outright disbelief is often perceived as a threat to the religious enterprise on the whole. As a result, followers of Cārvāka often endured intense persecution from politically and religiously orthodox institutions.

Like many ancient atheistic texts (see Introduction, "Which Voices Survive?"), the *Bārhaspatya-sūtras* as a complete text have been lost, surviving only in fragments related by secondary sources, most from the 8th to 12th century CE, and many of them critical. As with the atheist and agnostic literature of ancient Greece, the criticism itself helps to transmit the ideas historically in quoted fragments.

KEEP IN MIND AS YOU READ

The history of the subcontinent now known as India has long been marked by a degree of religious pluralism unparalleled in human history. As a result, tolerance of different beliefs is deeply woven into Indian culture and law. Even so, because they question the wisdom or sense of theistic belief itself, atheistic (or *nāstika*) systems like Cārvāka often receive greater criticism from the more dominant theistic systems around them than those systems direct at each other.

Document: Fragments from the Bārhaspatya-sūtras (India, Third Century BCE)

Brhaspati: Hindu god of wisdom and eloquence
Vedas: the oldest sacred scriptures of Hinduism

Jyotistoma rite: Hindu Vedic ritual involving animal sacrifice

Brahmins: members of the highest scholarly caste or class in India

Agnihotra: ancient Hindu vedic ritual in which an offering, usually milk or melted butter, is poured into a sacred flame

There is no means of knowledge for determining (the existence of) the other-world. There is no other-world because of the absence of any other-worldly being (i.e., the transmigrating self).

Religious act is not to be performed. (Religion's) instructions are not to be relied upon. There is no heaven, no final liberation, nor any soul in another world.

Brhaspati says—The Agnihotra, the three **Vedas**, the ascetic's three staves, and smearing one's self with ashes—(all these) are the livelihood of those destitute of knowledge and manliness.

If a beast slain in the **Jyotistoma rite** will itself go to heaven, why then does not the sacrificer forthwith offer his own father? If beings in heaven are gratified by (our offering) here, then why not give the food down below to those who are standing on the housetop?

While life remains, let a man live happily; nothing is beyond death. When once the body becomes ashes, how can it even return again? If he who departs from the body goes to another world, how is it that he comes not back again, restless for love of his kindred?

Hence it is only as a means of livelihood that **Brahmins** have established here. All these ceremonies for the dead—there is no other fruit anywhere.

The three authors of the Vedas were buffoons, knaves, and demons. O, the naked one (Jain), ascetic (Buddhist), dimwit, given to practicing physical hardship! Who has taught you this way to leading life?

Man consists of only as much as is within the scope of the senses. What the vastly learned ones speak of (as true) is but similar to (the statement) "Oh! Dear! Look at the footprint of the wolf"!

Penances are only various forms of torments, and abstinence is only depriving oneself of consuming (the pleasures of life). The rituals of **Agnihotra**, etc., appear only to be child's play.

Source: Bhattacharya, Ramkrishna. "Cārvāka Fragments: A New Collection." *Journal of Indian Philosophy* 30, no. 6 (December 2002): 597–640.

AFTERWARD

Perhaps in part because of its compelling voice and argumentative style, the influence of Cārvāka is felt throughout Indian literature and culture, including later Upanishads and other Hindu religious texts. Dale Riepe, a researcher specializing in Indian philosophy, challenged the claims by critical commentators in the Middle Ages that Cārvāka was the enemy of all good Vedic values. Instead, he said Cārvāka simply focused on the naturalistic and materialistic values within Vedic tradition: "It may be said from the available material that Cārvākas hold truth, integrity, consistency, and freedom of thought in the highest esteem."

ASK YOURSELF

Given the specific nature of the criticisms in the text fragments, who might have had both the incentive and the power to actively or passively prevent the transmission of Cārvāka texts to future generations?

TOPICS AND ACTIVITIES TO CONSIDER

What features of our current society protect the expression and transmission of minority points of view? What features impede that expression and transmission?

Further Information

Embree, Ainslie, ed. *Sources of Indian Tradition.* Vol. 1, *From the Beginning to 1800.* 2nd ed. New York: Columbia University Press, 1988.

Hiorth, Finngeir. *Atheism in India.* Mumbai: Indian Secular Society, 1998.

Web Site

"Lokāyata/Cārvāka—Indian Materialism," Internet Encyclopedia of Philosophy: http://www.iep.utm.edu/indmat.

4. Atheism and Agnosticism in Ancient Greece and Rome (Second Century BCE– Second Century CE)

INTRODUCTION

Classical and Hellenistic Greece (fifth–second centuries BCE) and early imperial Rome (44 BCE–third century CE) contributed a significant amount of original philosophical thought. Such diverse areas as the natural world, beauty, ethics, logic, politics, and metaphysics were the subject of serious thought and debate in several schools of philosophy, each embodying a unique perspective.

Only a small fraction of the voices active during this period survived through the ages to reach the present day (see Introduction, "Which Voices Survive?"). Among the least likely to survive were those that challenged the prevailing opinions of the time, and no idea in ancient Greece and Rome was more unorthodox than disbelief in the existence of gods. As a result, the thoughts and words of ancient Greek and Roman atheists and agnostics were among the least likely to survive into modern times.

The first of three documents offered below from this period is a 42-line passage known as the Sisyphus Fragment, an excerpt from a play titled *Sisyphus* that has otherwise not survived. Considered the oldest known description of the naturalistic view of religion (that the idea of gods was created by humans), the fragment suggests that the concept of the divine was first invented to prevent the commission of immoral or violent acts in secret. Though Sextus attributes the passage to Critias (460–403 BCE), an uncle of Plato and one of the Thirty Tyrants of Athens, recent scholarship has favored the playwright Euripides (480–406 BCE).

Regardless of authorship, the question of whether the famous passage reflects the author's point of view or simply that of the character who delivers it is an open one.

In an essay titled "On the Gods," Greco-Roman philosopher Sextus Empiricus (160–210 CE) listed five Greek philosophers he called the most prominent atheists of their time: Protagoras of Kos, Protagoras of Abdera, Diagoras of Melos, Theodorus of Cyrene, and Euhemerus of Crete. Some are probably better described as agnostic, though the term was not yet coined; all were said to have expressed deep skepticism about the existence or knowability of the gods.

But only tantalizing fragments of the works of these writers and thinkers have made their way through the centuries to us. Included among these is the opening sentence of Protagoras's *On the Gods*, the only fragment of that work to be preserved in several late classical sources: "Concerning the gods, I have no means of knowing whether they exist or not or of what sort they may be. Many things prevent knowledge including the obscurity of the subject and the brevity of human life."

In his treatise "On the Nature of the Gods," Roman philosopher and orator Marcus Tullius Cicero (106–43 BCE) likewise listed several Greek atheists and agnostics still well known in his time, and spelled out his own theological position as well, which is perhaps best described as pragmatic skepticism. His treatise is addressed to his friend Brutus, famed for his part in the assassination of Julius Caesar.

KEEP IN MIND AS YOU READ

Though the reader is invited to draw his or her own conclusions, Euripides, Sextus, and Cicero were all careful to distance themselves from the atheist opinions on which they reported. But Cicero spelled out his opinion more clearly, if still cautiously, later in *De Natura Deorum*:

> In this subject of the nature of the gods the first question is: do the gods exist or do they not? It is difficult, you will say, to deny that they exist. I would agree, if we were arguing the matter in a public assembly, but in a private discussion of this kind it is perfectly easy to do so. Now I myself hold a religious office, and believe that public religious worship and ritual ought to be reverently observed: so that I could wish to be certainly persuaded on this first question, that the gods exist, as a matter of fact and not of faith. I confess that many doubts arise to perplex me about this, so that at times I wonder whether they exist at all. But I will meet you halfway. I shall not attack you on assertions such as this, in which you are in agreement with the other schools of philosophy. Almost all philosophers agree—and I as much as any—that gods exist. I will not dispute this. But I challenge the cogency of the arguments which you have adduced to prove it.

Cicero's statement that "in a private discussion . . . it is perfectly easy" to deny the existence of gods neatly parallels Sextus's description of the Greek philosopher Epicurus, who he said "leaves God undisputed when addressing himself to the public, but not where the real nature of things is the issue."

Document: Euripides, The Sisyphus Fragment

A time there was when disorder ruled
Human lives, which were then, like lives of beasts,
Enslaved to force; nor was there then reward
For the good, nor for the wicked punishment.

Next, it seems to me, humans established laws
For punishment, that justice might rule
Over the tribe of mortals, and wanton injury be subdued;
And whosoever did wrong was penalized.

Next, as the laws held [mortals] back from deeds
Of open violence, but still such deeds
Were done in secret,—then, I think,
Some shrewd man first, a man in judgment wise,
Found for mortals the fear of gods,

Thereby to frighten the wicked should they
Even act or speak or scheme in secret.

Hence it was that he introduced the divine
Telling how the divinity enjoys endless life,
Hears and sees, and takes thought
And attends to things, and his nature is divine,

So that everything which mortals say is heard
And everything done is visible.
Even if you plan in silence some evil deed
It will not be hidden from the gods: for discernment
Lies in them. So, speaking words like these,
The sweetest teaching did he introduce,
Concealing truth under untrue speech.

The place he spoke of as the gods' abode
Was that by which he might awe humans most,—
The place from which, he knew, terrors came to mortals
And things advantageous in their wearisome life—
The revolving heaven above, in which dwell
The lightnings, and awesome claps
Of thunder, and the starry face of heaven,

Beautiful and intricate by that wise craftsman Time,—
From which, too, the meteor's glowing mass speeds
And wet thunderstorm pours forth upon the earth.
Such were the fears with which he surrounded mortals,
And to the divinity he gave a fitting home,
By this his speech, and in a fitting place,
And [thus] extinguished lawlessness by laws.

Source: Sextus Empiricus, *Sextus Empiricus III: Against the Physicists, Against the Ethicists*. Translated by R. G. Bury. Cambridge, MA: Harvard University Press, 1936.

Document: Marcus Tullius Cicero, De Natura Deorum (On the Nature of the Gods)

There are a number of branches of philosophy that have not as yet been by any means adequately explored; but the inquiry into the nature of the gods, which is both highly interesting in relation to the theory of the soul, and fundamentally important for the regulation of religion, is one of special difficulty and obscurity, as you, Brutus, are well aware.

The multiplicity and variety of the opinions held upon this subject by eminent scholars are bound to constitute a strong argument for the view that philosophy has its origin and starting-point in ignorance, and that the Academic School were well-advised in "withholding assent" from behests that are uncertain: for what is more unbecoming than ill-considered haste? and what is so ill-considered or so unworthy of the dignity and seriousness proper to a philosopher as to hold an opinion that is not true, or to maintain with unhesitating certainty a proposition not based on adequate examination, comprehension and knowledge?

As regards the present subject, for example, most philosophers have affirmed that the gods exist, and this is the most probable view and the one to which we are all led by nature's guidance; but **Protagoras [of Abdera]** declared himself uncertain, and **Diagoras of Melos** and **Theodorus of Cyrene** held that there are no gods at all. Moreover, the upholders of the divine existence differ and disagree so widely, that it would be a troublesome task to recount their opinions. Many views are put forward about the outward form of the gods, their dwelling-places and abodes, and mode of life, and these topics are debated with the oddest variety of opinion among philosophers; but as to the question upon which the whole issue of the dispute principally turns, whether the gods are entirely idle and inactive, taking no part at all in the direction and government of the world, or whether on the contrary all things both were created and ordered by them in the beginning and are controlled and kept in motion by them throughout eternity, here there is the greatest disagreement of all. And until this issue is decided, mankind must continue to labour under the profoundest uncertainty, and to be in ignorance about matters of the highest moment.

There are and have been philosophers who hold that the gods exercise no control over human affairs whatever. But if their opinion is the true one, how can piety, reverence or religion exist? For all these are tributes which it is our duty to render in purity and holiness to the divine powers solely on the assumption that they take notice of them, and that some service has been rendered by the gods to the race of men. But if on the contrary the gods have neither the power nor the will to aid us, if they pay heed to us at all and take no notice of our actions, if they can exert no possible influence upon the life of men, what ground have we for rendering any sort of worship, honor or prayer to the immortal gods? Piety, however, like the rest of the virtues, cannot exist in mere outward show and pretence; and with piety, reverence and religion must likewise disappear. And when these are gone, life soon becomes a welter of disorder and confusion. In all probability disappearance of piety towards the gods will entail the disappearance of loyalty and social union among men as well, and of justice itself, the queen of all virtues.

There are however other philosophers, and those of eminence and note, who believe that the whole world is ruled and governed by divine intelligence and reason . . . the weather and the seasons and the changes of the atmosphere by which all products of the soil are ripened and matured are the gift of the immortal gods to the human race; and they adduce a number of things, which will be recounted in the books that compose the present treatise, that are of such a nature as almost to appear to have been expressly constructed by the immortal gods for the use of man. This view was controverted at great length by **Carneades**, in such a manner as to arouse in persons of active mind a keen desire to discover the truth. There is in fact no subject upon which so much difference of opinion exists, not only

Protagoras of Abdera (490–420 BCE): Pre-Socratic Greek philosopher, author of earliest known agnostic statement

Diagoras "Atheos" of Melos (5th c. BCE): Greek poet known for criticizing belief in Greek gods and Roman Eleusinian mysteries (see sidebar)

Theodorus "Atheos" of Cyrene (340–250 BCE): one of two famous Theodori of Cyrene in modern-day Libya (the other was a prominent mathematician). "Theodorus the Atheist" was a philosopher who believed the goal of life was joy, and that joy was primarily found in knowledge. Primarily known for atheism articulated in his lost book *On the Gods*

Carneades (213–128 BCE): Greek Skeptic philosopher who called into question the ability to truly know anything

among the unlearned but also among educated men; and the views entertained are so various and so discrepant, that, while it is no doubt a possible alternative that none of them is true, it is certainly impossible that more than one should be so.

Source: Cicero, Marcus Tullius. *De Natura Deorum.* Edited by Joseph Mayor. Cambridge: Cambridge University Press, 1885.

Document: Sextus Empiricus, "On the Gods," *from* Against the Physicists

Of those, then, who have examined the question of the existence of God, we have some who assert his existence, some who assert his non-existence, and some who say he is "no more" existent than non-existent. That he exists is the contention of most of the **dogmatists** and is the general preconception of ordinary men. That he does not exist is the contention of those who are nicknamed "atheists," such as **Euhemerus**, "A boastful old man who scribbles wicked books,"[1] and Diagoras of Melos, and **Prodicus of Ceos**, and Theodorus, and multitudinous others. Of these Euhemerus said that those who were believed to be gods were actually certain men of power who for this reason had been deified by the others, and then were thought to be gods. Prodicus said that whatever benefits life was understood to be God—things such as sun, moon, rivers, lakes, meadows, crops and everything of that kind. . . . And Critias, one of the tyrants of Athens, seems to be from the ranks of the atheists when he says that the lawgivers of ancient times invented God as a kind of overseer of the right and wrong actions of men. Their purpose was to prevent anyone from wronging his neighbors secretly, as he would incur the risk of vengeance at the hands of the gods. . . .

> **Dogmatist:** in this context, anyone who articulates a system of belief. The term carries a pejorative implication today that was not present in classical antiquity
> **Euhemerus (Fourth c. BCE):** compiler of mythology and legend for Cassander, King of Macedonia. Identified with early naturalistic explanations of belief in gods. See "Euhemerism" sidebar
> **Prodicus of Ceos (465–395 BCE):** Greek Sophist philosopher

Theodorus, "the Atheist," is also in agreement with these men, and according to some, Protagoras of Abdera. The former, in his treatise *On Gods*, demolished with various arguments the theological beliefs of the Greeks, while Protagoras in one passage wrote expressly: "In regard to the gods I can say neither whether they exist nor of what sort they are, for many are the things that prevent me." The Athenians condemned him to death for this, but he escaped, and then perished, lost at sea. . . . And Epicurus, according to some, leaves God undisputed when addressing himself to the public, but not where the real nature of things is the issue.

Source: Hallie, Philip P. *Sextus Empiricus: Selections from the Major Writings on Scepticism, Man, & God.* Edited by Philip P. Hallie. Indianapolis, IN: Hackett, 1985, 188–90.

---

[1] From the *Iambi* of Callimachus, a Greek poet in the third century BCE.

EUHEMERISM

In his *Sacred History*, a work now lost, Euhemerus of Crete (fourth century BCE) provided one of the earliest known naturalistic explanations of religion. He suggested that the gods of the Greek pantheon—Zeus, Apollo, Athena, Poseidon, Hermes, and the rest—had originally been historical kings and heroes whose cults of adoration assumed supernatural dimensions after their deaths.

"Euhemerism" became a term of art for any attempt to describe a supernatural belief in natural, rational terms. In addition to those who have called all gods into question, Euhemerism has served the purposes of many religious leaders who wished to paint earlier local religions as sanctified history. The early Christian theologian Clement of Alexandria engaged in Euhemerism when he addressed believers in pagan deities, saying, "Those to whom you bow were once men like yourselves."

The 13th-century Icelandic Christian historian Snorri Sturluson provided a similar explanation for the Norse gods in the prologue to the *Prose Edda*, a collection of Norse mythology. The Norse gods, he said, were most likely ancient Trojan warriors who emigrated to Northern Europe after the defeat of that city in the Trojan War, impressing the locals with their superior war craft, metallurgy, and skill.

DIAGORAS THE ATHEIST

"The poet Diagoras of Melos was perhaps the most famous atheist of the fifth century [BCE]. Although he did not write about atheism, anecdotes about his unbelief suggest he was self-confident, almost teasing, and very public. He revealed the secret rituals of the Eleusinian mystery religion to everyone and 'thus made them ordinary,' that is, he purposefully demystified a cherished secret rite, apparently to provoke his contemporaries into thought. In another famous story, a friend pointed out an expensive display of votive gifts and said, 'You think the gods have no care for man? Why, you can see from all these votive pictures here how many people have escaped the fury of storms at sea by praying to the gods who have brought them safe to harbor.' To which Diagoras replied, 'Yes, indeed, but where are the pictures of all those who [prayed, but still] suffered shipwreck and perished in the waves?'"

—From *Doubt: A History*, by Jennifer Michael Hecht

AFTERWARD

The names of the ancient Greek atheists continued to echo down the centuries long after Sextus and Cicero. Early Christian church fathers frequently used the presence of such opinions in Greek thought in their denunciations of pagan culture in the third and fourth centuries CE. Ironically, even as the church fathers attacked Euhemerus as an atheist, they frequently adopted his technique of positing naturalistic origins for other belief systems.

ASK YOURSELF

1. The process by which voices from the past are handed down to the present is complex and capricious. How many reasons can you think of that any given thought in ancient Greece might not have made it to our time?

2. As a political figure, was Cicero free to express his own religious convictions if they differed from the mainstream? Do you think politicians today are more or less free to do so than in Cicero's time, or is it much the same? Why?

TOPICS AND ACTIVITIES TO CONSIDER

Mock historical selection (10 groups of two–three people each):

Each small group represents one historical generation. On separate index cards, ask the group to write down the names of five favorite songs, five favorite books, and five favorite movies, including as wide a range of taste and type as possible. Have the first "generation" pass the stack of 15 cards to the next generation, who in turn will pass on only the songs, books, and films they themselves think are worth preserving. Continue through the 10 groups/generations. Show the cards that survive (usually 3–4) to the first generation, asking if what remains is an accurate reflection of the music, literature, and film of their time. Note that 10 generations is equivalent to just 10 percent of the time since ancient Greece. Discuss what was learned about historical selection.

Follow-up questions: (1) How does this exercise help you reevaluate what we think we know about past eras? (2) What from our time do you think is most likely to survive historical selection? What is least likely?

Further Information

Bett, Richard, ed. *The Cambridge Companion to Ancient Scepticism (Cambridge Companions to Philosophy)*. Cambridge: Cambridge University Press, 2010.

Web Sites

Ancient Skepticism: http://plato.stanford.edu/entries/skepticism-ancient/.
"Atheism and Skepticism with Greek Philosophers": http://atheism.about.com/od/athcism history/a/AncientGreeceSkepticism.htm.
"Cicero," Internet Encyclopedia of Philosophy: http://www.iep.utm.edu/cicero.

THE "MIDDLE AGES"
IN FOUR CULTURES

5. Unbelief in Medieval India—*Mahapurana* of Jinasena (Ninth Century CE)

INTRODUCTION

The sixth century BCE was a time of great innovation in Hinduism, giving rise to diverse new schools of thought. Among these was Jainism, a nontheistic religion based on natural law, pacifism, and nonviolence toward all living things. Jainism rejects the idea that the universe was created or is sustained by supernatural beings and includes direct criticisms of supernatural belief in many of its texts.

Mahapurana is one of the most important Jain texts. Written primarily by the Acharya (religious teacher) Jinasena and finished by his student Gunabhadra in the ninth century CE, this text gives a thorough description of Jain tradition and belief, including what historian Vipan Chandra has called "the finest and most audacious ancient defense of atheism." That famous passage, presented below, echoes the arguments of Epicurus and Diagoras and presages those of the 18th-century Enlightenment.

KEEP IN MIND AS YOU READ

A *purana* ("of ancient times" in Sanskrit) is an important type of religious text found in several Indian religious traditions, including Jainism. While other sacred texts are compilations of hymns, proverbs, or sacred verse, the *purana* is intended to provide descriptions of the history of the universe.

Document: Acharya Jinasena, Mahapurana 4.16–31 (Ninth Century CE)

Some foolish men declare that Creator made the world.

The doctrine that the world was created is ill-advised, and should be rejected.

If God created the world, where was he before creation? If you say he was transcendent then, and needed no support, where is he now?

No single being had the skill to make the world—for how can an immaterial god create that which is material?

How could God have made the world without any raw material?

If you say he made this first, and then the world, you are faced with an endless regression.

If you declare that the raw material arose naturally you fall into another fallacy, for the whole universe might thus have been its own creator, and have risen equally naturally.

If God created the world by an act of will, without any raw material, then it is just his will and nothing else—and who will believe this silly stuff?

If he is ever perfect, and complete, how could the will to create have arisen in him?

If, on the other hand, he is not perfect, he could no more create the universe than a potter could.

If he is formless, actionless, and all-embracing, how could he have created the world? Such a soul, devoid of all modality, would have no desire to create anything.

If you say that he created to no purpose, because it was his nature to do so then God is pointless. If he created in some kind of sport, it was the sport of a foolish child, leading to trouble. . . .

If he created out of love for living things and need of them he made the world; why did he not make creation wholly blissful, free from misfortune? . . .

Thus the doctrine that the world was created by God makes no sense at all.

And God commits great sin in slaying the children whom he himself created.

If you say that he slays only to destroy evil beings, why did he create such beings in the first place? . . .

Good men should combat the believer in divine creation, maddened by an evil doctrine.

Know that the world is uncreated, as time itself is, without beginning and end, and is based on the principles [natural law], life, and the rest.

Source: Embree, Ainslie, ed. *Sources of Indian Tradition.* Vol. 1, *From the Beginning to 1800,* 2nd ed. New York: Columbia University Press, 1988, 80–82.

DHARMAKĪRTI

The scholar Dharmakīrti (seventh century CE) was among the great figures in the tradition of Buddhist philosophical logic. While teaching at Nalanda University, an ancient seat of Buddhist learning in northeastern India, he wrote seven treatises on knowledge and perception that laid the foundation for Buddhist logical philosophy for centuries to come. Included was *Nyāyabinduprakaraṇa* (Drop of Reasoning), a treatise describing an entirely naturalistic and atheistic system of logical reasoning.

Dharmakīrti represented both the pinnacle of Buddhist logicians in the "Middle Ages" and the last major figure before Buddhist philosophical logic, along with Buddhism itself, went into a period of rapid decline as Hinduism exerted greater influence in the Indian subcontinent.

NONTHEISTIC SCHOOLS OF THOUGHT WITHIN HINDUISM

Despite the diversity of expressions within Christianity, it is difficult to imagine a Christian denomination rejecting the idea of God while retaining its Christian identity. Yet the stunning collection of distinct traditions that make up Hinduism include explicitly atheistic branches—not as dissenting groups on the margin, but right in the heart of orthodox Hinduism.

Though Carvaka was the most strongly atheistic branch of Hinduism, adherents of Samkhya, the oldest of the six orthodox schools of Hindu philosophy, also rejected the idea of gods entirely, while texts of the early Poorva Mimamsa school from the third to first centuries BCE were essentially agnostic, declaring that the evidence for gods is simply insufficient, and that gods are at any rate unnecessary for human flourishing.

RELIGIOUS PLURALISM IN INDIA

Though most laypeople in the West associate India with Hinduism, the subcontinent is in fact the home and even the point of origin for countless religious traditions and identities. Four major world faiths were born and continue to thrive in India (Buddhism, Hinduism, Sikhism, and Jainism), and over 25 million Christians, 125 million Muslims, and 60 million nonreligious persons currently call India home.

A wide diversity of traditions and beliefs exists within each of these labels. Hinduism is especially diverse, with no single point of origin or founder and no single authoritative text. Complete freedom of belief is a given; such concepts as blasphemy or heresy are essentially unknown. Depending on which branch of the religion they follow, both Hindus and Buddhists might believe in one god, many gods, or no gods at all. As a result of an ancient (and given the close-quarters diversity, pragmatic) tolerance, India has what is surely the most heterogeneous landscape of worldviews on Earth, as well as a particularly accepting cultural context for unbelief.

AFTERWARD

A number of later texts, including other *puranas* in Jainism, Buddhism, and Hinduism, were deeply influenced by the themes and content of the *Mahapurana*. It remains to this day one of the most comprehensive accounts of Jain tradition ever created.

ASK YOURSELF

Do you find the arguments in the *Mahapurana* convincing? Why or why not?

TOPICS AND ACTIVITIES TO CONSIDER

Atheists in modern times have the benefit of scientific explanations for much of what we see and experience. If you were born into a prescientific culture, do you think you would have been able to accept a nontheistic position such as that espoused by the *Mahapurana*?

Further Information

Embree, Ainslie, ed. *Sources of Indian Tradition*. Vol. 1, *From the Beginning to 1800*, 2nd ed. New York: Columbia University Press, 1988.

Web Site

BBC Religions—A Guide to Jainism: http://www.bbc.co.uk/religion/religions/jainism.

6. The Unbeliever in Islam—Ibn al-Rawāndī (Persia, ca. 815–ca. 860)

INTRODUCTION

As Europe continued to struggle through a period of relative intellectual stagnation in the late 8th to early 14th centuries, the Arab world experienced striking advances in science, technology, medicine, art and philosophy in what has been called the Islamic Golden Age (see The Islamic Golden Age sidebar). Though overtly radical and unorthodox opinions were still few, it was during this period that the most notable challenges to Islamic orthodoxy were heard.

Several Muslim theologians of the period wrote treatises titled "Against the Unbelievers," addressing heretics and outright nonbelievers in separate and distinct arguments. This amounts to the same kind of evidence as Psalm 14:1 regarding the presence not only of heterodox religious opinion but of atheism during this time. One such work by Zaydi theologian al-Qāsim b. Ibrāhim (fl. 860) begins with an extensive proof that the world in fact had a Creator—an argument generally reserved for atheists rather than heretics, and further evidence of the existence of articulated atheism in the Islamic Golden Age.

Among the most radical voices in this period was that of Abu al-Hasan Ahmad ibn Yahya ibn Ishaq al-Rawāndī (ca. 815–ca. 860), an Islamic theologian who broke with the beliefs of his Mu'tazilite sect to become a vocal critic of Islam, of Muhammad, of prophecy, and of all revealed religion. His tone was often contemptuous, including suggestions that Muhammad was a "liar" and that the Allah depicted in the Qur'an behaves "like a wrathful, murderous enemy," is petty and cruel, and "does not know how to add two to four to make six."[1] As is often the case with dissenting voices, Ibn al-Rawāndī's written works have not survived except in quotation by sources attempting to refute his arguments. It is through these secondary sources that Ibn al-Rawāndī's most important work, *The Book of the Emerald*, survived to be quoted here.

KEEP IN MIND AS YOU READ

Because his own works survive only in fragments filtered through highly critical secondary sources, and these consist of attacks on orthodoxy rather than the description of a proposed

---

[1] Quoted in Ibn al-Jawzi, *Muntazam*, via Sarah Stroumsa, *Freethinkers of Medieval Islam: Ibn al-Rawāndī, Abū Bakr al-Rāzī and Their Impact on Islamic Thought* (Boston: Brill, 1999), 73–74.

replacement, both historians and Ibn al-Rawāndī's contemporaries disagree about his actual beliefs. Some assert that he was a heretic rather than an unbeliever, since no direct refutations of belief in a god are present in his surviving quotations, while others, including the Islamic philosophy scholar Friedrich Niewöhner, consider Ibn al-Rawāndī to be a "radical atheist."

As in Inquisitional Europe, heresy was considered to be a greater threat to orthodox religion than complete unbelief. For this reason, Ibn al-Rawāndī's arguments against specific elements of belief, including the validity of prophecy, would have found their way more reliably into the texts of his critics than would any renunciation of belief in the existence of God.

Document: Excerpts from Ibn al-Rawāndī, The Book of the Emerald, *as quoted in the* Tathbit *of ʿAbd al-Jabbar and the* Intisar *of al-Hayyat*

The book known as *Kitab al-Zumurrud*, in which he [i.e., Ibn al-Rawāndī] mentioned the miracles of the prophets, peace upon them, such as the miracles of Abraham, Moses, Jesus and Muhammad, God's blessing on them. He disputed the reality of these miracles and claimed that they were fraudulent tricks and that the people who performed them were magicians and liars; that the Qur'an is the speech of an unwise being, and that it contains contradictions, errors and absurdities. He included in it a chapter entitled: "Against the Muhammadans in particular," meaning the community of Muhammad, God's blessing on him. . . .

[Ibn al-Rawāndī] denied the created nature of bodies and rejected it. He claimed that there is no indication in the affect for the existence of its cause, nor in the act of its existence for its agent. The world and everything in it . . . is pre-eternal; it has neither a maker nor a governor, neither an initiator nor a creator.

Source: Al-Hayyat, *Al-Intisar*, quoted in Stroumsa, Sarah, *Freethinkers of Medieval Islam: Ibn al-Rawāndī, Abū Bakr al-Rāzī and Their Impact on Islamic Thought.* Boston: Brill, 1999, 47, 127.

[Ibn al-Rawāndī] said, "The ability of [Moses and Jesus] to predict the coming of Muhammad is similar to the ability of astrologers to predict the future." He was told, "And since when can astrologers predict something like this, that is to say, something like the advent of Muhammad, the date of his appearance, the content of his message, his country of provenance, the generation to which he belongs and his ancestry, in the same detailed manner that this was announced? This kind of prediction is not to be found in the announcements of the most proficient astrologers. They cannot even come close to it or do anything of a similar nature. Only by chance [the astrologers] may happen to hit on a general, marginal thing, after a thousand cases of errors and mistakes.

Then these [non-Muslims] say: The only reason why [the Jews] did not wish for death [as Muhammad challenged them to do, to prove that a glorious afterlife awaited Jews] is that, had they expressed such a wish, [Muhammad] would have

> ## THE ISLAMIC GOLDEN AGE
>
> Beginning around 750 CE, Islamic culture experienced a remarkable flourishing of art, philosophy, science, medicine, and technology, a period of several centuries often referred to as the Islamic Golden Age. Islamic scientists made rapid advances in astronomy, optics, and medicine, building on translated works from ancient Greece during a time when Christian Europe was suspicious of pagan sources and therefore at a relative standstill in science and natural philosophy.
>
> Greek texts were translated into Arabic, preserved, recopied, studied, and enlarged upon by such Arab scholars as ibn Rushd and Avicenna during the early period of the Abbasid Caliphate (750–1258). Without this active preservation of Greek culture and learning, it is likely that most of the Greek sources that were to provide the spark for the European Renaissance and scientific revolution, including Aristotle, Plato, and Euclid, would have been lost.
>
> Though scholars tend to agree on the flourishing of art, science, and culture in the Abbasid Caliphate, there is some disagreement over whether the period should be known as an Islamic Golden Age (which identifies with the religion) or an Arab Golden Age (which identifies with the culture).
>
> The end of the Golden Age is often dated to the invasions and conquests by the Mongol Empire under Genghis Khan, especially the destruction of Baghdad by Hulagu Khan, Genghis' grandson, in 1258.

answered that he had meant them to wish it in their hearts. Had they said to him, "We did wish it in our hearts," he would have answered "Gabriel told me that you did not."

Source: Al-Jabbar, 'Abd. *Tathbit*. As quoted in Stroumsa, Sarah, *Freethinkers of Medieval Islam: Ibn al-Rawāndī, Abū Bakr al-Rāzī and Their Impact on Islamic Thought*. Boston: Brill, 1999, 60–61.

AFTERWARD

Though little is known of the life of Ibn al-Rawāndī, the effect of his challenges on Islam was far-reaching. The number of refutations of his work that have survived in print, written in the course of centuries after his death, shows that his criticisms were not lightly dismissed and were even feared for their potential to undercut the faith of others. Fully 200 years after Ibn al-Rawāndī's death, the Persian theologian Al-Muayyad al-Shirazi devoted scrupulous attention to refuting Ibn al-Rawāndī's arguments that truth can be discovered through application of human intellect without recourse to prophecy or other supernatural religious practices.

ASK YOURSELF

1. Why does the presence of voices challenging religious orthodoxy so often correspond to periods of intellectual and cultural ferment—in China, in Europe, in the Arab World, and elsewhere?
2. How do you think a critic of Islam like Ibn al-Rawāndī would be received by the Islamic world today? What is the basis of your opinion?
3. Just as Ibn al-Rawāndī's opinions were filtered through critical observers, Western knowledge of Arab culture is currently filtered through the lens of the news and our own preconceptions, both of which are affected by sensational and unusual

examples. How confident are you in your ability to objectively assess Arab culture and the Islamic religion?

TOPICS AND ACTIVITIES TO CONSIDER

Conduct research to identify current freethinkers living and working within predominantly Islamic countries. How do these countries vary in their tolerance of religious dissent?

Further Information

Stroumsa, Sarah. *Freethinkers of Medieval Islam: Ibn al-Rawāndī, Abū Bakr al-Rāzī and Their Impact on Islamic Thought.* Boston: Brill, 1999.

7. A Continuing Thread of Doubt in China—Chang Tsai (1020–1077)

INTRODUCTION

Neo-Confucianism was a philosophical movement of the 9th to 14th centuries CE that worked to revitalize Confucianism after centuries of neglect by cleansing it of the supernatural elements it had accrued since the death of Confucius in the 6th c. BCE. Chang Tsai (1020–1077), one of the most influential thinkers in the movement, saw original Confucianism as a rational, secular philosophy of ethics and self-improvement that was later corrupted by the influence of Buddhism and Taoism.

Chang did not reject all aspects of these other systems of thought. "The words [of the Buddhists] . . . resemble the correct [Way]," he wrote, but had been seriously diminished by their association with superstition and mysticism. *Correcting the Unenlightened*, written the year before his death, was the book in which Chang most carefully and completely laid out his vision for the restoration of a rational Confucianism.

KEEP IN MIND AS YOU READ

Like Xun Zi more than a millennium before, Chang spends considerable time and effort examining the concept of *t'ien* (heaven). And like Xun, Chang makes it clear that his is a conception without supernatural elements. When he argues that men must be guided by the dictates of heaven, he is advocating an adherence to the natural order, not to a divine consciousness. Concerning human nature, Chang differed from Xun Zi, arguing that both humanity and heaven/nature were essentially good, and that the former was most good when in harmony with the latter.

Document: Chang Tsai, Correcting the Unenlightened *(1076), Including an Introduction by Fan Yü and an Excerpt from Their Correspondence*

The words of *Correcting the Unenlightened* were spoken because there is no choice. Truly, there is only one Way . . . That by which heaven moves, the earth supports [things], the sun and moon are bright, ghosts and spirits are mysterious, wind and clouds change, and the rivers flow . . . from root to branches and top to bottom, are strung together in the one Way.

Fan Yü, disciple of Chang Tsai, in his introduction to *Correcting the Unenlightened*

In a letter to his disciple, Chang lays out a strictly naturalistic approach to interrogating the world. If something seems "weird" or mysterious, pursue it to its source, and you will find a rational explanation:

As for your inquiry on weird things and mysterious monstrosities—this is not hard to explain . . . [It is like] what **Mencius** said [about] knowing the nature and knowing heaven. When a man's study reaches the point of knowing heaven, then he should continually see the source whence things emerge. When he knows whence [things] emerge, then he will always understand in his mind whether every thing should or should not exist.

> **Mencius (ca. 372–289 BCE):** an important Confucian philosopher who believed human nature was essentially good

Letter from Chang Tsai to Fan Yü

In Correcting the Unenlightened, *Chang Tsai echoes Xun Zi before him, taking great care to dissociate the concept "heaven" from the idea of a god or other consciousness:*

> **"the hundred things":** a Confucian term for the diversity of life on Earth

The way of heaven proceeds through the four seasons and **the hundred things** are born.

That which moves the myriad things but does not share the concerns of the sage—this we refer to directly as "heaven." Heaven is thus without consciousness.

[Heaven] moves the myriad things and produces [everything, but] it is without a mind by which to sympathize with them.

Heaven thus is without consciousness, without [purposive] action. There is nothing which directs it. It is forever thus.

When there are two, there must be interaction; but what thoughts or concerns do the interactions of heaven have? There is nothing that is not spontaneous.

Source: Kasoff, Ira. *The Thoughts of Chang Tsai (1020–1077).* Cambridge: Cambridge University Press, 1984.

NONTHEISTIC PHILOSOPHY IN CHINA

Nontheistic perspectives have held center stage in Chinese philosophy, culture, and government throughout its history. Though several religions coexist in both theistic and nontheistic forms, including Buddhism and Taoism, it is Confucianism, with its rational, secular philosophy of ethics, that has served as the foundation of Chinese thought and national character for most of its history.

AFTERWARD

By the 13th century, secular Confucianism had reemerged as the foundational philosophy of Chinese culture and government, a position it has retained for most of the nation's history.

ASK YOURSELF

Most religions and philosophies develop schisms, splintering into diverse beliefs and practices, often soon after the death of the founder or founders. Chang Tsai suggested that Confucianism was originally nontheistic, while others have argued the opposite. A similar discussion has continued for centuries over Buddhism's founding characteristics. Even a much more recent founding such as that of the United States is subject to intense debate regarding its religious versus secular intent. What are the obstacles to discovering the true intentions of such founding moments? What is the best way to proceed in determining the truth?

Further Information

Kasoff, Ira. *The Thoughts of Chang Tsai (1020–1077)*. Cambridge: Cambridge University Press, 1984.

8. INQUISITION INTERROGATIONS FROM THE FOURNIER REGISTER (FRANCE, 1318–1325)

INTRODUCTION

Born in southern France in the late 13th century, Jacques Fournier became a Cistercian monk before rising to Bishop of Pamiers in 1317, just a dozen miles from his place of birth. Within a year of his appointment, Fournier was instructed to undertake local interrogations to root out adherents of Catharism, an unorthodox sect that had been spreading through the region.

Fournier took the unusual step of having each of the hundreds of individual interrogations he conducted transcribed in detail.

KEEP IN MIND AS YOU READ

Nonbelievers were not the main target or concern of the late medieval Inquisitions. All of the major Inquisitional campaigns were primarily designed to root out heretical sects—Christian movements whose beliefs were not entirely in keeping with Roman Catholic doctrine, including the Waldensians (who ordained independent clergy without Roman authority) and the Cathars (who believed among other things that not God but a lesser, evil deity created the world). Such sects often spread rapidly and were perceived to be a threat to Catholic religious and political power on the continent.

The three interrogations excerpted below were of individuals identified by others or by themselves not only as heretics but as unbelievers in the existence of God at some recent point prior to their appearance before the bishop. It was understandably the idea of interrogation itself that often brought a change of heart. One of the subjects recorded below, a villager named Guillemette, testified that she had returned to an orthodox opinion regarding the nature of the soul because "I heard tell that My Lord the Bishop of Pamiers wanted to carry out an investigation against me about it. I was afraid of My Lord Bishop because of that, and I changed my opinion after that time."

Document: Jacques Fournier, Inquisition Interrogation Transcripts from the Fournier Register (1318–1325)

Confession of Guillemette, Widow of Bernard Benet of Ornolac

In the year of our Lord 1319, the 11th of May, Alazaïs, wife of Pierre Munier of Ornolac, sworn witness to the event of the heretical words that it is said were uttered by Guillemette, widow of Bernard Benet of Ornolac, said:

A year ago, in relationship to the present time in which I am testifying, when the leaves of the elm trees grow, myself and Guillemette, widow of Bernard Benet of Ornolac, were sitting under the elm of Ornolac, and we were talking about this and that. Among other things, I said, "May God guard your soul, and with your body let God do what he will!" Guillemette said to me, "Idiot, idiot, what are you afraid of?" I told her that I was afraid for my soul because we sin often, and I asked her: "And you, aren't you afraid?" She responded that she was not. I asked her why she was not afraid for her soul, and she responded: "The soul, the soul! Idiot! Our soul is no more than blood." Hearing this, I told her to never again say such a thing, for it could make misfortune befall her. She responded that she would say it in front of anyone she liked: "And what would happen to me, if I said it?"

That year, around Lent, I was in a house that is next to Guillemette's house, and Raimond Benet, her son-in-law, was in her house, and he was speaking to her (I overheard it). He was saying: "My good woman, preserve your soul!" "Idiot, idiot, what soul? The soul is nothing more than blood." Afterwards, I spoke of these words to Raimond Benet, who repeated them to me.

[When] questioned if it is out of hatred, love, fear, prayer, the promise of a sum of money, or another bribe that she testifies so, she responded no, it was only because it is the truth.

The same year and day as above, Gentille, the daughter of the late Guillaume Rous d'Ornolac, witness sworn and interrogated on that which precedes, said:

About a year ago, it seems to me, I was in the garden I have at Ornolac, which is next to the garden of Guillemette, the widow of Bernard Benet of Ornolac; she was in her garden, and we began to speak about the dead and the souls of the deceased. She said then: "The soul, the soul! Personally, I don't see anything come out of men or women when they die. If I saw the soul or some other thing come out, I would know what the soul is, but so far I haven't seen anything come out, and that is why I don't know what the soul is." Based on these words, I believe and I believed that she thought that the soul does not survive after the death of the body.

In the same place, she said that when men and woman live in the present life, their life is but blood. I understood by these words that she was saying that the soul is but blood.

I often heard her making such remarks, in my house as well as elsewhere.

—*Have you revealed this to anyone?*

No.

—*Do you believe that what she said was true?*

No.

[When] questioned if it is out of hatred, love, fear, prayer, the promise of a sum of money, or another bribe that she testifies so, she responded no, it was only because it is the truth.

The same year as above, Raimond Benet of Ornolac, witness sworn and interrogated on that which precedes, said:

Less than a year ago, though I remember neither the day nor the season, Guillemette, my mother-in-law, and Raimonde, my wife, were sleeping together in my house, while I slept in another. In the morning, my mother-in-law told me that she and my wife had heard something that cried "ha," and asked me if I had heard it. I replied that no, I had not heard it, but that cats often cry in this way when they fight with each other. She told me that it could very well have been the soul of a dead person, for she had heard tell that when souls are not in a good place, they cry and go in the wind, and that one can see them. I told her: "How can you say that one can see the soul and that it goes in the wind?" She responded: "You don't see that, when men die, one doesn't see them do anything but exhale? This exhalation is nothing but wind. If the soul were something other than this exhalation, one would see something come out of the body. Now, one only sees this exhalation; that is why the soul goes in the wind."

I often heard her say, when one asked her to give alms for her soul: "Arma, arma!" ["Soul, soul!"]

That year, I had cut the head off of a goose, and that goose lived and cried still, until its blood had left its body. Guillemette said: "The goose cried as long as it had blood, and the same thing would happen for a man or a woman: they would live as long as they had blood." But I do not remember having heard her say that the human soul is nothing but blood.

If I remember anything else, I will come and find My Lord the Bishop, and I will reveal it to him.

[When] questioned if it is out of hatred, love, fear, prayer, the promise of a sum of money, or another bribe that she testifies so, she responded that no, it was only because it is the truth.

Confession of Guillemette, Widow of Bernard Benet

The year of our Lord 1320, the 16th of July. Whereas it came to the attention of Revered Father in Christ, My Lord Jacques, by the grace of God bishop of Pamiers, that Guillemette, the widow of Bernard Benet of Ornolac, had said in front of diverse persons that the human soul, while it is in the human body, is but blood, and that when the man dies, only wind comes out of the body; that after the death of the body, the human soul ceases to exist, and is neither good or evil in its merits or faults, but that it dies at the death of the body; whereas My Lord Bishop had received information on these points, he summoned her to his presence on Monday, the 15th of July.

On the said day, the said Guillemette appeared before him in the Chamber of the Episcopal seat of Pamiers, and it was asked of her by My Lord the Bishop simply, and without oath, if she had said, in public, or in private, that which was the purpose of taking her into custody, if she had believed it or believed it to be true. She said that she no longer remembered, but wanted to think about it until the next day, a time of reflection which My Lord the Bishop accorded to her until the following morning.

The next day, at the said hour, she appeared in the presence of the said bishop, in the Chamber of the seat of Pamiers. As she did not wish to admit to any of that which precedes simply, the said Lord Bishop received from her physically the oath to tell the truth, unmitigated by any falsehood, on the above said events and others concerning the Catholic faith, concerning herself as defendant and others, living or dead, as a witness.

This oath sworn, the said articles having been explained to her anew in the common tongue, she denied having said or believed them in totality or in part. And immediately My said Lord Bishop, considering her a suspect as a consequence of the information given against her, arrested her, ordering her to surrender herself immediately at the Castle des Allemans, and to go to the dungeons of My said Lord Bishop, and to not leave without his authorization and his order.

After which, in the year of our Lord 1320, the 11th of August, the said Guillemette, appearing in the Chamber of the bishopric of Pamiers in the presence of My said Lord Bishop attended by Brother Gaillard de Pomiès, said and confessed:

Three years ago the next grape-harvesting season, I was in my garden at Ornolac, and I fell to the ground from a wall and hurt my nose, to the point that blood came out of it. When I fell, Gentille, the daughter of the late Guillaume Rous of Ornolac, came to help me, and as I saw that blood was coming out of my nose, I said: "The soul, the soul! The soul is but blood."

A year ago at the end of April, when the elms were beginning to put out their leaves, I was under the elm of Ornolac, which is near the land of Pierre Bordas of Ornolac, I do believe. We were speaking together, saying that one must do good, life enduring, for one's soul, and that one must fear God for the salvation of one's soul. I said then that the soul of the man and the woman is but blood, and that when the man or the woman dies, their soul dies also.

That year, around Easter, Raimond Benet had a newborn child who was dying. He called me, when I was going to the woods in the forest, so that I could look after his dying son. I looked after him from morning to night, and I was watching if I could see something come out of the child's mouth when he died. As I saw nothing come out except an exhalation, I said, in front of Gentille den Rous, already subpoenaed: "Watch, watch, when a man dies, you don't see anything but wind come out of his mouth. If I saw something else come out, I would believe that the soul is something. But since only wind came out, I do not believe that it is anything."

—Did you say these words about the soul in possession of all your senses, and believing this in your heart, in the meaning of these words?

Yes, and I have believed it for two years, although I have not remained continuously in this belief, only intermittingly. It seems to me that it was during a half a year, in those two years, that I was of that opinion, believing that the human soul was nothing but blood when the man lives in his body, and that it would die when the man or the human body dies.

—At the time when you believed that the human soul dies with the body, did you believe that there was a hell or a heaven, or that souls were punished or rewarded after death?

During that time, I did not believe that there was a hell or a heaven, or any other world but the present; I also believed that souls would not be punished or rewarded in the other world.

—Why did you believe that the human soul was but the blood of the living man, and that it would die with the body?

Firstly, I believed it because I saw that when all the blood has left the body of a living thing, it dies. I believed it secondly because I didn't see anything come out of the men who were dying, except wind.

—During the time when you were in this believe about the mortality of the soul, did you believe that the souls of Saint Peter, Paul, and of the other saints and of all deceased men were dead?

Yes, except that I always believed in the existence of God, of the Virgin Mary, and of Saint John the Evangelist, for the Virgin Mary and Saint John neither died, nor were killed. But for the others, some died, and some were even killed.

—From the moment that you believed that human souls die with the body, did you believe that men would be resurrected or would live again after death?

I did not believe in the resurrection of human bodies, for I believed that just as the body is buried, the soul is also buried with it. And as I saw the human body rot, I believed that it could never live again.

—Did you have someone who taught this to you, did you learn it from someone?

No. I thought it over and believed it by myself.

—Do you believe that the soul of Jesus Christ, who died on the cross, is dead or with his body?

Yes, for, although God cannot die, Jesus Christ died, all the same. Therefore, although I believed that God has always been, I did not believe that Christ's soul lived and subsisted after his death.

—Do you believe then that Christ was resurrected?

Yes, and it is God who did that.

—Do you currently believe that the human soul is anything other than blood, that it does not die at the death of the body, that it is not buried with the body, that there is a hell and a heaven, where souls are punished or rewarded, and there will be a resurrection of all men, and that the soul of Christ did not die with his body?

Yes, and I have believed it since the last holiday of the Ascension of the Lord because at that time I heard tell that My Lord the Bishop of Pamiers wanted to carry out an investigation against me about it. I was afraid of My Lord Bishop because of that, and I changed my opinion after that time.

Confession of Aude, Wife of Guillaume Fauré, of Merviel (1318)

Year of our Lord 1318, the Saturday before the holiday of Saint Mary Magdalene (July 15th 1318). As it reached the knowledge of Revered Father in Christ My Lord Jacques, Bishop of Pamiers by divine Providence, that Aude, the daughter of the late Guillaume de Maucasal, of Lafage in the diocese of Mirepoix, and the spouse of Guillaume Fauré of Merviel, in the diocese of Pamiers, was suspected of heresy, and even strongly so, by reason of certain words and declarations uttered, as it has been said, by her in the presence of certain people against the Catholic Faith, and that moreover, as it has been said, this Aude was publicly slandered, My said Lord Bishop, wishing thus to take the responsibility of investigating the truth of these events with the said Aude and others, had her brought into his presence, wishing, as he has said, to investigate with her regarding the truth of these above-mentioned accusations.

My said Lord Bishop, having summoned the venerable and discrete persons My Lord Pierre du Verdier, Archdeacon of Majorque; master Hugues de Bilhères, appellate Judge of Pamiers; master Guillaume de Saint-Julien, jurist of Pamiers; master Bernard Gaubert, jurist of the diocese of Narbonne; and Guillaume de Pardailhan, public apostolic notary, to assist him in this investigation, physically swearing them in, ordered them under the faith of the oath in virtue of holy obedience to keep the secrets of this investigation and to bring him help and council, all things which they promised to do according to the conventions of law hereabove.

After which My said Lord Bishop one day asked the said Aude in the name of simple information if she had fallen into error on the articles of faith and the sacraments of the Church, and on which of them, as it had been reported to My Lord the Bishop. She responded immediately:

I believe that our Lord Jesus Christ was born of the flesh of the Holy Virgin Mary, and that he suffered, and was crucified for the human race, that he was resurrected, and ascended to heaven, and that he will return to judge the good people and the bad people; I profess and believe the faith and the sacraments as they are observed by the Holy Roman Catholic Church.

Interrogated subsequently, she nevertheless said:

About eight years ago, I contracted a marriage with Guillaume Fauré, my husband, and I was taken to his house in Merviel around All Saints'. As I had never received the body of the Lord, even though I was 17 or 18, I confessed my sins to a priest, but at the following Easter, I did not receive the Body of Christ. My husband asked me why and reproached me for it. I told him that in Lafage, where I am from originally, young men and women did not usually receive the body of Christ.

Then, the following year, again on Easter Day, I received the body of Christ. And as I had omitted to confess a serious sin that I had committed before marrying my said husband, I was completely terrified and upset because I had received the body of Christ without having confessed this sin.

Finally, after the following three years had gone by, I fell into the following error: I did believe that God was all-powerful in heaven, but I did not believe that God was in the sacrament on the altar, or that by virtue of the holy words spoken by the priest, it became the body of Christ. I was in this error and persisted in it without interruption until now that I have been taken to My Lord Bishop for it.

In the presence of which she said that the Holy Virgin Mary had inspired her in her heart to again believe that the flesh and the blood of Christ are the in sacrament on the altar, and that she believed that which a good Christian must believe.

—Did anyone, man or women, lead you to this error?

No, but it came to me, I believe, from the persistence of the sin I spoke of because I had not confessed it.

—Have you met any of the heretics or spoken with them?

No, to my knowledge, I have never seen a heretic.

—Have you confessed this error to a priest or to anyone else?

No, until recently, when I was gravely ill. In the grip of that sickness, I revealed this error to Guillaume Fauré, my husband, and to Ermengarde Garaud, of Merviel. And first to my husband in these terms: "Sir, how is it possible that I cannot believe in our Lord!" My husband said to me, scolding me: "What, damn woman, are you saying this in your right mind?" I responded: "Yes." My husband told me then that if I had not confessed, I had better, because otherwise I could not stay with him, and he would send me away.

—*When you said these words to your husband, were you in your right mind?*

Yes, and even now I remember all that very well.

In this same sickness, I sent for Ermengarde Garaud of Merviel. When she had arrived in my house, I told her: "Aunt, how can it be that I cannot believe in our Lord, and that I cannot believe that the host that is raised on the altar by the priest is the body of Christ?" Then Ermengarde reprimanded me strongly and suggested many things to encourage me to believe, among them, the following example:

"A long time ago, there was a Goodwoman who made a loaf of bread, which was then consecrated by the priest on the altar. This consecrated loaf was then made into the body of Christ. The priest used it to give Communion to the congregation. The woman who had made it began to laugh when she saw this. The priest noticed, and when she approached to receive the Communion, he told her, 'You, stay behind,' and asked her why she had laughed. She responded: 'Sir, the body of Christ can be made out of the loaf that I kneaded! That's what I'm laughing about.' Immediately the priest began to pray with the congregation so that God might work a miracle on it. Once this prayer was done, when he tried to give this consecrated bread to this woman, the consecrated bread that he offered to her for Communion looked like the finger of a child, and the consecrated wine in the Chalice like coagulated blood. Seeing this, the frightened woman began to pray. The priest and the congregation did the same. After this prayer, the woman was thus converted, believing that the body of Christ was in this sacrament, and this finger and this blood regained their first appearance of bread and wine as before, and this woman received Communion devoutly."

After that story, I said, "O aunt, your words are so good, and you have comforted me so much!"

—*Have you confessed this error to a priest?*

I don't remember.

After which, the Monday before the holiday of Saint Mary Magdalene, the 17th of July, 1318, the said Aude appeared in person before My said Lord Bishop in the Episcopal House of Pamiers, in the presence of My said lords Pierre du Verdier, Archdeacon of Majorque; master Barnard Gaubert, and me, Guillaume de Pardailhan, aforementioned notary, the assistants of My said Lord Bishop. Aude swore on the Gospel of God, touching it physically with her right hand, to tell the whole and pure truth and to respond truthfully to the questions that she would be posed. Interrogated about all the aforementioned events and about each one separately under oath, she persisted in her previous confession, except for the following corrections and rectifications, to the effect that during the first year that she came to her husband's house, she received the body of the Lord at Easter, and after having received it, she fell immediately, so she says, into the said error, because she had not confessed a serious sin that she had committed before having contracted marriage with her said husband.

And from that moment until last Saturday, she had persisted without interruption in that error. Not long ago, however, so she says, she had abandoned it and firmly believed all the articles of faith and all the sacraments of the Church, these having been explained to her one by one by My said Lord Bishop.

She also said that she had recently confessed this error in her illness, one month ago, to the priest of the Holy Cross and that he had imposed a certain penance on her; she herself offered, so she says, to accomplish this penance, and even an even bigger one at that; this priest estimated that that penance was too severe, so he imposed a certain gentler penance.

Diligently interrogated, she said nothing more of pertinence.

Next, the same Monday, My Lord the Bishop being assisted by the same, to supplement the inquiry and the obtaining of the truth on that which precedes, he had Ermengarde Garaud of Merviel brought before him, who swore on the Gospel of God physically touching it with her right hand to tell the pure and entire truth on that which precedes, in the principal capacity and as witness. She said and testified as follows:

That year, around the last day of Saint John the Baptist, I do not remember the day, Aude was very ill in her husband's house in Merviel. She sent someone to find me. When I arrived near her, she asked me if there was anyone else in the room. I told her there was not. She told me then that she wanted to confess something to me; I asked her what it was that she wanted to tell me, and she said: "Tia, how can it be that I cannot believe in God, and that when the body of Christ is raised on the altar, I can neither pray to it nor believe that it is the body of Christ?" I responded to her: "There are no traitors here, for this country and this house have always been pure from all evil and all heresy. Take care to not bring it from elsewhere and spoil our country." Aude said to me then: "Tia, what might I do to believe in God, and to believe that the body of Christ is really on the altar, when the priest performs the Elevation of the Host?"

I told her to believe strongly that the Lord and the body of Christ were really above the altar when the priest performs the Elevation, after he speaks the words prescribed by the Lord, and that she mustn't doubt it in the least. Otherwise she would be lost.

Later, she asked me again: "Tia, how do you pray to God, and what words do you say during the Elevation of the body of Christ, when the priest raises it above the altar?" I told her: "Personally, here is how I pray to God, and the prayer that I say: 'Oh Lord, true God and true man, all-powerful, born of the body of the Virgin Mary without sin, and accepted death and suffering on the tree of the True Cross, nailed by his hands and feet, his head crowned with thorns and his side pierced with a spear, shed blood and water, gave to redeem all from sin, Lord, grant me a single tear to cleanse my heart of all ugliness and of all sin. Into your hands, Lord, I commend my spirit; You have redeemed me, the one true Lord God.' "

Aude told me again: "Aunt, what words do you say, in the morning when you get out of bed?" I told her that I said the prayer: "Lord God Almighty, you protect my heart and soul; Lord, you keep me from sinning and from failing and from further sin, and from myself and from bearing false witness, and lead me to the True Faith." After which Aude said: "Aunt, you have comforted me well! You have such good words and you know how to pray to God so well! Without you, I was lost, and if I were to die, my body would rot in the Church of Saint Christopher, and devils would take away my soul." At that I repeated to her again: "No, traitoress, take care to believe strongly in God, and believe that the body of Christ is in the sacrament on the altar, and listen to the example that I am going to tell you.

(*And she recounted the example placed above in the confession of Aude.*)

And, continuing:

Then Aude began to strike her face with her hands and cried; she told me and asked me, for the love of God, to come see her often to comfort her.

As a result of the terror that I felt when she revealed her error to me, I fell very seriously ill, and I still am at the present time; during that illness, I revealed what she had told me to a priest, my lord Guillaume of the Infirmary, to clear my conscience, and so that no one could reproach me in any way. I believe that it was this priest who revealed me to My Lord Bishop.

(*Interrogated about herself, she said:*)

I strongly believe in all the articles of faith and sacraments of the Church as the Holy Church of God keeps and observes them. Never have I seen or heard any heretic or any suspect against the faith, nor have I frequented any of them.

—*Have you given this deposition for favor, affection, hatred, or fear?*

No, only because it is the truth.

—*Are you a relative of Aude?*

No.

And she said nothing more of any pertinence.

Testimony of Raimond Séguy de Tignac against Raimond De l'Aire, alias Bour de Tignac (1322)

The year as above (1322), the sixth of February, Raimond Séguy de Tignac, summoned by the Reverend Father in Christ, by the grace of God Bishop of Pamiers, as a witness against Raimond de l'Aire, alias Bour, de Tignac, in the matter of heresy, appearing judicially before him in the Chamber of the Bishopric of Pamiers, in the presence of religious persons Brothers Gaillard de Pomiès, Arnaud du Carla, O.P. of the convent of Pamiers, and myself, Guillaume Peyre-Barthe, notary of My said Lord the Bishop, as a witness for those convened, swore on the four holy Gospels of God to tell the pure and entire truth in the aforementioned matter of heresy, regarding himself as a defendant as well as others, living or dead, as a witness. This oath taken, he said, confessed, and testified as follows:

It could have been 10 or 12 years ago, I do not remember the time or the season, I was at the square of Tignac one day, and Guillaume Carrière, Vital de l'Aire, and Raimond de l'Aire, alias en Bour, were with me. This Raimond de l'Aire said to me, "Do you know how God [Christ] was made?" I said that I did not really know, but that I believed that he was made in a good way, to save us. And, addressing Raimond, I said, "And you? Do you know how [Christ] was made?" He responded, "I'm going to tell you: [Christ] was made by fucking," striking one hand against the other as he said so. I told him that he was speaking evil, and he deserved to be killed. He fell silent.

—*Did you agree with these heretical and blasphemous words of Raimond? Or were you approving of them, at that time or otherwise?*

No, to the contrary. They displeased me very much.

Around the same time, Raimond de l'Aire and I were on a street in Tignac, I do not remember the place, nor what we had begun speaking about, but we were talking together. He said that when the blood has left the man, there is no other soul for him. And I understood what he meant to say: that one has no soul other than blood. I told him that he was just speaking evil.

—*When Raimond said these words to you, was he in his right mind?*

Yes, as it appeared to me.

—*Did you believe these errors that you heard?*

No.

—*Why have you hidden these remarks of Raimond for so long?*

I confessed it in sacramental confession, a long time ago, to a priest in the church of Unac, and I believed that this was enough, and that it was not necessary to confess it to anyone else or to reveal these remarks to My Lord the Bishop or My Lord the Inquisitor.

And given that Raimond had testified against him to the effect that he himself had said similar things with him regarding the manner in which Christ was created, and that he denied it, the aforesaid Raimond de l'Aire was summoned and told in person, with assurances and under oath, that he had made these remarks against him. But he continued to persist in his denial. He was given a period to reflect on these remarks and the heretical remarks that he had intended to hold against the late Pierre Rauzy de Caussou, from this day until the following Monday.

Source: Fournier, Jacques. *The Fournier Register (1318—1325).* Original manuscript currently in the Vatican Library, Lat. MS. 4030. Previously unpublished English translations by Dareth Pray, assisted by Nancy P. Stork, Department of English, San Jose State University (2006 and 2011). Occitan prayer translations by Anastasia Makeeva and Tony Patricolo. Reprinted with permission from Dareth Pray.

THE INQUISITION

Inquisitio Haereticae Pravitatis ("the inquiry into heretical depravity"), commonly known as the Inquisition, was a series of campaigns by the Roman Catholic Church to eliminate unorthodox belief movements across Europe. Though heresy had always been dealt with severely by the Church, the 12th century marked the introduction of a new intensity and the use of new interrogation techniques, including torture and execution, to expose and punish heresy.

The first Inquisition began in 1184 in the south of France to halt the spreading influence of Catharism, a Christian sect whose unorthodox beliefs included the existence of two gods—one corporeal and evil, who had created the world, the other spiritual and good. Subsequent campaigns—including the Medieval, Spanish, Portuguese, and Roman Inquisitions—addressed the rise of heretic movements across Europe over the course of more than 600 years with the purpose of securing Roman Catholic dominance over the continent. The last of the tribunals, the Roman Inquisition, created to combat the spread of Protestantism, was essentially ended in the 18th century when Italian secular authorities began disputing the right of the Church to conduct trials.

AFTERWARD

Of the 578 individuals interrogated by Fournier, 5 heretics were sentenced to be burned at the stake. Most of the remainder were imprisoned or sentenced to wear a double yellow cross on their backs for the remainder of their lives as a mark of shame. Both Guillemette and Aude received this lesser punishment. The fate of Raimond de l'Aire is unknown.

Jacques Fournier went on to become a cardinal in 1327 and Pope Benedict XII in 1334. He died in 1342.

ASK YOURSELF

1. What was the primary motivation for this Inquisition? What was the intended purpose of the punishments?
2. Why do you think Fournier had transcripts made of his interrogations? Who was his intended audience?
3. How reliable do you think statements are when made in an interrogation of this kind?

TOPICS AND ACTIVITIES TO CONSIDER

- Stage a reenactment of one or more of the Fournier interrogations posted at the San Jose State University Web site: http://www.sjsu.edu/people/nancy.stork/courses/c4/. Include the testimony of friends, neighbors, and spouses included with each primary interview.
- The U.S. Senate's Army-McCarthy hearings in 1954 have been compared to the Inquisitions of the medieval period. Visit http://www.americanrhetoric.com/speeches/welch-mccarthy.html for a video and transcript of the most famous exchange of those hearings, then write an essay comparing and contrasting the McCarthy exchange with the Fournier interrogation of your choice.
- Prepare a research paper or debate on the reliability of eyewitness testimony.

Further Information

Given, James B. *Inquisition and Medieval Society*. New York: Cornell University Press, 2001.

Ladurie, Emmanuel LeRoy. *Montaillou: The Promised Land of Error*. New York: Vintage, 1979.

Secret Files of the Inquisition, a PBS documentary. Available at http://www.pbs.org/inquisition/.

Stark, Rodney. *For the Glory of God*. Princeton, NJ: Princeton University Press, 2003.

Web Site

Additional translations of Fournier interrogations at San Jose State University: http://www.sjsu.edu/people/nancy.stork/courses/c4/.

AGE OF ENLIGHTENMENT

9. A Clandestine Manuscript—Toland's (?) *Treatise of the Three Impostors* (ca. 1680s)

INTRODUCTION

One of the most fascinating and maddening documents in the history of unbelief is the *Traité des Trois Imposteurs* (*Treatise of the Three Impostors*). It began as a rumor, a mythical document attacking religious belief and assailing Moses, Jesus, and Muhammad equally as impostors and frauds who deceived their followers, and one that called the very existence of God into question.

As early as the 13th century, the legend of such a book's existence was whispered down the ages, even though none of the whisperers seemed to possess a copy or know where one might be found. The book's authorship was attributed variously to humanist and heretic Michael Servetus (1511–1553), French printer and skeptic Étienne Dolet (1509–1546), Islamic polymath Ibn Rusd (known in Europe as Averroes, 1126–1198), and even the powerful Holy Roman Emperor, Frederick II (1194–1250), among others. To further confuse things, a Latin document titled *De Tribus Impostoribus* had existed for centuries prior to the 18th century, though its content was completely unrelated.

Close textual scholarship has determined that the *Treatise of the Three Impostors* did not exist in physical form prior to the late 17th century, at which point someone—historians now point to the Irish philosopher and satirist John Toland (1670–1722) as the most likely suspect—brought the myth to life, creating an anonymous manuscript with the same title and purpose, and circulating it widely throughout Europe.

The English translation, privately printed and issued to "The Subscribers" under the pseudonym "Alcofribas Nasier, The Later," attempts (perhaps with tongue in cheek) to perpetuate the document's origin myth by placing "1230 A.D." beneath the title.

KEEP IN MIND AS YOU READ

Though the document was subtitled "In the Spirit of Spinoza," its conclusions are decidedly more atheistic than those of the 17th-century philosopher Baruch Spinoza. Though Spinoza is rightly considered one of the primary forebears of the Enlightenment, of the French Revolution, and of modern secularism, his views were essentially deistic (see Deism sidebar).

The translator/editor of the private 1904 English edition was apparently aware of the pitfalls of "creative translation" and offered this cautionary (yet self-excusing) preamble:

In Volney's *Lectures on History,* it is said; "If a work be translated it always receives a coloring which is more or less faint or is vivid according to the opinions and ability of the Translator." From an examination of other translations of this Treatise, I am assured that Volney's statement above has actuated and governed all who have been previously engaged with this work. I can assure the readers hereof, that the Treatise contained herein is a literal translation of the manuscript and the notes found therein, and no liberties have been taken with the text.

Document: The Three Impostors: L'Esprit de Spinosa *(1680s, English Translation 1904)*

CHAPTER I. OF GOD

I

However important it may be for all men to know the Truth, very few, nevertheless, are acquainted with it, because the majority are incapable of searching it themselves, or perhaps, do not wish the trouble. Thus we must not be astonished if the world is filled with vain and ridiculous opinions, and nothing is more capable of making them current than ignorance, which is the sole source of the false ideas that exist regarding the Divinity, the soul, and the spirit, and all the errors depending thereon.

The custom of being satisfied with born prejudice has prevailed, and by following this custom, mankind agrees in all things with persons interested in supporting stubbornly the opinions thus received, and who would speak otherwise did they not fear to destroy themselves.

II

What renders the evil without remedy, is, that after having established these silly ideas of God, they teach the people to receive them without examination. They take great care to impress them with aversion for philosophers, fearing that the Truth which they teach will alienate them. The errors in which the partisans of these absurdities have been plunged, have thrived so well that it is dangerous to combat them. It is too important for these impostors that the people remain in this gross and culpable ignorance than to allow them to be disabused. Thus they are constrained to disuse the truth, or to be sacrificed to the rage of false prophets and selfish souls.

III

If the people could comprehend the abyss in which this ignorance casts them, they would doubtless throw off the yoke of these venal minds, since it is impossible for Reason to act without immediately discovering the Truth. It is to prevent the good effects that would certainly follow, that they depict it as a monster incapable of inspiring any good sentiment, and however we may censure in general those who are not reasonable, we must nevertheless be persuaded that Truth is quite perverted. These enemies of Truth fall also into such perpetual contradictions that it is difficult to perceive what their real pretensions are. In the meanwhile it is true that Common Sense is the only rule that men should follow, and the world should not be prevented from making use of it. . . .

CHAPTER II. REASONS WHICH HAVE CAUSED MANKIND TO CREATE FOR THEMSELVES AN INVISIBLE BEING WHICH HAS BEEN COMMONLY CALLED GOD

I

Those who ignore physical causes have a natural fear born of doubt. Where there exists a power which to them is dark or unseen, from thence comes a desire to pretend the existence of invisible Beings, that is to say their own phantoms which they invoke in adversity, whom they praise in prosperity, and of whom in the end they make Gods. And as the visions of men go to extremes, must we be astonished if there are created an innumerable quantity of Divinities? It is the same perceptible fear of invisible powers which has been the origin of Religions, that each forms to his fashion. Many individuals to whom it was important that mankind should possess such fancies, have not scrupled to encourage mankind in such beliefs, and they have made it their law until they have prevailed upon the people to blindly obey them by the fear of the future.

II

The Gods having thus been invented, it is easy to imagine that they resembled man, and who, like them, created everything for some purpose, for they unanimously agree that God has made nothing except for man, and reciprocally that man is made only for God. [Man is the noblest work of God—but nobody ever said so but man. —**Fra Elbertus**.] This conclusion being general, we can see why man has so thoroughly accepted it, and know for that reason that they have taken occasion to create false ideas of good and evil, merit and sin, praise and blame, order and confusion, beauty and deformity— and similar qualities.

> **Fra Elbertus:** a pen name of American writer and satirist Elbert Green Hubbard (1856–1915)

III

It should be agreed that all men are born in profound ignorance, and that the only thing natural to them is a desire to discover what may be useful and proper, and evade what may be inexpedient to them. Thence it follows first, that we believe that to be free it suffices to feel personally that one can wish and desire without being annoyed by the causes which dispose us to wish and desire, because we do not know them. Second, it consequently occurs that men are contented to do nothing but for one object, that is to say, for that object which is preferable above all, and that is why they have a desire only to know the final result of their action, imagining that after discovering this they have no reason to doubt anything. Now as they find in and about themselves many means of procuring what they desire: having, for example, ears to hear, eyes to see, animals to nourish, a sun to give light, they have formed this reasoning, that there is nothing in nature, which was not made for them, and of which they may dispose and enjoy. Then reflecting that they did not make this world, they believe it to be a well-founded proposition to imagine a Supreme Being who has made it for them such as it is, for after satisfying themselves that they could not have made it, they conclude that it was the work of one or several Gods who intended it for the use and pleasure of man alone. On the other hand, the nature of the Gods whom man has admitted, being unknown, they have concluded in their own minds that these Gods susceptible of the same passions as men, have made the earth only for them, and that man to them was extremely precious. But as each one has different inclinations it became proper to adore God according to the humor of each, to attract his blessings and to cause Him to make all Nature subject to his desires.

IV

By this method this precedent becomes Superstition, and it is implanted so that the grossest natures are believed capable of penetrating the doctrine of final causes as if they had perfect knowledge. Thus in place of showing that nature has made nothing in vain, they show that God and Nature dream as well as men, and that they may not be accused of doubting things, let us see how they have put forth their false reasoning on this subject.

Experience causing them to see a myriad of inconveniences marring the pleasure of life, such as storms, earthquakes, sickness, famine and thirst, they draw the conclusion that nature has not been made for them alone. They attribute all these evils to the wrath of the Gods, who are vexed by the offences of man, and they cannot be disabused of these ideas by the daily instances which should prove to them that blessings and evils have been always common to the wicked and the good, and they will not agree to a proposition so plain and perceptible.

The reason for that is, it is more easy to remain in ignorance than to abolish a belief established for many centuries and introduce something more probable.

V

This precedent has caused another, which is the belief that the judgments of God were incomprehensible, and that for this reason, the knowledge of truth is beyond the human mind; and mankind would still dwell in error were it not that mathematics and several other sciences had destroyed these prejudices.

VI

By this it may be seen that Nature or God does not propose any end, and that all final causes are but human fictions. A long lecture is not necessary since this doctrine takes away from God the perfection ascribed to him, and this is how it may be proved. If God acted for a result, either for himself or another, he desires what he has not, and we must allow that there are times when God has not the wherewith to act; he has merely desired it and that only creates an impotent God. To omit nothing that may be applied to this reasoning, let us oppose it with those of a contrary nature. If, for example, a stone falls on a person and kills him, it is well known they say, that the stone fell with the design of killing the man, and that could only happen by the will of God. If you reply that the wind caused the stone to drop at the moment the man passed, they will ask why the man should have passed precisely at the time when the wind moved the stone. If you say that the wind was so severe that the sea was also troubled since the day before while there appeared to be no agitation in the air, and the man having been invited to dine with a friend, went to keep his appointment. Again they ask, for the man never got there, why he should be the guest of his friend at this time more than another, adding questions after questions, finally avowing that it was but the will of God, (which is a true "**asses' bridge**") and the cause of this misfortune.

> **asse's bridge (pons asinorum):** in this usage, an awkward or invalid transition between an argument and conclusion

Again when they note the symmetry of the human body, they stand in admiration and conclude how ignorant they are of the causes of a thing which to them appears so marvelous, that it is a supernatural work, in which the causes known to us could have no part.

Thence it comes that those who desire to know the real cause of supposed miracles and penetrate like true scholars into their natural causes without amusing themselves with the prejudice of the ignorant, it happens that the true scholar passes for impious and heretical by the malice of those whom the vulgar recognize as the expounders of Nature and of God. These mercenary individuals do not question the ignorance which holds the people in astonishment, upon whom they subsist and who preserve their credit.

VII

Mankind being thus of the ridiculous opinion that all they see is made for themselves, have made it a religious duty to apply it to their interest, and of judging the price of things by the profit they gain. Thence proceed the ideas they have formed of good and evil, of order and confusion, of heat and cold, of beauty and ugliness, which serve to explain to them the nature of things, which in the end are not what they imagine. Because they pride themselves in having free will they judge themselves capable of deciding between Praise and blame, sin and merit, calling everything good which redounds to their profit and which concerns divine worship, and to the contrary denominate as evil that which agrees with neither. Because the ignorant are not capable of judging what may be a little abstruse, and having no idea of things only by the aid of imagination which they consider understanding, these folk who know not what represents order in the world believe all that they imagine. Man being inclined in such a manner that they think things well or ill ordered as they have the facility or trouble to conclude when good sense would teach differently. Some are more pleased to be weary of the means of investigation, being satisfied to remain as they are, preferring order to confusion, as if order was another thing than a pure effect of the imagination of man, so that when it is said that God has made everything in order, it is recognizing that he has that faculty of imagination as well as man. If it was not so, perhaps to favor human imagination they pretend that God created this world in the easiest manner imaginable, although there are an hundred things far above the force of imagination, and an infinity which may be thrown into disorder by reason of weakness. . . .

CHAPTER XIV. OF SPIRITS WHICH ARE CALLED DEMONS
VII

As Jesus Christ was a Jew, and consequently imbued with these silly opinions [about the existence of demons], we read everywhere in the Gospels, and in the writings of his Disciples, of the Devil, of Satan and Hell as if they were something real and effective. While it is true, as we have shown, that there is nothing more imaginary, and when what we have said is not sufficient to prove it, but two words will suffice to convince the most obstinate. All Christians agree unanimously that God is the first principle and the foundation of all things, that he has created and preserves them, and without his support they would fall into nothingness. Following this principle it is certain that God must have created what is called the Devil, and Satan, as well as the rest, and if he has created both good and evil, why not all the balance, and if by this principle all evil exists, it can only be by the intervention of God.

Now can one conceive that God would maintain a creature, not only who curses him unceasingly, and who mortally hates him, but even who endeavors to corrupt his friends, to have the pleasure of being cursed by a multitude of mouths. How can we comprehend that God should preserve the Devil to have him do his worst to dethrone him if he could, and to alienate from his service his elect and his favorites? What would be the object of God in such conduct? Now what can we say in speaking of the Devil and Hell. If God does all, and nothing can be done without him how does it happen that the Devil hates him, curses him, and takes away his friends? Now he is either agreeable, or he is not. If he is agreeable, it is certain that the Devil in cursing him only does what he should, since he can only do what God wills. Consequently, it is not the Devil, but God in person who curses himself; a situation to my idea more absurd than ever.

If it is not in accord with his will then it is not true that he is all powerful. Thus there are two principles, one of Good, the other of Evil, one which causes one thing and the other that does quite the contrary. To what does this reasoning lead us? To avow without contradiction that there is no God such as is conceived, nor Devil, nor Soul, nor Paradise, such as has been depicted, and that the Theologians, that is to say, those who relate fables for truth, are persons of bad faith who maliciously abuse the credulity of the ignorant by telling them what

---

CLANDESTINA

The first European texts written from an explicitly atheistic perspective began appearing in the mid-17th century. Referred to collectively as the "clandestina" or clandestine documents, the texts were mostly handwritten, mostly in French, and mostly circulated anonymously. In *Radical Enlightenment*, Jonathan Israel notes that the main audience (and suspected authors) of the clandestina were "members of the nobility . . . army officers, diplomats, and [other] officials . . . mixed with a sprinkling of medical men and other highly literate persons" who bought, read, and discussed the literature in secret.

The first significant clandestine manuscript in Europe was *Theophrastus redivivus*, a collection of skeptical, atheist, and agnostic writings from antiquity to the early modern period that made its first appearance in the 1650s. In an introduction, the compiler of *Theophrastus* made the claim that even though they sometimes hid their true opinions, every great philosopher in every era has been an atheist.

Theophrastus was followed by another anonymous atheist tract, *Symbolum sapientiae* ("The Creed of Wisdom"), in or around 1700. The two documents represented the earliest books written from an explicitly atheistic perspective.

These and over 200 similar anonymous manuscripts were circulated mainly in handwritten form and consequently escaped censorship. Most of the main atheist arguments of the French Enlightenment are anticipated in the clandestina.

they please, as if the people were capable of nothing but chimera or who should be fed with insipid food in which is found only emptiness, nothingness and folly, and not a grain of the salt of truth and wisdom. Centuries have passed, one after the other, in which mankind has been infatuated by these absurd imaginations which have been combatted; but during all the period there have also been found sincere minds who have written against the injustice of the Doctors in Tiaras, Mitres and Gowns, who have kept mankind in such deplorable blindness which seems to increase every day.

Source: Briggs, Samuel, ed. *The three impostors : translated (with notes and comments) from a French manuscript of the work written in 1716* [*sic*]. Cleveland, OH: Private print edition, 1904. Reproduced online by the Secular Web, http://www.infidels.org.

AFTERWARD

The Treatise of the Three Impostors became the most widely read of the clandestine documents of the 17th and 18th centuries (see Clandestina sidebar), and along with the others helped to set the ideological stage for the *philosophes* of the French Revolution.

ASK YOURSELF

Historian Jonathan Israel has suggested that members of the upper classes would have been the main readers, owners, and discussers of clandestine documents during this time. What might account for this?

TOPICS AND ACTIVITIES TO CONSIDER

Choose an era in history with which you are familiar. Write a brief essay on a topic that would have been scandalous or even illegal during the time—a criticism of the Roman Emperor, Nero, in 65 CE, for example, or of Hitler in 1942, or an abolitionist tract in the American South shortly before the Civil War. How would you get your clandestine document into the hands of sympathetic readers? How would you meet to discuss ways to put the ideas into action?

Further Information

Israel, Jonathan. *Radical Enlightenment: Philosophy and the Making of Modernity 1650–1750*. Oxford: Oxford University Press, 2001.

Web Site

Full text of *Three Impostors* at the Secular Web: http://www.infidels.org/library/historical/unknown/three_impostors.html.

10. "War Song of an Atheist Priest"—The *Testament* of Jean Meslier (1729)

INTRODUCTION

What follows is an excerpt from one of the most extraordinary documents in the history of unbelief: a heartfelt and complete renunciation of religious belief by a Catholic priest in 18th-century France.

When Jean Meslier became the parish priest in the French village of Étrépigny in 1689, the nation had yet to fully recover from nearly a century of religious warfare between Catholics and Protestants. Meslier assumed his clerical duties at age 25—"to please my parents," he says—but "hardly ever had the slightest belief" in the religion in which he spent 40 years as a curate. Though he never left the pulpit physically, the document below makes it clear that he had left mentally and emotionally before he even entered it.

In 1719, as he entered what would be the final decade of his life, Meslier began to write an astonishing document in secret. Titled simply *Memoir of the Thoughts and Sentiments of Jean Meslier*, it was in the book's subtitle that his subject was revealed: *Clear and Evident Demonstrations of the Vanity and Falsity of All the Religions of the World.*

Working alone every night in his vicarage, a village priest in 18th-century France was writing what would become the first book-length articulation of the atheist position by a named author in modern times.

And decisively atheistic it is. Despite an attempt by the philosopher Voltaire to mischaracterize Meslier as a believer in the deistic God (see Afterward) by omitting all references to the author's atheism, the original text is extraordinarily clear, including the phrase "there is no God" four times, as well as hundreds of pages renouncing and refuting all grounds for religious belief.

The lengthy arguments themselves—93 chapters in all—are impossible to summarize in this anthology and so must be sought out in the new translation cited at the end of this section. This excerpt is intended to capture Meslier's general opinions, and to illuminate for the reader the incredible situation in which he found himself and the way in which he responded to it.

KEEP IN MIND AS YOU READ

Meslier necessarily wrote his *Testament* in secret, as blasphemy was still punishable by death in France during his lifetime. Still, Meslier, wracked with guilt over his part in their deception, sought to ensure that his parishioners would have access to his thoughts by registering the existence of the manuscript with the parish clerks and giving instructions to deliver the copies to the people of the parish immediately upon his death.

Document: Jean Meslier, Memoir of the Thoughts and Sentiments of Jean Meslier *(1729)*

My dear friends, seeing that I would not be permitted and the consequences would be too dangerous and distressing for me to tell you openly during my lifetime what I think about the conduct of the government of men and about their religions and morals, I have decided, at least, to tell you after my death. I would much rather say these things aloud to you before I die, if I saw the end of my days approaching and still had the free use of speech and judgment, but since in those final days or moments I may not have the presence of mind that would be necessary to tell you what I think, I am going to tell you now in writing and at the same time give you clear and convincing proofs of everything I have to say in order to try to open your eyes. . . .

Perhaps you will think, my dear friends, that with such a large number of false religions in the world, my intention is to make an exception for the Christian, Apostolic, and Roman religion that we profess and that we call the only one that teaches the truth, the only one that knows and properly worships the true God, and the only one that leads men on the true path to salvation and eternal happiness.

But, do not fool yourselves, my dear friends, open your eyes to this and in general to everything that your pious morons or mocking, self-interested priests and scholars are eager to tell you and make you believe on the false pretext of the infallible certainty of their so-called holy and divine religion. You are no less seduced and abused than those who are the most seduced and most abused; you are no less in error than those who are most deeply plunged. Your religion is no less vain or superstitious than any other; it is no less false in its principles, no less ridiculous or absurd in its dogma and maxims. You are no less idolatrous than those whom you yourselves accuse and condemn of idolatry; the idols of pagans are different only in name and shape. In short, everything that your priests and scholars preach to you with so much eloquence concerning the grandeur, excellence, and sanctity of the mysteries they make you worship, everything they tell you so seriously about the certainty of their so-called miracles, and everything they recite with so much zeal and assurance concerning the grandeur of the rewards of heaven and the terrible punishments of hell, are, in fact, only illusions, errors, lies, fictions, and impostures invented at first by the shrewd and crafty politicians, continued by the seducers and imposters, then received and blindly believed by the ignorant and vulgar people, and finally maintained by the rulers and sovereigns of the earth who encourage the abuses, errors, superstitions, and impostures and even authorize them by their laws in order to keep a tight rein on the community of men and make them do whatever they want. . . .

You will say, perhaps that it is partly against myself that I am speaking since I myself am in the ranks of those whom I call here the greatest abusers of the people. It is true that I am speaking against my profession, but not at all against the truth and not at all against my inclination or my own sentiments. For as I have hardly ever had the slightest belief or hardly been inclined to bigotry and superstition and I have never been so stupid as to think highly of the mysterious delusions of religion, so I have never had the inclination to do my duties or even speak of them to my advantage or with honor. On the contrary, I would always rather have openly shown the contempt I had, if it had been permitted to me . . .

I do not believe, dear friends, that I have ever given you reason to think that I shared these sentiments. On the contrary, you could have noticed several times that I was completely opposed to them and I was extremely sensitive to your pains. You could have noticed that I was not very attached to that pious **lucre** of the payments of my ministry, since I often neglected and abandoned it when I could have profited from it, and I never canvassed for **benefices** or asked for masses and offerings. I certainly would always have taken more pleasure in giving than in receiving, if I had had the means to follow my inclination. . . .

> **Lucre:** monetary gain, especially by shameful means
> **Benefice:** a revenue or tax used to support a parish priest or minister

I was, nevertheless, obligated to teach you about your religion and to talk to you about it sometimes, at least, for better or for worse, to do the false duty that I committed myself to as priest of your parish. And ever since then I have seen myself in this annoying obligation of acting and speaking entirely against my own sentiments; I have had the displeasure of keeping you in the stupid errors, the vain superstitions, and the idolatries that I hated, condemned, and detested to the core.

But I declare to you that I was never without pain and extreme loathing for what I was doing. That is also why I hated all the vain functions of my ministry, and particularly all the idolatrous and superstitious celebrations of masses, and the vain and ridiculous administrations of sacraments that I had to do for you. I cursed them thousands of times to the core when I had to do them, and particularly when I had to do them with a little more attention and solemnity than normal when I saw you come to your churches with a little more devotion to attend some vain solemnities or to hear with a little more devotion what they make you believe to be the word of God, it seemed to me that I was abusing your good faith much more shamefully and that I was, consequently, much more worthy of reproach and condemnation, which increased my hatred of these kinds of ceremonies . . . so much that I was hundreds and hundreds of times on the point of indiscreetly bursting out with indignation, almost not able to hide my resentment any longer or keep to myself the indignation I felt. However, I did, in a way, keep it to myself, and I struggled to keep it to myself to the end of my days, not wanting to expose myself during my life to the indignation of the priests or to the cruelty of the tyrants who, it seemed to me, would not have found cruel enough tortures to punish me for such so-called recklessness.

I am pleased to die, my dear friends, as peacefully as I lived. Moreover, having never given you reason to want to harm me or to enjoy any harm that might come to me, I also do not believe that you would be happy to see me persecuted and tyrannized for this matter. That is why I resolved to keep silent to the end of my days.

But as this reason forces me to keep silent at present, I will at least, in a way, speak to you after my death. It is with this in mind that I began to write: to open your eyes, as I said, as far as it is in my power, to all the errors, abuses, and superstitions with which you have been raised and fed, and that you have, so to speak, been suckling on. . . .

Let the priests, preachers, scholars, and all the instigators of such lies, errors, and impostures be scandalized and angered as much as they want after my death; let them treat me, if they want, like an impious apostate, like a blasphemer and an atheist; let them insult me and curse me as they want. I do not really care since it will not bother me in the least.

Likewise, let them do what they want with my body: let them tear it apart, cut it to pieces, roast it or fricassee it and then eat it, if they want, in whatever sauce they want, it will not trouble me at all. I will be entirely out of their reach; nothing will be able to frighten me.

After this introduction, the heart of the book—fully 93 chapters—examines nearly every imaginable aspect of religious belief and practice: the exaltation of ancient emperors to god status, the connection between politics and religion, religion as the cause of war and division, questionable historical claims, contradictions in the Gospels, the character of Jesus Christ, scriptural immorality, the doctrines of the Trinity and transubstantiation, the contradiction of wealthy clergy vis-à-vis the example of Christ, even specific counterarguments to major theistic treatises of the day. It is an astonishing accomplishment, its breadth and depth made all the more impressive by the fact that it was done in isolation, as philosopher Michel Onfray notes, "[w]ithout friends, without sophisticated conversations, without libraries, salons, or correspondence."

We conclude with some of Meslier's own closing thoughts.

All these arguments are as conclusive as they can be: it is enough just to pay a little attention to see the evidence. And so it is clearly demonstrated . . . that all of the religions of the world are . . . only human inventions. . . .

I would like to be able to make my voice heard from one end of the kingdom to the other, or rather from one extremity of the earth to the other. I would cry out with all my force: O men, you are crazy! You are crazy to let yourselves be led in this way and to believe so blindly in so many stupidities. . . .

Your salvation is in your hands. Your deliverance will depend only on if you can understand everything well. You have all the means and all the forces necessary to set yourselves free and make slaves of your tyrants. For, as powerful and formidable as they may be, your tyrants have no power over you without you yourselves. . . .

You do not need these people. You will manage without them easily, but they will not be able to manage without you at all . . . Unite, then, in the same sentiments to deliver yourselves from this hateful and insupportable yoke of their tyrannical rule, as well as from the vain and superstitious practices of their false religions. . . .

If everyone who knew as well as me or rather who knew even much better than me the vanity of human things, the errors and impostures of religions, the abuses and injustices of the government of men would say at least at the end of their days what they thought: if they would reproach, condemn, and curse them at least before they die at least as much as they deserve to be reproached, condemned, and cursed, you would soon see the world change face. You would soon mock all the errors and all the vain and superstitious practices of religions and you would soon see all that haughty grandeur and proud fierceness of tyrants fall. . . .

After this, let people think, judge, say, and do whatever they want in the world; I do not really care.

Let men adapt themselves and be governed as they want, let them be wise or crazy, let them be good or vicious, let them say or do with me whatever they want after my death: I really do not care in the least.

I already take almost no part in what is done in the world. The dead, whom I am about to join, no longer worry about anything, they no longer take part in anything, and they no longer care about anything.

So, I will finish this with nothing.

I am hardly more than nothing and soon I will be nothing.

Source: From Jean Meslier, *Testament: Memoir of the Thoughts and Sentiments of Jean Meslier.* Translated by Michael Shreve. Amherst, NY: Prometheus Books, 2009, 27, 35–36, 39–44, 577–78, 585, 590, 593. English-language translation copyright © 2009 by Michael Shreve. Used with permission of the publisher, http://www.prometheusbooks.com.

AFTERWARD

That Meslier's *Testament* was discovered almost immediately upon his death, and that it displeased the ecclesiastical authorities, is evidenced by the strange circumstances of his burial. Rather than being interred in the churchyard, he was buried in an unmarked grave in an unknown location—possibly (guesses philosopher Onfray, in his 2009 preface to the English translation of Meslier's book) the yard of the vicarage in which he lived, with "no tombstone, no plaque or sign, no trace, not even a notice in the parish register."

Meslier left behind four handwritten copies of the *Testament*, of which countless abridged extracts were secretly copied out and circulated. In 1762, Voltaire published his own extract, selectively culling passages to make it appear that Meslier was not an atheist —something Voltaire detested—but a deist like himself (see Deism sidebar). Voltaire concluded his version by saying it was the "testimony of a priest who asks forgiveness of God."

Despite this falsification of Meslier's work, it was Voltaire's abridgement that deeply influenced the French Enlightenment *philosophes*, who subsequently laid the philosophical groundwork for the French Revolution.

ASK YOURSELF

1. Meslier believed that he could do more good for the people of his parish by continuing in his role as priest despite his convictions that religion was false. Do you agree? If you were in his position, do you think you would have made the same choice?

2. Michel Onfray suggests in the Preface that anger comes through as the dominant emotion of the work. The same has been said of atheist writers in the 21st century. What might account for the anger in voices such as Meslier's?
3. If you were a member of Meslier's parish, how might you have felt upon learning after his death that he never believed in God nor considered religion a force for good?

TOPICS AND ACTIVITIES TO CONSIDER

Blasphemy remains a crime in many countries around the world with punishments ranging from fines to death. Pakistani law prohibits blasphemy against any "recognized" religion, though it has been used only in protection of Islam. At this writing, several European countries have enacted or are considering new or enhanced laws against what is commonly called "religious hate speech." An existing 1937 blasphemy statute in Ireland was strengthened in 2010 by a new law threatening anyone who "publishes or utters matter that is grossly abusive or insulting in relation to matters held sacred by any religion, thereby causing outrage among a substantial number of the adherents of that religion" with a fine of up to 25,000 euros ($35,000). A group called Atheist Ireland immediately posted 25 quotes critical of religion online to challenge the new law. At this writing, nearly 18 months later, no action has been taken against the group.

Six U.S. states have existing laws against blasphemy (Massachusetts, Michigan, Oklahoma, South Carolina, Wyoming, and Pennsylvania), though when challenged, federal courts have consistently struck down such laws as unconstitutional abridgements of free expression.

Meslier was convinced that publishing his *Testament* during his 18th-century lifetime would have been "dangerous and distressing," and the reaction of authorities after his death seems to support this. How would the book's reception have been different in 21st-century Ireland? Pakistan? Pennsylvania?

Further Information

New Humanist article "Thinker: Jean Meslier," http://newhumanist.org.uk/1425/thinker-jean-meslier.

Web Site

Atheist Ireland challenges new blasphemy law: http://www.atheist.ie/campaigns/blasphemy-law/.

11. ATHEISM IN PREREVOLUTIONARY FRANCE— BARON D'HOLBACH'S *GOOD SENSE* (1772)

INTRODUCTION

The Enlightenment was an intellectual period devoted to the promotion of reason as the most reliable means to both truth and social justice. Centered in 18th-century Europe, the period was defined by the works of such thinkers as Voltaire, Diderot, Hobbes, Locke, Hume, Kant, and Rousseau, who created a philosophical framework that challenged orthodoxy and traditional authority, including the authority and doctrines of the Christian church, and advocated reason and science as the best means of achieving a better world.

Paul-Henri Thiry, better known as Baron d'Holbach (1723–1789), was among the most influential Enlightenment philosophers of the age. Born in Germany but raised and educated in Paris, d'Holbach created a *salon* in Paris, a place for the meeting of minds and exchange of ideas. Many members of d'Holbach's *salon*, including the baron himself, contributed extensive articles to the *Encyclopédie*, a groundbreaking 35-volume reference work of over 70,000 articles by scores of contributors—designed (according to its primary editor, the atheist philosopher Denis Diderot) "to change the way people think."

D'Holbach published what was to become his best-known and most influential work, *The System of Nature*, under a pseudonym. The work denied the existence of God and described the universe as entirely materialistic and subject to comprehensible physical laws. In addition to seeking an accurate view of reality, d'Holbach's critique of Christian religion had a moral purpose: he saw the Church as an impediment to human happiness and flourishing. The ideas in the *System* were published in 1772 in a shorter, more accessible form as *Good Sense, or Natural Ideas Opposed to Supernatural*, an excerpt of which appears below.

KEEP IN MIND AS YOU READ

Even in France during the Enlightenment, d'Holbach found it prudent to publish his atheistic writings under a false name. *The System of Nature* drew stinging rebuttals from theologians, from the deistic Voltaire, and even from Frederick the Great of Prussia. The Catholic Church threatened to withdraw financial support from the French monarchy unless the book was suppressed.

D'Holbach himself had a reputation for generosity and kindness, including the anonymous financial support of many friends and projects. The Christian philosopher

Jean-Jacques Rousseau is believed to have modeled the character of Jean de Wolmar, an atheist of exemplary moral character, on Baron d'Holbach.

Document: Thiry, Paul-Henri, Baron d'Holbach, Good Sense, or Natural Ideas Opposed to Supernatural (Bon Sens, on idées naturelles opposees aux idées surnaturelles) (1772)

Author's Preface

When we examine the opinions of men, we find that nothing is more uncommon than common sense; or, in other words, they lack judgment to discover plain truths, or to reject absurdities, and palpable contradictions. We have an example of this in Theology, a system revered in all countries by a great number of men; an object regarded by them as most important, and indispensable to happiness. An examination of the principles upon which this pretended system is founded, forces us to acknowledge, that these principles are only suppositions, imagined by ignorance, propagated by enthusiasm or knavery, adopted by timid credulity, preserved by custom which never reasons, and revered solely because not understood.

In a word, whoever uses common sense upon religious opinions, and will bestow on this inquiry the attention that is commonly given to most subjects, will easily perceive that Religion is a mere castle in the air. Theology is ignorance of natural causes; a tissue of fallacies and contradictions. In every country, it presents romances void of probability, the hero of which is composed of impossible qualities. His name, exciting fear in all minds, is only a vague word, to which, men affix ideas or qualities, which are either contradicted by facts, or inconsistent.

Notions of this being, or rather, *the word* by which he is designated, would be a matter of indifference, if it did not cause innumerable ravages in the world. But men, prepossessed with the opinion that this phantom is a reality of the greatest interest, instead of concluding wisely from its incomprehensibility, that they are not bound to regard it, infer on the contrary, that they must contemplate it, without ceasing, and never lose sight of it. Their invincible ignorance, upon this subject, irritates their curiosity; instead of putting them upon guard against their imagination, this ignorance renders them decisive, dogmatic, imperious, and even exasperates them against all, who oppose doubts to the reveries which they have begotten.

What perplexity arises, when it is required to solve an insolvable problem; unceasing meditation upon an object, impossible to understand, but in which however he thinks himself much concerned, cannot but excite man, and produce a fever in his brain. Let interest, vanity, and ambition, co-operate ever so little with this unfortunate turn of mind, and society must necessarily be disturbed. This is the reason that so many nations have often been the scene of extravagances of senseless visionaries, who, believing their empty speculations to be eternal truths, and publishing them as such, have kindled the zeal of princes and their subjects, and made them take up arms for opinions, represented to them as essential to the glory of the Deity. In all parts of our globe, fanatics have cut each other's throats, publicly burnt each other, committed without a scruple and even as a duty, the greatest crimes, and shed torrents of blood. For what? To strengthen, support, or propagate the impertinent conjectures of some enthusiasts, or to give validity to the cheats of impostors, in the name of a being, who exists only in their imagination, and who has made himself known only by the ravages, disputes, and follies, he has caused.

Savage and furious nations, perpetually at war, adore, under divers names, some God, conformable to their ideas, that is to say, cruel, carnivorous, selfish, blood-thirsty. We find, in all the religions, "a God of armies," a "jealous God," an "avenging God," a "destroying God," a "God," who is pleased with carnage, and whom his worshippers consider it a duty to serve. Lambs, bulls, children, men, and women, are sacrificed to him. Zealous servants of this barbarous God think themselves obliged even to offer up themselves as a sacrifice to him. Madmen may everywhere be seen, who, after meditating upon their terrible God, imagine that to please him they must inflict on themselves, the most exquisite torments. The gloomy ideas formed of the deity, far from consoling them, have every where disquieted their minds, and prejudiced follies destructive to happiness.

How could the human mind progress, while tormented with frightful phantoms, and guided by men, interested in perpetuating its ignorance and fears? Man has been forced to vegetate in his primitive stupidity: he has been taught stories about invisible powers upon whom his happiness was supposed to depend. Occupied solely by his fears, and by unintelligible reveries, he has always been at the mercy of priests, who have reserved to themselves the right of thinking for him, and of directing his actions.

Thus, man has remained a slave without courage, fearing to reason, and unable to extricate himself from the labyrinth, in which he has been wandering. He believes himself forced under the yoke of his gods, known to him only by the fabulous accounts given by his ministers, who, after binding each unhappy mortal in the chains of prejudice, remain his masters, or else abandon him defenceless to the absolute power of tyrants, no less terrible than the gods, of whom they are the representatives.

Oppressed by the double yoke of spiritual and temporal power, it has been impossible for the people to be happy. Religion became sacred, and men have had no other Morality, than what their legislators and priests brought from the unknown regions of heaven. The human mind, confused by theological opinions, ceased to know its own powers, mistrusted experience, feared truth and disdained reason, in order to follow authority. Man has been a mere machine in the hands of tyrants and priests. Always treated as a slave, man has contracted the vices of slavery.

Such are the true causes of the corruption of morals. Ignorance and servitude are calculated to make men wicked and unhappy. Knowledge, Reason, and Liberty, can alone reform and make men happier. But every thing conspires to blind them, and to confirm their errors. Priests cheat them, tyrants corrupt and enslave them. Tyranny ever was, and ever will be, the true cause of man's depravity, and also of his calamities. Almost always fascinated by religious fiction, poor mortals turn not their eyes to the natural and obvious causes of their misery; but attribute their vices to the imperfection of their natures, and their unhappiness to the anger of the gods. They offer to heaven vows, sacrifices, and presents, to obtain the end of sufferings, which in reality, are attributable only to the negligence, ignorance, and perversity of their guides, to the folly of their customs, and above all, to the general want of knowledge. Let men's minds be filled with true ideas; let their reason be cultivated; and there will be no need of opposing to the passions, such a feeble barrier, as the fear of gods. Men will be good, when they are well instructed; and when they are despised for evil, or justly rewarded for good, which they do to their fellow citizens.

In vain should we attempt to cure men of their vices, unless we begin by curing them of their prejudices. It is only by showing them the truth, that they will perceive their true interests, and the real motives that ought to incline them to do good. Instructors have long enough fixed men's eyes upon heaven; let them now turn them upon earth. An incomprehensible theology, ridiculous fables, impenetrable mysteries, puerile ceremonies, are to be no longer endured. Let the human mind apply itself to what is natural, to intelligible objects, truth, and useful knowledge.

Does it not suffice to annihilate religious prejudice, to shew, that what is inconceivable to man, cannot be good for him? Does it require any thing, but plain common sense, to perceive, that a being, incompatible with the most evident notions—that a cause continually opposed to the effects which we attribute to it—that a being, of whom we can say nothing, without falling into contradiction—that a being, who, far from explaining the enigmas of the universe, only makes them more inexplicable—that a being, whom for so many ages men have vainly addressed to obtain their happiness, and the end of sufferings—does it require, I say, any thing but plain, good sense, to perceive—that the idea of such a being is an idea without model, and that he himself is merely a phantom of the imagination? Is any thing necessary but good sense to perceive, at least, that it is folly and madness for men to hate and damn one another about unintelligible opinions concerning a being of this kind? In short, does not every thing prove, that Morality and Virtue are totally incompatible with the notions of a God, whom his ministers and interpreters have described, in every country, as the most capricious, unjust, and cruel of tyrants, whose pretended will, however, must serve as law and rule the inhabitants of the earth?

To discover the true principles of Morality, men have no need of theology, of revelation, or of gods: They have need only of good sense. They have only to commune with themselves, to reflect upon their own nature, to consider the objects of society, and of the individuals, who compose it; and they will easily perceive, that virtue is advantageous, and vice disadvantageous to themselves. Let us persuade men to be just, beneficent, moderate, sociable; not because such conduct is demanded by the gods, but, because it is pleasant to men. Let us advise them to abstain from vice and crime; not because they will be punished in another world, but because they will suffer for it in this.—*These are*, says Montesquieu, *means to prevent crimes—these are punishments; these reform manners—these are good examples.*

The way of truth is straight; that of imposture is crooked and dark. Truth, ever necessary to man, must necessarily be felt by all upright minds; the lessons of reason are to be followed by all honest men. Men are unhappy, only because they are ignorant; they are ignorant, only because every thing conspires to prevent their being enlightened; they are wicked only because their reason is not sufficiently developed.

By what fatality then, have the first founders of all sects given to their gods ferocious characters, at which nature revolts? Can we imagine a conduct more abominable, than that which Moses tells us his God showed towards the Egyptians, where that assassin proceeds boldly to declare, in the name and by the order of *his God*, that Egypt shall be afflicted with the greatest calamities, that can happen to man? Of all the different ideas, which they give us of a supreme being, of a God, creator and preserver of mankind, there are none more horrible, than those of the impostors, who represented themselves as inspired by a divine spirit, and "Thus saith the Lord."

Why, O theologians! do you presume to inquire into the impenetrable mysteries of a being, whom you consider inconceivable to the human mind? You are the blasphemers, when you imagine that a being, perfect according to you, could be guilty of such cruelty towards creatures whom he has made out of nothing. Confess, your ignorance of a creating God; and cease meddling with mysteries, which are repugnant to *Good Sense*.

Apologue

There is a vast empire, governed by a monarch, whose strange conduct is to confound the minds of his subjects. He wishes to be known, loved, respected, obeyed; but never shows himself to his subjects, and everything conspires to render uncertain the ideas formed of his character.

The people, subjected to his power, have, of the character and laws of their invisible sovereign, such ideas only, as his ministers give them. They, however, confess, that they have no idea of their master; that his ways are impenetrable; his views and nature totally incomprehensible. These ministers, likewise, disagree upon the commands which they pretend have been issued by the sovereign, whose servants they call themselves. They defame one another, and mutually treat each other as impostors and false teachers. The decrees and ordinances, they take upon themselves to promulgate, are obscure; they are enigmas, little calculated to be understood, or even divined, by the subjects, for whose instruction they were intended. The laws of the concealed monarch require interpreters; but the interpreters are always disputing upon the true manner of understanding them. Besides, they are not consistent with themselves; all they relate of their concealed prince is only a string of contradictions. They utter concerning him not a single word that does not immediately confute itself. They call him supremely good; yet many complain of his decrees. They suppose him infinitely wise; and under his administration everything appears to contradict reason. They extol his justice; and the best of his subjects are generally the least favoured. They assert, he sees everything; yet his presence avails nothing. He is, say they, the friend of order; yet throughout his dominions, all is in confusion and disorder. He makes all for himself; and the events seldom answer his designs. He foresees everything; but cannot prevent anything. He impatiently suffers offence, yet gives everyone the power of offending him. Men admire the wisdom and perfection of his works; yet his works, full of imperfection, are of short duration. He is continually doing and undoing; repairing what he has made; but is never pleased

---

DEISM

Deism is the general belief that a supernatural entity created the universe, endowed it with physical and ethical laws, then allowed it to run with no further intervention. Deism generally rejects the idea of prayer, salvation, miracles, prophecy, and any other implied interaction between the deity and humankind.

Though the idea of a nonintervening god existed in previous eras, the term "deism" was first used in the early 17th century as the scientific revolution was profoundly altering views of the universe and the place of humanity in it. Many philosophers and other well-known political and intellectual figures of the 17th and 18th centuries identified as deists, including Voltaire, David Hume, Benjamin Franklin, George Washington, Thomas Jefferson, Napoleon Bonaparte, Thomas Paine, James Madison, and John Locke. Many deists voiced strong criticism of conventional religious belief, leading many to be misidentified as atheists.

Deism influenced the development of a number of progressive religious identities in the early 19th century, including Unitarianism, and the growth of these identities led to a decline in deism as an independent label.

---

with his work. In all his undertakings, he proposes only his own glory; yet is never glorified. His only end is the happiness of his subjects; and his subjects, for the most part want necessaries. Those, whom he seems to favour are generally least satisfied with their fate; almost all appear in perpetual revolt against a master, whose greatness they never cease to admire, whose wisdom to extol, whose goodness to adore, whose justice to fear, and whose laws to reverence, though never obeyed!

This empire is the world; this monarch GOD; his ministers are the priests; his subjects mankind.

Source: Thiry, Paul-Henri, Baron d'Holbach. *Good Sense, or Natural Ideas Opposed to Supernatural*, 1772. Translated from the French original by Anna Knoop, 1878.

AFTERWARD

The ideas and writing of Baron d'Holbach had a deep influence on the development of Enlightenment philosophy and the universal human rights movement. Over 20 revolutions in the late 18th and early 19th centuries had their origins in Enlightenment concepts of human rights and the rejection of traditional power structures. Documents including the U.S. Bill of Rights and the French Declaration of the Rights of Man and of the Citizen, which in turn formed the foundation of later international human rights agreements, were directly rooted in Enlightenment principles.

ASK YOURSELF

1. Do you agree with d'Holbach that Christianity was or is an obstacle to morality and human flourishing?
2. Do you agree that people can be "persuade[d] to be just, beneficent, moderate, sociable" by reason, or "good sense"?
3. Does our current system for ensuring peace and public safety rely on the existence of God, on reason, on something else—or on a combination of these?

TOPICS AND ACTIVITIES TO CONSIDER

D'Holbach's work calls into question many values and assumptions that people of his time considered acceptable or good. Later writers who argued for the abolition of slavery, women's rights, animal rights, and a number of other causes were likewise met with outrage and hostility. Choose a current practice or belief that is generally unexamined or held to be good and argue for reconsideration of its value or morality. Possibilities:

- Eating meat
- Keeping pets
- Laws that limit child labor
- Military draft
- Immigration laws
- Death penalty
- Voting, driving, drinking age restrictions

Further Information

Blom, Philipp. *A Wicked Company: The Forgotten Radicalism of the European Enlightenment.* New York: Basic Books, 2005.

Edelstein, Dan. *The Enlightenment: A Genealogy.* Chicago: University of Chicago Press, 2010.

Web Site

Baron d'Holbach page at British Humanist Association: http://www.humanism.org.uk/humanism/humanist-tradition/enlightenment/baron-d-holbach.

THE 19TH CENTURY

12. "Thro' Deficiency of Proof"—Shelley's *The Necessity of Atheism* (1811)

INTRODUCTION

Percy Bysshe Shelley (1792–1822), considered one of the greatest poets in the English language, was also an advocate of radical social reform and a strong critic of religion.

In 1811, while a student at University College, Oxford, the 19-year-old Shelley published and distributed an anonymous pamphlet titled *The Necessity of Atheism*, a short treatise arguing that atheism is the only reasonable position on the question of God's existence.

KEEP IN MIND AS YOU READ

Blasphemy, including the denial of the existence of God, was still an actionable crime in early 19th-century England. Thirty years after *The Necessity of Atheism*, a British publisher was convicted of blasphemy—coincidentally for publishing an unabridged poem of Shelley's that included denials of God (see Afterward).

Document: Percy Bysshe Shelley, The Necessity of Atheism *(1811)*

A close examination of the validity of the proofs adduced to support any proposition, has ever been allowed to be the only sure way of attaining truth, upon the advantages of which it is unnecessary to descant; our knowledge of the existence of a Deity is a subject of such importance, that it cannot be too minutely investigated; in consequence of this conviction, we proceed briefly and impartially to examine the proofs which have been adduced. It is necessary first to consider the nature of Belief.

When a proposition is offered to the mind, it perceives the agreement or disagreement of the ideas of which it is composed. A perception of their agreement is termed belief; many obstacles frequently prevent this perception from being immediate; these the mind attempts to remove in order that the perception may be distinct. The mind is active in the investigation, in order to perfect the state of perception which is passive; the investigation being confused with the perception has induced many falsely to imagine that the mind is active in belief, that belief is an act of volition, in consequence of which it may be regulated by the mind; pursuing, continuing this mistake they have attached a degree of criminality to disbelief of which in its nature it is incapable; it is equally so of merit.

The strength of belief, like that of every other passion, is in proportion to the degrees of excitement.—The degrees of excitement are three.—The senses are the sources of all knowledge to the mind, consequently their evidence claims the strongest assent.—The decision of the mind founded upon our own experience derived from these sources, claims the next degree.—The experience of others which addresses itself to the former one, occupies the lowest degree,—Consequently no testimony can be admitted which is contrary to reason, reason is founded on the evidence of our senses.—Every proof may be referred to one of these three divisions; we are naturally led to consider what arguments we receive from each of them to convince us of the existence of a Deity.

1st. The evidence of the senses.—If the Deity should appear to us, if he should convince our senses of his existence; this revelation would necessarily command belief;—Those to whom the Deity has thus appeared, have the strongest possible conviction of his existence.

Reason claims the 2nd place, it is urged that man knows that whatever is, must either have had a beginning or existed from all eternity, he also knows that whatever is not eternal must have had a cause.—Where this is applied to the existence of the universe, it is necessary to prove that it was created, until that is clearly demonstrated, we may reasonably suppose that it has endured from all eternity.—In a case where two propositions are diametrically opposite, the mind believes that which is less incomprehensible, it is easier to suppose that the Universe has existed from all eternity, than to conceive a being capable of creating it; if the mind sinks beneath the weight of one, is it an alleviation to increase the intolerability of the burden?—The other argument which is founded upon a man's knowledge of his own existence stands thus.—A man knows not only he now is, but that there was a time when he did not exist, consequently there must have been a cause.—But what does this prove? we can only infer from effects causes exactly adequate to those effects;—But there certainly is a generative power which is effected by particular instruments; we cannot prove that it is inherent in these instruments, nor is the contrary hypothesis capable of demonstration; we admit that the generative power is incomprehensible, but to suppose that the same effect is produced by an eternal, omniscient Almighty Being, leaves the cause in the same obscurity, but renders it more incomprehensible.

The 3rd and last degree of assent is claimed by Testimony—it is required that it should not be contrary to reason.—The testimony that the Deity convinces the senses of men of his existence can only be admitted by us, if our mind considers it less probable that these men should have been deceived, then that the Deity should have appeared to them—our reason can never admit the testimony of men, who not only declare that they were eye-witnesses of miracles but that the Deity was irrational, for he commanded that he should be believed, he proposed the highest rewards for faith, eternal punishments for disbelief—we can only command voluntary actions, belief is not an act of volition, the mind is even passive, from this it is evident that we have not sufficient testimony, or rather that testimony is insufficient to prove the being of a God, we have before shewn that it cannot be deduced from reason,—they who have been convinced by the evidence of the senses, they only can believe it.

From this it is evident that having no proofs from any of the three sources of conviction: the mind *cannot* believe the existence of a God, it is also evident that as belief is a passion of the mind, no degree of criminality can be attached to disbelief, they only are reprehensible who willingly neglect to remove the false medium thro' which their mind views the subject.

It is almost unnecessary to observe, that the general knowledge of the deficiency of such proof, cannot be prejudicial to society: Truth has always been found to promote the best interests of mankind.—Every reflecting mind must allow that there is no proof of the existence of a Deity. **Q.E.D.**

Thro' deficiency of proof, AN ATHEIST

> **Q.E.D.:** "Therefore it is proven"

Source: Shelley, Percy Bysshe. *The Necessity of Atheism.* Quoted in *The Works of Percy Bysshe Shelley in Verse and Prose.* Edited by H. Buxton Forman. London: Reeves & Turner, 1880.

AFTERWARD

Though the pamphlet was signed only "AN ATHEIST," the whispered phrase "It must have been Shelley" quickly made its way around Oxford University. When confronted by shocked university administrators, Shelley did not deny authoring the pamphlet and as a consequence was "rusticated" (e.g., suspended from college). Shelley was given the choice to be reinstated after his father, a member of Parliament, intervened, on the condition that he would recant his atheism. His refusal to do so led to estrangement from his father, and Shelley was permanently expelled from Oxford.

By the time of his death by drowning at age 29, Shelley had established himself as one of the finest lyric poets in the English language. Long after his death, his radical social and religious opinions continued to scandalize Victorian England. When his widow, Mary Shelley, published his collected poetry in 1839, she removed several atheistic passages from *Queen Mab*, his first large-scale poem. Two years later publisher Edward Moxon restored the expunged passages for a second edition. A sample passage:

> The name of God
> Has fenced about all crime with holiness,
> Himself the creature of his worshippers,
> Whose names and attributes and passions change,
> Seeva, Buddh, Foh, Jehovah, God, or Lord,
> Even with the human dupes who build his shrines,
> Still serving o'er the war-polluted world
> Earth groans beneath religion's iron age,
> And priests dare babble of a God of peace,
> Even whilst their hands are red with guiltless blood,
> Murdering the while, uprooting every germ
> Of truth, exterminating, spoiling all,
> Making the earth a slaughter-house!

Moxon was prosecuted and convicted of blasphemous libel, and the passages in question were once again expunged.

ASK YOURSELF

1. Shelley attempts to prove, in the form of a formal argument, that atheism is a "necessary" position. Is his argument convincing? Why or why not?
2. Can you think of topics that, if advocated verbally or in writing, might draw a similar reaction of shock and anger today? If so, what topics, and from whom would the anger most likely come? Would it be justified?
3. Can you think of other topics that were once shocking or forbidden but are now freely expressed?
4. Are there ideas that are simply too dangerous to express or defend today, even in an open society?

TOPICS AND ACTIVITIES TO CONSIDER

In a group discussion, share any stories of being punished or criticized for expressing an unconventional idea. Did you know in advance that the idea would draw such a reaction? If not, would you have expressed it had you known? If so, why did you think the idea was important enough to express? Would you do it again?

Further Information

Shelley, Percy Bysshe. *The Necessity of Atheism and Other Essays*. Amherst, NY: Prometheus Books, 1993.

Web Site

Expanded 1813 version of *Necessity*: http://www.infidels.org/library/historical/percy _shelley/necessity_of_atheism.html.

13. "What Does She Believe?"—Frances Wright's Lectures (1828–1829)

INTRODUCTION

Frances Wright (1795–1852) was a pioneering feminist, abolitionist, and social reformer who publicly articulated an agnostic perspective two generations before the term was coined by Thomas Huxley. "With respect to myself," she said, "my efforts have been strenuously directed to ascertain what I *know*, to understand, what *can be known*, and to increase my *knowledge* as far as possible."

A friend of Thomas Jefferson and other influential figures of the time, the Scottish-born Wright cofounded the *Free Inquirer* newspaper and engaged in a controversial series of public lectures around the United States, from which the following document is drawn.

KEEP IN MIND AS YOU READ

Frances Wright was the first woman to speak publicly to a mixed audience of men and women in the United States, the first to publicly advocate women's equality, and the first to openly question religion and denounce the power of the clergy. During her lecture tour, she was forcefully condemned by the press and clergy alike, who called her "the great Red Harlot of Infidelity" and the "Whore of Babylon." She was often under threat of violence and on more than one occasion had to flee the scene of a lecture under the protection of bodyguards.

Document: Frances Wright, Excerpts from the Public Lectures of 1828–1829

I have seen an honest teacher of religion, born and bred within the atmosphere of sectarian faith, and whose hairs have grown white in the labors of sectarian ministries, open his mind to more expanded views, his heart to more expanded feelings, and as the light dawned upon his own reason, steadily proclaim it to his followers. And what hath been the reward of his honesty? They who should have blessed, have risen up against him; the young in years, but old in false-hood, even among his followers, have sought their own popularity, by proclaiming his heresy; nor rested from plots and persecutions until they drove him from his own pulpit, and shut the doors of his own church, upon his venerable person.

Such being the reward of sincerity, who then shall marvel at its absence. . . .

I am here to speak what I believe the truth. I am here to speak that for which some have not the courage and others not the independence. I am here, not to flatter the ear, but to probe the heart; not to minister to vanity, but to urge self-examination; assuredly, therefore, not to court applause, but to induce conviction. . . .

I must entreat you to inquire what the knowledge is, that you learn from your spiritual teachers. "The knowledge by faith," they will answer for you. "And faith," they will add, "is the knowledge of things unseen."

Can there be any such knowledge? I put it to your reason. Knowledge we have shown to be ascertained facts. Things unseen! Can human understanding know any thing about them? . . . And do ye hire teachers to teach you non-existent knowledge, impossible knowledge, and knowledge which, even under the supposition of its possibility, could serve no conceivable purpose? We are on the earth, and they tell us of heaven; we are human beings, and they tell us of angels and devils; we are matter, and they tell us of spirit; we have five senses whereby to admit truths, and a reasoning faculty by which to build our belief upon them; and they tell us of dreams dreamed thousands of years ago, which all our experience flatly contradicts.

Again I must entreat your patience—your gentle hearing. I am not going to question your opinions. I am not going to meddle with your belief. I am not going to dictate to you mine. All that I say is, examine; enquire. Look into the nature of things. Search out the ground of your opinions, the *for* and the *against*. Know *why* you believe, understand *what* you believe, and possess a reason for the faith that is in you.

But your spiritual teachers caution you against enquiry—tell you not to read certain books; not to listen to certain people; to beware of profane learning; to submit your reason, and to receive their doctrines for truths. Such advice renders them suspicious counselors. By their own creed, you hold your reason from their God. Go! Ask them why he gave it.

Be not afraid! If that being which they tell us of exist, we shall find him in his works. If that revelation be his which they tell us to revere, we shall find all nature and its occurrences, all matter and its phenomena, bearing testimony to its truth. Be not afraid! In admitting a creator, refuse not to examine his creation; and take not the assertions of creatures like yourselves, in place of the evidence of your senses and the conviction of your understanding.

"But," you will say, "the clergy preach against these things." And when did mere preaching do any good? Put something in the place of these things. Fill the vacuum of the mind. Awaken its powers, and it will respect itself. Give it worthy objects on which to spend its strength . . . Do the clergy do this? Do they not rather demand a prostration of the intellect—a humbling and debasing of the spirit? . . . Preach they not the innate corruption of our race? Away with this libel of our nature! Away with this crippling, debasing, cowardly theory! Long, long enough hath this foul slander obscured our prospects, paralyzed our efforts, crushed the generous spirit within us! Away with it! . . . Fit yourself for the examination of your opinions, then *examine your opinions*. . . .

Perhaps, at this very moment, the question, *what does she believe*, is uppermost in the thoughts of two-thirds of my hearers. Should such be their thoughts, I will reply to them.

With respect to myself, my efforts have been strenuously directed to ascertain what I *know*, to understand, what *can be known*, and to increase my *knowledge* as far as possible. In the next place, I have endeavoured to communicate my *knowledge* to my fellow creatures; and strictly laid down to myself the rule, never to speak to them of that of which I have *not* knowledge.

Source: Wright, Frances. *Course of Popular Lectures as Delivered by Frances Wright, with Three Addresses on Various Public Occasions*. New York: The Free Enquirer, 1829.

AFTERWARD

Wright's lecture tour took place in the midst of a collapsing personal dream. An idealistic multiracial farming commune she had built in Nashoba, Tennessee, near Memphis was nearing financial ruin. The year after her lecture tour, Wright arranged for the transport of 30 freed slaves from the commune to Haiti, where they could live as free citizens of the new country. Her influence waned in her final years, due in part to declining health, and she died and was buried in Cincinnati, Ohio, in 1852. Because her speeches and thoughts had been committed to writing and had developed steadfast support among early feminist activists, Wright's work continued to exert a powerful influence on subsequent generations.

ASK YOURSELF

Wright's oratorical style alternates between diplomacy and direct challenge of the assumptions of her listeners. Find three passages that exemplify each. Why did she choose this approach?

TOPICS AND ACTIVITIES TO CONSIDER

Select a topic on which you have deeply felt, emotionally charged opinions. Find two essays online that opposed your position, one that is direct and accusatory, another that is diplomatic in its approach. Are you as easily able to consider the points made in both? Why or why not?

Further Information

Gaylor, Annie Laurie, ed. *Women without Superstition: No Gods, No Masters*. Madison, WI: Freedom From Religion Foundation, 1997.

Morris, Celia. *Fanny Wright: Rebel in America*. Cambridge, MA: Harvard University Press, 1984.

Web Sites

Frances Wright's reception at Monticello: http://www.monticello.org/site/research-and-collections/frances-wright.

Freethought quotes by Frances Wright: http://www.positiveatheism.org/hist/quotes/wright.htm.

14. "Sit Down before Fact as a Little Child"— T. H. Huxley's Letter to Rev. Kingsley (1860)

INTRODUCTION

The Victorian era (1837–1901) was a time of great intellectual activity in the UK. Many age-old assumptions were overturned by scientific advances, from the age of the Earth to the kinship of all living things. Defenders of religious orthodoxy decried what they saw as unacceptable contradictions to scripture. But other religious leaders were advocates of science even when it challenged long-standing church doctrines.

Among these was Charles Kingsley, a chaplain-in-ordinary to Queen Victoria and a Cambridge historian who endorsed Charles Darwin's theory of evolution by natural selection. "All I have seen of it awes me," he wrote to Darwin after viewing an advance copy of *On the Origin of Species*. "If you be right, I must give up much that I have believed & written." His advocacy brought him into contact with biologist Thomas Henry Huxley, who was to become the most famous public advocate of Darwin's earthshaking theory.

In September of 1860, the Huxley family suffered the death of their four-year-old son Noel—"our delight and our joy," as Huxley wrote in his diary—from scarlet fever. "Thursday he and I had a great romp together. On Friday his restless head, with its bright blue eyes and tangled golden hair, tossed all day upon his pillow. On Saturday night the fifteenth, I carried him here into my study, and laid his cold still body here where I write." Writing to console Huxley in the depths of his grief, Charles Kingsley asked if Huxley might reconsider his religious doubts to accept the comforts that belief in an afterlife would provide. Huxley's reply, excerpted below, is considered one of the great personal testaments to scientific integrity and the courageous quest for knowledge even when the implications of knowledge are difficult or painful.

KEEP IN MIND AS YOU READ

Discrimination against religious doubters was still institutionalized in 19th-century Britain. Huxley's statement in the letter that "my evidence . . . would not be received" in a court of law reflects the fact that testimony from witnesses who were unwilling to swear a Christian oath was not legally accepted at the time (see The Bradlaugh Affair in England sidebar).

Many Anglicans in the 19th century believed their church was becoming too secular. A movement called Tractarianism aiming to restore traditional elements of ritual and identity created a split in the denomination that is still evident today. In this tense environment, Kingsley and other clergy who granted that they might have to "give up much that [they] have believed" in the face of scientific advances were often under strong pressure to reaffirm orthodoxy.

Document: Letter from Thomas Henry Huxley to Rev. Charles Kingsley, September 23, 1860

My dear Kingsley—I cannot sufficiently thank you, both on my wife's account and my own, for your long and frank letter, and for all the hearty sympathy which it exhibits. To myself your letter was especially valuable, as it touched upon what I thought even more than upon what I said in my earlier letter to you.

My convictions, positive and negative, on all the matters of which you speak, are of long and slow growth and are firmly rooted. But the great blow which fell upon me seemed to stir them to their foundation, and had I lived a couple of centuries earlier I could have fancied a devil scoffing at me—asking me what profit it was to have stripped myself of the hopes and consolations of the mass of mankind? To which my only reply was and is—Oh devil! truth is better than much profit. I have searched over the grounds of my belief, and if wife and child and name and fame were all to be lost to me one after the other as the penalty, still I will not lie.

I neither deny nor affirm the immortality of man. I see no reason for believing in it, but, on the other hand, I have no means of disproving it. Surely it must be plain that an ingenious man could speculate without end on both sides, and find analogies for all his dreams. Nor does it help to tell me that the aspirations of mankind—that my own highest aspirations even—lead me towards the doctrine of immortality. I doubt the fact, to begin with, but if it be so even, what is this but in grand words asking me to believe a thing because I like it.

Science has taught to me the opposite lesson. She warns me to be careful how I adopt a view which jumps with my preconceptions, and to require stronger evidence for such belief than for one to which I was previously hostile. My business is to teach my aspirations to conform themselves to fact, not to try and make facts harmonise with my aspirations.

Science seems to me to teach in the highest and strongest manner the great truth which is embodied in the Christian conception of entire surrender to the will of God. Sit down before fact as a little child, be prepared to give up every preconceived notion, follow humbly wherever and to whatever abysses nature leads, or you shall learn nothing. I have only begun to learn content and peace of mind since I have resolved at all risks to do this.

If at this moment I am not a worn-out, debauched, useless carcass of a man, if it has been or will be my fate to advance the cause of science, if I feel that I have a shadow of a claim on the love of those about me, if, in the supreme moment when I looked down into my boy's grave, my sorrow was full of submission and without bitterness, it is because these ideas have worked upon me, and not because I have ever cared whether my poor personality shall remain distinct for ever from the All from whence it came and whither it goes.

And thus, my dear Kingsley, you will understand what my position is. I may be quite wrong, and in that case I know I shall have to pay the penalty for being wrong. But I can only say with Luther, "Gott helfe mir, Ich kann nichts anders" [God help me, I cannot do otherwise].

I know right well that 99 out of 100 of my fellows would call me atheist, infidel, and all the other usual hard names. As our laws stand, if the lowest thief steals my coat, my evidence (my opinions being known) would not be received against him.

But I cannot help it. One thing people shall not call me with justice and that is—a liar. As you say of yourself, I too feel that I lack courage; but if ever the occasion arises when I am bound to speak, I will not shame my boy.

I have spoken more openly and distinctly to you than I ever have to any human being except my wife.

If you can show me that I err in premises or conclusion, I am ready to give up these as I would any other theories. But at any rate you will do me the justice to believe that I have not reached my conclusions without the care befitting the momentous nature of the problems involved. . . .

I don't profess to understand the logic of yourself, **Maurice**, and the rest of your school, but I have always said I would swear by your truthfulness and sincerity, and that good must come of your efforts. The more plain this was to me, however, the more obvious the necessity to let you see where the men of science are driving, and it has often been in my mind to write to you before.

If I have spoken too plainly anywhere, or too abruptly, pardon me, and do the like to me. My wife thanks you very much for your volume of sermons.

Ever yours very faithfully,
T. H. Huxley.

Maurice: John Frederick Denison Maurice (1805–1872), Anglican theologian and education reformer admired by Kingsley

Source: Huxley, Leonard. *Life and Letters of Thomas Henry Huxley*. Vol. 1. London: Macmillan, 1900.

AGNOSTICISM

In the same way that atheism uses the prefix "a" to express a negation (a + theism = "without god belief"), agnosticism joins the "a" prefix to the Greek word "gnosis" ("knowledge") to mean "without knowledge." It is used most often in relation to knowledge of the existence and nature of a god or gods. In actual usage, the term designates the stronger suggestion that a given concept is not only unknown but unknowable.

Though agnostic positions had been described as early as classical Greece, the word "agnostic" was coined by the biologist Thomas Henry Huxley in 1869 to describe his own position. In his 1889 essay titled "Agnosticism," Huxley offered this explanation:

When I reached intellectual maturity and began to ask myself whether I was an atheist, a theist, or a pantheist; a materialist or an idealist; Christian or a freethinker; I found that the more I learned and reflected, the less ready was the answer; until, at last, I came to the conclusion that I had neither art nor part with any of these denominations, except the last. The one thing in which most of these good people were agreed was the one thing in which I differed from them. They were quite sure they had attained a certain "gnosis,"—had, more or less successfully, solved the problem of existence; while I was quite sure I had not, and had a pretty strong conviction that the problem was insoluble. So I took thought, and invented what I conceived to be the appropriate title of "agnostic." It came into my head as suggestively antithetic to the "gnostic" of Church history, who professed to know so much about the very things of which I was ignorant. To my great satisfaction the term took.

AFTERWARD

Huxley and Kingsley continued their friendship and correspondence for years, touching on topics large and small. "I have a great respect for all the old bottles," Huxley wrote to Kingsley in 1863, referring to old religious assumptions, "and if the new wine can be got to go into them and not burst them I shall be very glad." But, he added, "I confess I do not see my way to it." During the same year, Kingsley authored "The Great Hippocampus Question." This gentle satire of the debate over evolution helped popularize the theory. He became a canon of Westminster Abbey in 1873 and died in 1875.

Huxley coined the term "agnostic" in 1869 (see Agnosticism sidebar). In 1869 and 1870, a series of acts of Parliament ended the Christian oath requirement to which Huxley referred. But the reform was incomplete, as evidenced in the Bradlaugh affair (see The Bradlaugh Affair in England sidebar).

ASK YOURSELF

1. What are some sound guidelines when communicating across lines of difference in religious belief? Does Huxley follow them?
2. After reading this letter and learning its context, how do you think it would have been received by Charles Kingsley?
3. By calling himself agnostic rather than atheist, Huxley irritated many of his fellow nonbelievers. By endorsing evolutionary theory, Kingsley outraged many of his fellow clergy. What effect might these positions have had on their friendship?
4. In his letter to Darwin praising the *Origin*, Kingsley wrote, "Let us know what *is*, & follow up the villainous shifty fox of an argument, into whatsoever unexpected bogs & brakes he may lead us." Can you find a passage in Huxley's letter, written the following year, that parallels this idea?

TOPICS AND ACTIVITIES TO CONSIDER

- ✎ View the 2009 film *Creation*, which depicts events in the life of Charles Darwin. In the film, Huxley's character says, "You've killed God, sir . . . and I for one say good riddance to the vindictive old bugger." After reading Huxley's correspondence with Kingsley, do you think this is an accurate reflection of his position?
- ✎ Select a friend you respect who has different religious views from your own. Create a correspondence like that of Huxley and Kingsley, honestly exploring your differences while affirming your common ground.

Further Information

Blinderman, Charles S. "Huxley and Kingsley." *Victorian Newsletter* 20 (1961): 25–28.

Irvine, William. *Apes, Angels, and Victorians: A Joint Biography of Darwin and Huxley.* London: Weidenfeld and Nicolson, 1955.

Kingsley, Charles, with Frances Eliza Grenfell Kingsley. *Charles Kingsley: His Letters and Memories of His Life* [1908]. Ithaca, NY: Cornell University Press, 2009.

Web Site

T. H. Huxley, letters and diary entries, including full text of Kingsley correspondence: http://aleph0.clarku.edu/huxley/lindex.html.

15. "A Defence of Atheism" on the Eve of War—Ernestine Rose (1861)

INTRODUCTION

Like Frances Wright before her, Ernestine Rose (1810–1892) was an atheist, a pioneering feminist, and a committed abolitionist. Born to a Russian Jewish family, Rose lost her mother at 16 and was immediately promised in marriage by her father to a Jewish friend. When the man refused to release her from the pledge (probably because of her wealthy family), Rose pleaded her own case in court and won.

After living in Germany and England and working as a social reformer and public speaker, Rose emigrated with her new husband to New York in 1836 and began working for the abolition of slavery and improvement of women's rights. Like Wright, she was often threatened with physical violence at her speaking events, especially in the U.S. South. But not *only* in the South: a Maine newspaper editor in 1855 said she was "a female Atheist . . . a thousand times below a prostitute."

With the support of Susan B. Anthony, Rose was elected president of the National Women's Rights Convention in 1854. When several members of the Convention complained of Rose's atheism, Anthony insisted that "every religion—or none—should have an equal right on the platform."

KEEP IN MIND AS YOU READ

Religious fervor tends to increase dramatically in a time of war, as does the general call for unity and distrust of unorthodoxy. Rose's "A Defence of Atheism" was first delivered as a lecture in Boston in the midst of the extraordinary tension leading up to the American Civil War. The date of the lecture was April 10, 1861—just 36 hours before the first shots of the war were fired in Charleston Harbor.

Document: Ernestine Rose, "A Defence of Atheism" (1861)

MY FRIENDS: In undertaking the inquiry of the existence of a God, I am fully conscious of the difficulties I have to encounter. I am well aware that the very question produces in most minds a feeling of awe, as if stepping on forbidden ground, too holy and sacred for mortals to approach. The very question strikes them with horror, and it is owing to this prejudice so deeply implanted by education, and also strengthened by public sentiment, that so few are willing to give it a fair and impartial investigation,—knowing but too well that it casts a stigma and reproach upon any person bold enough to undertake the task, unless his previously known opinions are a guarantee that his conclusions would be in accordance and harmony with the popular demand. But believing as I do, that Truth only is beneficial, and Error, from whatever source, and under whatever name, is pernicious to man, I consider no place too holy, no subject too sacred, for man's earnest investigation; for by so doing only can we arrive at Truth, learn to discriminate it from Error, and be able to accept the one and reject the other.

Nor is this the only impediment in the way of this inquiry. The question arises, Where shall we begin? We have been told, that "by searching none can find out God," which has so far proved true; for, as yet, no one has ever been able to find him. The most strenuous believer has to acknowledge that it is only a belief, but he knows nothing on the subject. Where, then, shall we search for his existence? Enter the material world; ask the Sciences whether they can disclose the mystery? Geology speaks of the structure of the Earth, the formation of the different strata, of coal, of granite, of the whole mineral kingdom. It reveals the remains and traces of animals long extinct, but gives us no clue whereby we may prove the existence of a God.

Natural history gives us a knowledge of the animal kingdom in general; the different organisms, structures, and powers of the various species. Physiology teaches the nature of man, the laws that govern his being, the functions of the vital organs, and the conditions upon which alone health and life depend. . . . But in the whole animal economy—though the brain is considered to be a "microcosm," in which may be traced a resemblance or relationship with everything in Nature—not a spot can be found to indicate the existence of a God. . . .

The Universe of Matter gives us no record of his existence. Where next shall we search? Enter the Universe of Mind, read the millions of volumes written on the subject, and in all the speculations, the assertions, the assumptions, the theories, and the creeds, you can only find Man stamped in an indelible impress by his own mind on every page. In describing his God, he delineated his own character: the picture he drew represents in living and ineffaceable colours the epoch of his existence—the period he lived in. It was a great mistake to say that God made man in his image. Man, in all ages, made his God in his own image; and we find that just in accordance with his civilization, his knowledge, his experience, his taste, his refinement, his sense of right, of justice, of freedom, and humanity, so has he made his God. But whether coarse or refined; cruel and vindictive, or kind and generous; an implacable tyrant, or a gentle and loving father; it still was the emanation of his own mind—the picture of himself.

But, you ask, how came it that man thought or wrote about God at all? The answer is very simple. Ignorance is the mother of Superstition. In proportion to man's ignorance is he superstitious—does he believe in the mysterious. The very name has a charm for him. Being unacquainted with the nature and laws of things around him, with the true causes of the effects he witnessed, he ascribed them to false ones—to supernatural agencies. The savage, ignorant of the mechanism of a watch, attributes the ticking to a spirit. The so-called civilized man, equally ignorant of the mechanism of the Universe, and the laws which govern it, ascribes it to the same erroneous cause. Before electricity was discovered, a thunderstorm was said to come from the wrath of an offended Deity. To this fiction of man's uncultivated mind, has been attributed all of good and of evil, of wisdom and of folly. Man has talked about him, written about him, disputed about him, fought about him,—sacrificed himself, and extirpated his fellow man. Rivers of blood and oceans of tears have been shed to please him, yet no one has ever been able to demonstrate his existence.

But the Bible, we are told, reveals this great mystery. Where Nature is dumb, and Man ignorant, Revelation speaks in the authoritative voice of prophecy. Then let us see whether that Revelation can stand the test of reason and of truth. God, we are told, is omnipotent, omniscient, omnipresent—all wise, all just, and all good; that he is perfect. So far, so well; for less than perfection were unworthy of a God. The first act recorded of him is, that he created the world out of nothing; but unfortunately the revelation of Science-Chemistry—which is based not on written words, but demonstrable facts, says that Nothing has no existence, and therefore out of Nothing, Nothing could be made. . . .

The testimony of Revelation has failed. Its account of the creation of the material world is disproved by science. Its account of the creation of man in the image of perfection, is disproved by its own internal evidence. To test the Bible God by justice and benevolence, he could not be good; to test him by reason and knowledge, he could not be wise; to test him by the light of the truth, the rule of consistency, we must come to the inevitable conclusion that, like the Universe of matter and of mind, this pretended Revelation has also failed to demonstrate the existence of a God.

Methinks I hear the believer say, you are unreasonable; you demand an impossibility; we are finite, and therefore cannot understand, much less define and demonstrate the infinite. Just so! But if I am unreasonable in asking you to demonstrate the existence of the being you wish me to believe in, are you not infinitely more unreasonable to expect me to believe—blame, persecute, and punish me for not believing—in what you have to acknowledge you cannot understand?

But, says the Christian, the world exists, and therefore there must have been a God to create it. That does not follow. The mere fact of its existence does not prove a Creator.

Then how came the Universe into existence? We do not know, but the ignorance of man is certainly no proof of the existence of a God. Yet upon that very ignorance has it been predicated, and is maintained. From the little knowledge we have, we are justified in the assertion that the Universe never was created, from the simple fact that not one atom of it can ever be annihilated. To suppose a Universe created, is to suppose a time when it did not exist, and that is a self-evident absurdity. Besides, where was the Creator before it was created? Nay, where is he now? Outside of that Universe, which means the all in all, above, below, and around? That is another absurdity. Is he contained within? Then he can be only a part, for the whole includes all the parts. If only a part, then he could not be its Creator, for a part cannot create the whole. But the world could not have made itself. True; nor could God have made himself; and if you must have a God to make the world, you will be under the same necessity to have another to make him, and others still to make them, and so on until reason and common sense are at a stand-still.

The Universe is one vast chemical laboratory, in constant operation, by her internal forces. The laws or principles of attraction, cohesion, and repulsion, produce in never-ending succession the phenomena of composition, decomposition, and recomposition. The how, we are too ignorant to understand, too modest to presume, and too honest to profess. Had man been a patient and impartial inquirer, and not with childish presumption attributed everything he could not understand, to supernatural causes, given names to hide his ignorance, but observed the operations of Nature, he would undoubtedly have known more, been wiser, and happier.

As it is, Superstition has ever been the great impediment to the acquisition of knowledge. Every progressive step of man clashed against the two-edged sword of Religion, to whose narrow restrictions he had but too often to succumb, or march onward at the expense of interest, reputation, and even life itself.

But, we are told, that Religion is natural; the belief in a God universal. Were it natural, then it would indeed be universal; but it is not. We have ample evidence to the contrary. According to Dr. Livingstone, there are whole tribes or nations, civilized, moral, and virtuous; yes, so honest that they expose their goods for sale without guard or value set upon them, trusting to the honour of the purchaser to pay its proper price.

Yet these people have not the remotest idea of a God, and he found it impossible to impart it to them. And in all ages of the world, some of the most civilized, the wisest, and the best, were entire unbelievers; only they dared not openly avow it, except at the risk of their lives. Proscription, the torture and the stake, were found most efficient means to seal the lips of heretics; and though the march of progress has broken the infernal machines, and extinguished the fires of the Inquisition, the proscription, and more refined but not less cruel and bitter persecutions of an intolerant and bigoted public opinion, in Protestant countries, as well as in Catholic, on account of belief, are quite enough to prevent men from honestly avowing their true sentiments upon the subject. Hence there are few possessed of the moral courage of a Humboldt.

If the belief in a god were natural, there would be no need to teach it. Children would possess it as well as adults, the layman as the priest, the heathen as much as the missionary. We don't have to teach the general elements of human nature; the five senses, seeing, hearing, smelling, tasting, and feeling. They are universal; so would religion be were it natural, but it is not. On the contrary, it is an interesting and demonstrable fact, that all children are Atheists, and were religion not inculcated into their minds they would remain so. Even as it is, they are great sceptics, until made sensible of the potent weapon by which religion has ever been propagated, namely, fear—fear of the lash of public opinion here, and of a jealous, vindictive God hereafter. No; there is no religion in human nature, nor human nature in religion. It is purely artificial, the result of education, while Atheism is natural, and, were the human mind not perverted and bewildered by the mysteries and follies of superstition, would be universal.

But the people have been made to believe that were it not for religion, the world would be destroyed: man would become a monster, chaos and confusion would reign supreme. These erroneous notions conceived in ignorance, propagated by superstition, and kept alive by an interested and corrupt priesthood who fatten the credulity of the public, are very difficult to be eradicated.

But sweep all the belief in the supernatural from the face of the earth, and the world would remain just the same. The seasons would follow each other in their regular succession; the stars would shine in the firmament; the sun would shed his benign and vivifying influence of light and heat upon us; the clouds would discharge their burden in gentle and refreshing showers; and cultivated fields would bring forth vegetation; summer would ripen the golden grain, ready for harvest; the trees would bear fruits; the birds would sing in accordance with their happy instinct, and all Nature would smile as joyously around us as ever. Nor would man degenerate, Oh! no. His nature, too would remain the same. He would have to be obedient to the physical, mental, and moral laws of his being, or to suffer the natural penalty for their violation; observe the mandates of society, or receive the punishment. His affections would be just as warm, the love of self-preservation as strong, the desire for happiness and the fear of pain as great. He would love freedom, justice, and truth, and hate oppression, fraud, and falsehood, as much as ever.

Sweep all belief in the supernatural from the globe, and you would chase away the whole fraternity of spectres, ghosts, and hobgoblins, which have so befogged and bewildered the human mind, that hardly a clear ray of the light of Reason can penetrate it. You would cleanse and purify the heart of the noxious, poisonous weeds of superstition, with its bitter, deadly fruits—hypocrisy, bigotry, and intolerance, and fill it with charity and forbearance towards erring humanity. You would give man courage to sustain him in trials and misfortune, sweeten his temper, give him a new zest for the duties, the virtues, and the pleasures of life.

Morality does not depend on the belief in any religion. History gives ample evidence that the more belief the less virtue and goodness. Nor need we go back to ancient times to see the crimes and atrocities perpetrated under its sanction. We have enough in our own times. Look at the present crisis—at the South with 4,000,000 of human beings in slavery, bought and sold like brute chattels under the sanction of religion and of God, which the Reverend Van Dykes and the **Raphalls** of the North fully endorse, and the South complains that the reforms in the North are owing to Infidelity. Morality depends on an accurate knowledge of the nature of man, of the laws that govern his being, the principles of right, of justice, and humanity, and the conditions requisite to make him healthy, rational, virtuous, and happy.

> **Raphall:** Morris Raphall (1798–1868), a well-known rabbi of the time who wrote and spoke in defense of slavery using biblical precedent

[N]ot only have the priests tried to make the very term Atheism odious, as if it would destroy all of good and beautiful in Nature, but some of the reformers, not having the moral courage to avow their own sentiments, wishing to be popular, fearing least their reforms would be considered Infidel, (as all reforms assuredly are,) shield themselves from the stigma, by joining in the tirade against Atheism, and associate it with everything that is vile, with the crime of slavery, the corruptions of the Church, and all the vices imaginable. This is false, and they know it. Atheism protests against this injustice. No one has a right to give the term a false, a forced interpretation, to suit his own purposes, (this applies also to some of the Infidels who stretch and force the term Atheist out of its legitimate significance). As well might we use the terms Episcopalian, Unitarian, Universalist, to signify vice and corruption, as the term Atheist, which means simply a disbelief in a God, because finding no demonstration of his existence, man's reason will not allow him to believe, nor his conviction to play the hypocrite, and profess what he does not believe. Give it its true significance, and he will abide the consequence; but don't fasten upon it the vices belonging to yourselves. Hypocrisy is the prolific mother of a large family!

In conclusion, the Atheist says to the honest conscientious believer, Though I cannot believe in your God whom you have failed to demonstrate, I believe in man; if I have no faith in your religion, I have faith, unbounded, unshaken faith in the principles of right, of justice, and humanity. Whatever good you are willing to do for the sake of your God, I am full as willing to do for the sake of man. But the monstrous crimes the believer perpetrated in persecuting and exterminating his fellowman on account of difference of belief, the Atheist, knowing that belief is not voluntary, but depends on evidence, and therefore there can be no merit in the belief of any religions, nor demerit in a disbelief in all of them, could never be guilty of. Whatever good you would do out of fear of punishment, or hope of reward hereafter, the Atheist would do simply because it is good; and being so, he would receive the far surer and more certain reward, springing from well-doing, which would constitute his pleasure, and promote his happiness.

Source: Rose, Ernestine L. "A Defence of Atheism." Boston: J. P. Mendum, 1889.

AFTERWARD

In the years following the Civil War, Rose devoted herself to the movement to secure voting rights for African Americans, a process that culminated in the ratification of the Fifteenth Amendment to the U.S. Constitution. In 1869, Rose and her husband moved to England and began working for women's suffrage (voting rights) in the UK, just as that movement began to gain national momentum. Just six weeks before her death in 1892, Rose gave the publisher of the *London Freethinker* a copy of "A Defence of Atheism," published over 30 years earlier, and said she would not change a word.

ASK YOURSELF

Ernestine Rose embraced several positions—atheism, equal rights for women, abolition of slavery—that were extremely unpopular in her day. How large a role does the general popularity of a position play in your own willingness to publicly defend it?

TOPICS AND ACTIVITIES TO CONSIDER

Create a debate with Rose by alternating several of her arguments with your own rebuttals.

Further Information

Doress-Walters, Paula. *Mistress of Herself: Speeches and Letters of Ernestine Rose, Early Women's Rights Leader.* New York: Feminist Press at CUNY, 2008.
Gaylor, Annie Laurie, ed. *Women without Superstition: No Gods, No Masters.* Madison, WI: Freedom from Religion Foundation, 1997.

16. "The Great Agnostic"—Robert Green Ingersoll (1896)

INTRODUCTION

Despite a distinguished career in public service, Robert Ingersoll (1833–1899) was best known as an orator, a public speaker who drew enormous crowds to hear him advocate positions on the great issues of the day. He spoke on a tremendous variety of subjects, from literature to politics to religion. He was nicknamed "The Great Agnostic" for his frequent exploration of religious doubt in his talks.

Ingersoll's father, a Congregationalist minister, advocated the abolition of slavery and radical social reform, positions that often infuriated his more conservative congregations. The elder Ingersoll was removed from one pulpit after another or even put through "church trials" for unorthodoxy. Much of Robert's later criticism of traditional religion is thought to have been inspired by the mistreatment he saw his father endure.

The document below is an excerpt from "Why I Am an Agnostic," a speech devoted entirely to his religious opinions and observations. It continues to stand as one of the most complete discursions on agnosticism ever written or spoken.

KEEP IN MIND AS YOU READ

Though he distinguished himself in command of the 11th Illinois Cavalry Regiment during the Civil War and was active in Illinois state politics for many years, Robert Ingersoll's political career was severely limited by his radically progressive views on religion, women's rights, and slavery. At one point the state Republican Party urged him to run for governor but asked that he conceal his agnosticism. He refused, believing it unethical for a candidate to conceal information from the public, then turned to public oratory for the remainder of his career.

Document: Robert Green Ingersoll, "Why I Am an Agnostic" (1896)

For the most part we inherit our opinions. We are the heirs of habits and mental customs. Our beliefs, like the fashion of our garments, depend on where we were born. We are molded and fashioned by our surroundings. Environment is a sculptor—a painter.

If we had been born in Constantinople, the most of us would have said: "There is no God but Allah, and Mohammed is his prophet." If our parents had lived on the banks of the Ganges, we would have been worshipers of Siva, longing for the heaven of Nirvana. . . .

Like the most of you, I was raised among people who knew—who were certain. They did not reason or investigate. They had no doubts. They knew that they had the truth. In their creed there was no guess—no perhaps. They had a revelation from God. . . .

At the same time they knew that God created man in his own image and was perfectly satisfied with his work. They also knew that he had been thwarted by the Devil, who with wiles and lies had deceived the first of human kind. They knew that in consequence of that, God cursed the man and woman; the man with toil, the woman with slavery and pain, and both with death; and that he cursed the earth itself with briers and thorns, brambles and thistles. All these blessed things they knew . . . They knew that God, for the purpose of civilizing his children, had devoured some with earthquakes, destroyed some with storms of fire, killed some with his lightnings, millions with famine, with pestilence, and sacrificed countless thousands upon the fields of war. They knew that it was necessary to believe these things and to love God. They knew that there could be no salvation except by faith, and through the atoning blood of Jesus Christ.

All who doubted or denied would be lost. To live a moral and honest life—to keep your contracts, to take care of wife and child—to make a happy home—to be a good citizen, a patriot, a just and thoughtful man, was simply a respectable way of going to hell.

God did not reward men for being honest, generous and brave, but for the act of faith. Without faith, all the so-called virtues were sins, and the men who practiced these virtues, without faith, deserved to suffer eternal pain. . . .

I heard hundreds of these evangelical sermons—heard hundreds of the most fearful and vivid descriptions of the tortures inflicted in hell, of the horrible state of the lost. I supposed that what I heard was true and yet I did not believe it. I said: "It is," and then I thought: "It cannot be."

These sermons made but faint impressions on my mind. I was not convinced.

I had no desire to be "converted," did not want a "new heart" and had no wish to be "born again."

Free Will Baptist: a subgroup within the extended Baptist denomination that believes eternal life is granted solely upon acceptance of Christ as Savior (i.e., faith, not works).

But I heard one sermon that touched my heart, that left its mark, like a scar, on my brain. One Sunday I went with my brother to hear a **Free Will Baptist** preacher. He was a large man, dressed like a farmer, but he was an orator. He could paint a picture with words.

He took for his text the parable of "the rich man and Lazarus." He described Dives, the rich man—his manner of life, the excesses in which he indulged, his extravagance, his riotous nights, his purple and fine linen, his feasts, his wines, and his beautiful women.

Then he described Lazarus, his poverty, his rags and wretchedness, his poor body eaten by disease, the crusts and crumbs he devoured, the dogs that pitied him. He pictured his lonely life, his friendless death.

Then, changing his tone of pity to one of triumph—leaping from tears to the heights of exultation—from defeat to victory—he described the glorious company of angels, who with white and outspread wings carried the soul of the despised pauper to Paradise—to the bosom of Abraham.

Then, changing his voice to one of scorn and loathing, he told of the rich man's death. He was in his palace, on his costly couch, the air heavy with perfume, the room filled with servants and physicians. His gold was worthless then. He could not buy another breath. He died, and in hell he lifted up his eyes, being in torment.

Then, assuming a dramatic attitude, putting his right hand to his ear, he whispered, "Hark! I hear the rich man's voice. What does he say? Hark! 'Father Abraham! Father Abraham! I pray thee send Lazarus that he may dip the tip of his finger in water and cool my parched tongue, for I am tormented in this flame.'

"Oh, my hearers, he has been making that request for more than eighteen hundred years. And millions of ages hence that wail will cross the gulf that lies between the saved and lost and still will be heard the cry: 'Father Abraham! Father Abraham! I pray thee send Lazarus that he may dip the tip of his finger in water and cool my parched tongue, for I am tormented in this flame.'"

For the first time I understood the dogma of eternal pain—appreciated "the glad tidings of great joy." For the first time my imagination grasped the height and depth of the Christian horror. Then I said: "It is a lie, and I hate your religion. If it is true, I hate your God."

From that day I have had no fear, no doubt. For me, on that day, the flames of hell were quenched. From that day I have passionately hated every orthodox creed. That Sermon did some good.

IV

All the seeds of Christianity—of superstition, were sown in my mind and cultivated with great diligence and care.

All that time I knew nothing of any science—nothing about the other side—nothing of the objections that had been urged against the blessed Scriptures, or against the perfect Congregational creed. Of course I had heard the ministers speak of blasphemers, of infidel wretches, of scoffers who laughed at holy things. They did not answer their arguments, but they tore their characters into shreds and demonstrated by the fury of assertion that they had done the Devil's work. And yet in spite of all I heard—of all I read, I could not quite believe. My brain and heart said No.

For a time I left the dreams, the insanities, the illusions and delusions, the nightmares of theology. I studied astronomy, just a little—I examined maps of the heavens—learned the names of some of the constellations—of some of the stars—found something of their size and the velocity with which they wheeled in their orbits—obtained a faint conception of astronomical spaces—found that some of the known stars were so far away in the depths of space that their light, traveling at the rate of nearly two hundred thousand miles a second, required many years to reach this little world—found that, compared with the great stars, our earth was but a grain of sand—an atom—found that the old belief that all the hosts of heaven had been created for the benefit of man, was infinitely absurd.

I compared what was really known about the stars with the account of creation as told in Genesis. I found that the writer of the inspired book had no knowledge of astronomy—that he was as ignorant as a Choctaw chief—as an Eskimo driver of dogs. Does any one imagine that the author of Genesis knew anything about the sun—its size? that he was acquainted with Sirius, the North Star, with Capella, or that he knew anything of the clusters of stars so far away that their light, now visiting our eyes, has been traveling for two million years?

If he had known these facts would he have said that Jehovah worked nearly six days to make this world, and only a part of the afternoon of the fourth day to make the sun and moon and all the stars?

Yet millions of people insist that the writer of Genesis was inspired by the Creator of all worlds.

Now, intelligent men, who are not frightened, whose brains have not been paralyzed by fear, know that the sacred story of creation was written by an ignorant savage. The story is inconsistent with all known facts, and every star shining in the heavens testifies that its author was an uninspired barbarian.

I admit that this unknown writer was sincere, that he wrote what he believed to be true—that he did the best he could. He did not claim to be inspired—did not pretend that the story had been told to him by Jehovah. He simply stated the "facts" as he understood them.

After I had learned a little about the stars I concluded that this writer, this "inspired" scribe, had been misled by myth and legend, and that he knew no more about creation than the average theologian of my day. In other words, that he knew absolutely nothing. . . .

Then I studied geology—not much, just a little—Just enough to find in a general way the principal facts that had been discovered, and some of the conclusions that had been reached. . . .

Then I studied biology—not much—just enough to know something of animal forms, enough to know that life existed when the **Laurentian rocks** were made—just enough to know that implements of stone, implements that had been formed by human hands, had been found mingled with the bones of extinct animals, bones that had been split with these implements, and that these animals had ceased to exist hundreds of thousands of years before the manufacture of Adam and Eve.

Laurentian rocks: the lowest geologic stratum of the Archaean era (4.0 to 3.6 bya), which includes evidence of the earliest life forms on Earth

Then I felt sure that the "inspired" record was false—that many millions of people had been deceived and that all I had been taught about the origin of worlds and men was utterly untrue. I felt that I knew that the Old Testament was the work of ignorant men—that it was a mingling of truth and mistake, of wisdom and foolishness, of cruelty and kindness, of philosophy and absurdity—that it contained some elevated thoughts, some poetry,—a good deal of the solemn and commonplace,—some hysterical, some tender, some wicked prayers, some insane predictions, some delusions, and some chaotic dreams.

Of course the theologians fought the facts found by the geologists, the scientists, and sought to sustain the sacred Scriptures. They mistook the bones of the mastodon for those of human beings, and by them proudly proved that "there were giants in those days." They accounted for the fossils by saying that God had made them to try our faith, or that the Devil had imitated the works of the Creator.

They answered the geologists by saying that the "days" in Genesis were long periods of time, and that after all the flood might have been local. They told the astronomers that the sun and moon were not actually, but only apparently, stopped. And that the appearance was produced by the reflection and refraction of light.

They excused the slavery and polygamy, the robbery and murder upheld in the Old Testament by saying that the people were so degraded that Jehovah was compelled to pander to their ignorance and prejudice.

In every way the clergy sought to evade the facts, to dodge the truth, to preserve the creed.

At first they flatly denied the facts—then they belittled them—then they harmonized them—then they denied that they had denied them. Then they changed the meaning of the "inspired" book to fit the facts.

At first they said that if the facts, as claimed, were true, the Bible was false and Christianity itself a superstition. Afterward they said the facts, as claimed, were true and that they established beyond all doubt the inspiration of the Bible and the divine origin of orthodox religion.

Anything they could not dodge, they swallowed, and anything they could not swallow, they dodged.

I gave up the Old Testament on account of its mistakes, its absurdities, its ignorance and its cruelty. I gave up the New because it vouched for the truth of the Old. I gave it up on account of its miracles, its contradictions, because Christ and his disciples believe in the existence of devils—talked and made bargains with them, expelled them from people and animals. . . .

VI

My attention was turned to other religions, to the sacred books, the creeds and ceremonies of other lands—of India, Egypt, Assyria, Persia, of the dead and dying nations.

I concluded that all religions had the same foundation—a belief in the supernatural—a power above nature that man could influence by worship—by sacrifice and prayer.

I found that all religions rested on a mistaken conception of nature—that the religion of a people was the science of that people, that is to say, their explanation of the world—of life and death—of origin and destiny.

I concluded that all religions had substantially the same origin, and that in fact there has never been but one religion in the world. The twigs and leaves may differ, but the trunk is the same.

The poor African that pours out his heart to his deity of stone is on an exact religious level with the robed priest who supplicates his God. The same mistake, the same superstition, bends the knees and shuts the eyes of both. Both ask for supernatural aid, and neither has the slightest thought of the absolute uniformity of nature.

Apollo was a sun-god and he fought and conquered the serpent of night. Baldur was a sun-god. He was in love with the Dawn—a maiden. Chrishna was a sun-god. At his birth the Ganges was thrilled from its source to the sea, and all the trees, the dead as well as the living, burst into leaf and bud and flower. Hercules was a sun-god and so was Samson, whose strength was in his hair—that is to say, in his beams. He was shorn of his strength by Delilah, the shadow—the darkness. Osiris, Bacchus, and Mithra, Hermes, Buddha, and Quetzalcoatl, Prometheus, Zoroaster, and Perseus, Cadom, Lao-tsze, Fo-hi, Horus and Rameses, were all sun-gods.

All of these gods had gods for fathers and their mothers were virgins. The births of nearly all were announced by stars, celebrated by celestial music, and voices declared that a blessing had come to the poor world. All of these gods were born in humble places—in caves, under trees, in common inns, and tyrants sought to kill them all when they were babes. All of these sun-gods were born at the winter solstice—on Christmas. Nearly all were worshiped by "wise men." All of them fasted for forty days—all of them taught in parables—all of them wrought miracles—all met with a violent death, and all rose from the dead.

The history of these gods is the exact history of our Christ.

This is not a coincidence—an accident. Christ was a sun-god. Christ was a new name for an old biography—a survival—the last of the sun-gods. Christ was not a man, but a myth—not a life, but a legend.

I found that we had not only borrowed our Christ—but that all our sacraments, symbols and ceremonies were legacies that we received from the buried past. There is nothing original in Christianity.

Then I concluded that all religions had been naturally produced, and that all were variation, modifications of one,—then I felt that I knew that all were the work of man. . . .

Darwin, with his *Origin of Species*, his theories about Natural Selection, the Survival of the Fittest, and the influence of environment, shed a flood of light upon the great problems of plant and animal life. . . .

Theology looked more absurd than ever.

Huxley entered the lists for Darwin. No man ever had a sharper sword—a better shield. He challenged the world. The great theologians and the small scientists—those who had more courage than sense, accepted the challenge. Their poor bodies were carried away by their friends.

Huxley had intelligence, industry, genius, and the courage to express his thought. He was absolutely loyal to what he thought was truth. Without prejudice and without fear, he followed the footsteps of life from the lowest to the highest forms.

Theology looked smaller still.

Haeckel began at the simplest cell, went from change to change—from form to form—followed the line of development, the path of life, until he reached the human race. It was all natural. There had been no interference from without.

I read the works of these great men—of many others—and became convinced that they were right, and that all the theologians—all the believers in "special creation" were absolutely wrong.

The Garden of Eden faded away, Adam and Eve fell back to dust, the snake crawled into the grass, and Jehovah became a miserable myth. . . .

> **Haeckel:** Ernst Haeckel (1834–1919), a German biologist and naturalist whose work included hypotheses regarding the pace, stages, and nature of evolutionary change

Is there a God?

I do not know.

Is man immortal?

I do not know.

One thing I do know, and that is, that neither hope, nor fear, belief, nor denial, can change the fact. It is as it is, and it will be as it must be.

We wait and hope. . . .

XI

When I became convinced that the Universe is natural—that all the ghosts and gods are myths, there entered into my brain, into my soul, into every drop of my blood, the sense, the feeling, the joy of freedom. The walls of my prison crumbled and fell, the dungeon was flooded with light and all the bolts, and bars, and manacles became dust. I was no longer a servant, a serf or a slave. There was for me no master in all the wide world—not even in infinite space. I was free—free to think, to express my thoughts—free to live to my own ideal—free to live for myself and those I loved—free to use all my faculties, all my senses—free to spread imagination's wings—free to investigate, to guess and dream and hope—free to judge and determine for myself—free to reject all ignorant and cruel creeds, all the "inspired" books that savages have produced, and all the barbarous legends of the past—free from popes and priests—free from all the "called" and "set apart"—free from sanctified mistakes and holy lies—free from the fear of eternal pain—free from the winged monsters of the night—free from devils, ghosts and gods. For the first time I was free. There were no prohibited places in all the realms of thought—no air, no space, where fancy could not spread her painted wings—no chains for my limbs—no lashes for my back—no fires for my flesh—no master's frown or threat—no following another's steps—no need to bow, or cringe, or crawl, or utter lying words. I was free. I stood erect and fearlessly, joyously, faced all worlds.

And then my heart was filled with gratitude, with thankfulness, and went out in love to all the heroes, the thinkers who gave their lives for the liberty of hand and brain—for the freedom of labor and thought—to those who fell on the fierce fields of war, to those who died in dungeons bound with chains—to those who proudly mounted scaffold's stairs—to those whose bones were crushed, whose flesh was scarred and torn—to those by fire consumed—to all the wise, the good, the brave of every land, whose thoughts and deeds have given freedom to the sons of men. And then I vowed to grasp the torch that they had held, and hold it high, that light might conquer darkness still.

Let us be true to ourselves—true to the facts we know, and let us, above all things, preserve the veracity of our souls.

If there be gods we cannot help them, but we can assist our fellow-men. We cannot love the inconceivable, but we can love wife and child and friend.

We can be as honest as we are ignorant. If we are, when asked what is beyond the horizon of the known, we must say that we do not know. We can tell the truth, and we can enjoy the blessed freedom that the brave have won. We can destroy the monsters of superstition, the hissing snakes of ignorance and fear. We can drive from our minds the frightful things that tear and wound with beak and fang. We can civilize our fellow-men. We can fill our lives with generous deeds, with loving words, with art and song, and all the ecstasies of love. We can flood our years with sunshine—with the divine climate of kindness, and we can drain to the last drop the golden cup of joy.

Source: Ingersoll, Robert Green. "Why I Am an Agnostic." *The Works of Robert G. Ingersoll.* New York: Dresden/C. P. Farrell, 1920.

AFTERWARD

Soon after Ingersoll's death in 1899, his brother-in-law collected his best-known speeches for publication in a 12-volume set. By committing his spoken-word orations to the published page, this vital step allowed access to Ingersoll's ideas and powerful oratorical style by subsequent generations. He continues to be regarded as one of the most influential and important freethought voices in U.S. history.

ASK YOURSELF

1. Though Ingersoll's agnosticism drew sharp criticism from some, he was able to include clear and open statements of religious unbelief and direct criticisms of religion in his speeches and still draw large, enthusiastic crowds. Taking "Why I Am an Agnostic" as representative, what in Ingersoll's content or approach might account for this?
2. Do you think a public speech of this kind would be more or less acceptable to an audience in the United States in the 21st century?

TOPICS AND ACTIVITIES TO CONSIDER

Do you think public criticism of religious belief and institutions by Ingersoll and others is good or bad for those institutions in the long run? Do you think it is good or bad for the larger society in the long run to have such open critique of key institutions? Why?

Further Information

Greeley, Roger, ed. *The Best of Robert Ingersoll, Immortal Infidel: Selections from His Writings and Speeches.* Amherst, NY: Prometheus Books, 1993.
Jacoby, Susan. *Freethinkers: A History of American Secularism.* New York: Holt, 2004.
Page, Tim. *What's God Got to Do with It?: Robert Ingersoll on Free Thought, Honest Talk and the Separation of Church and State.* Hanover, NH: Steerforth Press, 2005.

Web Site

Historical writings of Ingersoll: http://www.positiveatheism.org/tochingr.htm.

17. Feminism and Freethought—Elizabeth Cady Stanton (1885)

INTRODUCTION

Like Frances Wright and Ernestine Rose, Elizabeth Cady Stanton (1815–1902) considered her direct and forceful criticisms of religion to be directly pertinent to her passions for social reform, women's rights, and the abolition of slavery. Her pamphlet "Has Christianity Benefited Woman?" answered its own title with a resounding no. It was one of several (including "The Degraded Status of Woman in the Bible," written when Stanton was 81) that cemented her reputation as one of the most outspoken 19th-century critics of the negative influence of Christian orthodoxy on women.

Stanton is also credited with launching the women's suffrage movement in the United States with her "Declaration of Sentiments," presented to the first women's rights convention in Seneca Falls, New York, in 1848.

KEEP IN MIND AS YOU READ

In retrospect, movements of all kinds—social, political, artistic, religious—often give an appearance of unity that close examination does not bear out. Though pioneering feminists were almost entirely religious skeptics to some degree, they differed over whether aligning that perspective with the cause of women's rights was strategically wise. Stanton clearly felt it was appropriate, while other leaders in the movement, including Susan B. Anthony, a Unitarian agnostic, expressed concern that it could further compel the enemies of women's rights to action against them.

Another rift occurred when Stanton and others chose to oppose the extension of voting rights to African Americans before all whites had secured those rights. That she made her case in language that was sometimes racially insulting was a further source of division. This rift was healed in 1890 with the creation of a single women's voting rights organization, the National American Woman Suffrage Association, with Stanton as president.

Document: Elizabeth Cady Stanton, "Has Christianity Benefited Woman?" (1885)

The assertion that woman owes all the advantages of her present position to the Christian church, has been repeated so often, that it is accepted as an established truth by those who would be unwilling to admit that all the injustice and degradation she has suffered might be logically traced to the same source. A consideration of woman's position before Christianity, under Christianity, and at the present time, shows that she is not indebted to any form of religion for one step of progress, or one new liberty; on the contrary, it has been through the perversion of her religious sentiments that she has been so long held in a condition of slavery. All religions thus far have taught the headship and superiority of man, the inferiority and subordination of woman. Whatever new dignity, honor, and self-respect the changing theologies may have brought to man, they have all alike brought to woman but another form of humiliation. History shows that the condition of woman has changed with different forms of civilization, and that she has enjoyed in some periods greater honor and dignity and more personal and property rights than have been accorded her in the Christian era. History shows, too, that the moral degradation of woman is due more to theological superstitions than to all other influences together. It is not to any form of religion that we are to look for woman's advancement, but to material civilization, to commerce, science, art, invention, to the discovery of the art of printing, and the general dissemination of knowledge. Buckle, in his "History of Civilization," calls attention to the fact that when woman became valuable in a commercial sense, in proportion as she secured material elevation and wealth through her property rights, she began to be treated with a deference and respect that the Christian church never accorded. In ancient Egypt, at the most brilliant period of its history, a woman sat upon the throne and directed the civilization of the country. In the marriage relation she was supreme in all things—a rule that, according to Wilkinson, was productive of lasting fidelity. As priestess she performed the most holy offices of religion, and to her is traced the foundation of Egyptian literature, the sacred songs of Isis, said by Plato to be ten thousand years old. Colleges for women were founded there twelve hundred years before Christ, and the medical profession was in the hands of women. It is a sad commentary on the Christianity of England and America, to find professors in medical colleges of the nineteenth century less liberal than those in the earliest civilizations. In 1876, four professors in the College of Surgeons in London resigned because three women were licensed for the practice of midwifery, and the whole Royal College of Physicians thanked them for it. In 1869, the professors in the University of Edinburgh refused to teach four highly respectable women that had matriculated, and the students, echoing the contempt of their teachers, mobbed them. Nor did the conduct of American students, when women were admitted to the clinics of the Pennsylvania and New York hospitals, reflect greater credit on American manhood. . . .

In harmony with the pagan worship of an ideal womanhood of sibyls, oracles, and priestesses, women held prominent positions in the church for several centuries after Christ. We have proof of this in the restrictions that at a later period were placed upon them by **canon laws**. The Council of Laodicea, three hundred and sixty-five years after Christ, forbade the ordination of women to the ministry, and prohibited them from entering the altar. The Council of Orleans, five hundred and eleven years after Christ, consisting of twenty-six bishops and priests, promul-

> **canon law:** regulations adopted by the leadership of a religious denomination to govern the organization and its members

gated a canon that, on account of their frailty, women must be excluded from the deaconship. Nearly three hundred years later we find the Council of Paris complaining that women serve at the altar, and even give to the people the body and blood of Jesus Christ. Through these canons we have the negative proof that for centuries women preached, baptized, administered the sacrament, and filled various offices of the church; and that ecclesiastics, through prohibitory canons, annulled these rights.

In the fifth century the church fully developed the doctrine of original sin, making woman its weak and guilty author. To St. Augustine, whose early life was licentious and degraded, we are indebted for this idea, which was infused into the canon law, and was the basis of all the persecutions woman endured for centuries, in the drift of Christian opinion from the extremes of polygamy to celibacy, from the virtues of chivalry to the cruelties of witchcraft, when the church taught its devotees to shun woman as a temptation and defilement. It was this persecution, this crushing out of the feminine element in humanity, more than all other influences combined, that plunged the world into the dark ages, shadowing the slowly rolling centuries till now with woman's agonies and death, paralyzing literature, science, commerce, education, changing the features of art, the sentiments of poetry, the ethics of philosophy, from the tender, the loving, the beautiful, the grand, to the stern, the dark, the terrible. Even the paintings representing Jesus were gradually changed from the gentle, watchful shepherd to the stern, unrelenting judge. Harrowing representations of the temptation, the crucifixion, the judgment-day, the Inferno, were intensified and elaborated by Dante and Milton. Painter and poet vied with each other in their gloomy portrayals, while crafty bishops coined these crude terrors into canons, and timid, dishonest judges allowed them to throw their dark shadows over the civil law.

The influence of the church on woman's civil position was equally calamitous. A curious old black-letter volume, published in London in 1632, entitled "The Laws and Resolutions of Woman's Rights," says, "The reason why women have no control in Parliament, why they make no laws, consent to none, abrogate none, is their Original Sin." This idea is the chief block in the way of woman's advancement at this hour. It was fully set forth by the canon law, with wearisome repetition, and when, in the fifteenth century, the sacred Scriptures were collected and first printed, the spirit of these canons and all that logically grew out of them were engrafted on its pages, making woman an afterthought in the creation, the author of sin, in collusion with the devil, sex a crime, marriage a condition of slavery for woman and defilement for man, and maternity a curse to be attended with sorrow and suffering that neither time nor knowledge could ever mitigate, a just punishment for having effected the downfall of man. And all these monstrous ideas, emanating from the bewildered brains of men in the dark ages, under an exclusively masculine religion, were declared to be the word of God, penned by writers specially inspired by his Spirit.

Just at the period when the civil code began to recognize the equality and independence of the wife in the marriage relation, the church, to which woman had reason to look for protection, either blindly or perversely gave the whole force of its power against woman's equality in the family, and in fact against her influence altogether. In chapter V. of Maine's "Ancient Law" we have a clear statement of the influence of canon law on the liberty of person and property that Roman women then enjoyed. Speaking of their freedom, he says:

"Christianity tended from the very first to narrow this remarkable liberty." "No society which preserves any tincture of Christian institution is likely to restore to married women the personal liberty conferred on them by middle Roman law." "The expositors of the canon law have deeply injured civilization." "There are many vestiges of a struggle between the secular and ecclesiastical principles, but the canon law nearly everywhere prevailed. In some of the French provinces married women of a rank below nobility, obtained all the powers of dealing with property which Roman jurisprudence had allowed, and this local law has been largely followed by the code Napoleon. The systems, however, which are least indulgent to married women are invariably those which have followed the canon law exclusively, or those which from the lateness of their contact with European civilization have never had their archaisms weeded out."

By the dishonoring of womanhood on the ground of original sin, by the dishonoring of all relations with her as carnal and unclean, the whole sex touched a depth of moral degradation that it had never known before. Rescued in a measure from the miseries of polygamy, woman was plunged into the more degrading and unnatural condition of celibacy. Out of this grew the terrible persecutions of witchcraft, which raged for centuries, women being its chief victims. They were hunted down by the clergy, tortured, burned, drowned, dragged into the courts, tried, and condemned, for crimes that never existed but in the minds of religious devotees. The clergy sustained witchcraft as Bible doctrine, far into the eighteenth century, until the spirit of rationalism laughed the whole thing to scorn and gave mankind a more cheerful view of life. The reformation brought no new hope to woman. The great head of the movement [Martin Luther], while declaring the right of individual conscience and judgment above church authority, as if to warn woman that she had no share in this liberty, was wont to say, "No gown worse becomes a woman than that she should be wise." Here is the key-note to the Protestant pulpit for three centuries, and it grates harshly on our ears to-day. The Catholic Church, in its holy sisterhoods, so honored and revered, and in its worship of the Virgin Mary, Mother of Jesus, has preserved some recognition of the feminine element in its religion; but from Protestantism it is wholly eliminated. Religions like the Jewish and Christian, which make God exclusively male and man supreme, consign woman logically to the subordinate position assigned her in Mohammed's. History has perpetuated this tradition, and her subjection has existed as an invariable element in Christian civilization. It could not be otherwise, with the Godhead represented as a trinity of males. The old masters in the galleries of art have left us their ideals of the Trinity in three bearded male heads. No heavenly Mother is recognized in the Protestant world.

The present position of woman in the spirit of our creeds and codes is far behind the civilization of the age, and unworthy the representative women of this day. And now, as ever, the strongest adverse influence to her elevation comes from the church, judging from its Biblical expositions, the attitude of the clergy, and the insignificant status that woman holds in the various sectarian organizations. For nearly forty years there has been an organized movement in England and America to liberalize the laws in relation to woman, to secure a more profitable place in the world of work, to open the colleges for higher education, and the schools of medicine, law, and theology, and to give woman an equal voice in the government and religion of the country. These demands, one by one, are slowly being conceded by the secular branch of the government, while the sectarian influence has been uniformly in the opposite direction. Appeals before legislative assemblies, constitutional conventions, and the highest courts have been respectfully heard and decided, while propositions for the consideration even of some honors to women in the church have uniformly been received with sneers and denunciations by leading denominations, who quote Scripture freely to maintain their position. Judges and statesmen have made able arguments in their respective places for woman's civil and political rights; but where shall we look for sectarian leaders that, in their general assemblies, synods, or other ecclesiastical conventions, have advocated a higher position for woman in the church? The attitude of the clergy is the same as in bygone centuries, modified somewhat, on this as on all other questions, by advancing civilization. The Methodists have a lay ministry, but they do not ordain women. Liberal clergymen in other sects have been arraigned and tried by their general assemblies for allowing women to preach in their pulpits. In imitation of the high churches in England, we have some in this country in which boys from twelve to fifteen supply the place of women in the choir, that the sacred altars may not be defiled by the inferior sex—an early Christian idea. The discourses of clergymen, when they enlarge on the condition of woman, read more like canons in the fifth century than sermons in the nineteenth, addressed to those who are their peers in religious thought and scientific attainment. The Rev. Morgan Dix's Lenten lectures last spring, and Bishop Littlejohn's last triennial sermon, are fair specimens. The latter recommends that all the liberal legislation of the past forty years for woman should be reversed, while the former is the chief obstacle in the way of woman's admission to Columbia College. And these fairly represent the sentiments of the vast majority, who never refer to the movement for woman's enfranchisement but with ridicule and contempt—sentiments that they insidiously infuse into all classes of women under their influence. None of the leading theological seminaries will admit women who are preparing for the ministry, and none of the leading denominations will ordain them when prepared. The Universalists, Unitarians, and Quakers are the only sects that ordain women. And yet women are the chief supporters of the church to-day. They make the surplices and gowns, get up the fairs and donation parties, and are the untiring beggars for its benefit. They supply its enthusiasm, and are continually making large bequests to its treasury; and their reward is still the echo of the old canon law of woman's subjection, from pulpit to pulpit throughout Christendom. Though England and America are the two nations in which the Christian religion is dominant, and can boast the highest type of womanhood, and the

Rev. Charles Kingsley (1819–1875): chaplain-in-ordinary to Queen Victoria and Cambridge historian. See also "Letter from Thomas Henry Huxley to Rev. Charles Kingsley, September 23, 1860" in this volume

John Stuart Mill (1806–1873): influential British philosopher and agnostic

greatest number in every department of art, science, and literature, yet even here women have been compelled to clear their own way for every step in progress. Not one wrong has been righted until women themselves made organized resistance against it. In the face of every form of opposition they are throwing off the disabilities of the old common law, which Lord Brougham said long ago "was in relation to woman the opprobrium of the age and Christianity." And not until they make an organized resistance against the withering influence of the canon law, will they rid themselves of the moral disabilities growing out of the theologies of our times. When I was standing near the last resting-place of **Rev. Charles Kingsley** not long ago, his warning words for woman, in a letter to **John Stuart Mill**, seemed like a voice from the clouds, saying with new inspiration and power, "This will never be a good world for woman until the last remnant of the canon law is civilized off the face of the earth."

Source: Stanton, Elizabeth Cady. "Has Christianity Benefited Woman?," *North American Review* 342 (May 1885).

AFTERWARD

Feminism and religious unbelief continued to show a high correlation into the 20th century, and several later feminist leaders including Simone de Beauvoir and Gloria Steinem cited Stanton as an influential predecessor.

ASK YOURSELF

Stanton and other critics of Christian religion are often accused of "cherry-picking" examples from Christian history and scripture—selecting those that support their argument and ignoring others. Do you agree with this criticism?

"NO GODS, NO MASTERS"—UNBELIEF AND EARLY FEMINISM

A little-known aspect of the women's rights movement is the fact that most of the major figures in the "first wave" of feminism—Ernestine Rose, Susan B. Anthony, Matilda Joslyn Gage, Margaret Sanger, and Elizabeth Cady Stanton, among others—were atheists or agnostics. In most cases this was not incidental; many of these women forcefully expressed the conviction that religion in general and the Bible in particular had been used to keep women disempowered for centuries. "The Bible and the church have been the greatest stumbling blocks in the way of woman's emancipation," said Stanton. Anthony said, "To no form of religion is woman indebted for one impulse of freedom," while Margaret Sanger adopted "No Gods, No Masters" as her personal motto.

Atheists and agnostics continued to dominate the ranks of feminism throughout the 20th century and into the 21st, including journalist/activists Gloria Steinem, Barbara Ehrenreich, and Katha Pollitt.

TOPICS AND ACTIVITIES TO CONSIDER

- ఈ Taking her title as her thesis, create a concise, bulleted summary of several of Stanton's major points. Which do you think most strongly supports the thesis? Which is weakest? Why?
- ఈ Write a response to Stanton's article arguing that Christianity has indeed benefited women. Address some of Stanton's individual points when possible.
- ఈ Have class members write letters to the editor of the *North American Review* from the perspective of an 1885 reader of Stanton's article. Limit responses to 150 words, and have each student identify him or herself in the text (e.g., "As a long-standing member of the Christian church," or "As an educated woman," etc.).

Further Information

Gaylor, Annie Laurie, ed. *Women without Superstition: No Gods, No Masters.* Madison, WI: Freedom From Religion Foundation, 1997.

Web Site

Not for Ourselves Alone: The Story of Elizabeth Cady Stanton and Susan B. Anthony, a documentary film by Ken Burns and Paul Barnes: http://www.pbs.org/stantonanthony.

18. Erasing Unbelief—Charles Darwin's *Autobiography* (1887, 1958)

INTRODUCTION

In May 1876, Charles Darwin sat down to write what he called "recollections of the development of my mind and character," driven in part by realizing "that it would have interested me greatly to have read even so short and dull a sketch of the mind of my grandfather [Erasmus Darwin] written by himself, and what he thought and did and how he worked." He thought the attempt at such a thing "would amuse me, and might possibly interest my children or their children."

The *Autobiography* first appeared publicly in 1887 as part of *Life and Letters of Charles Darwin*, edited by his son Francis. Among the explorations of his own life and opinions, Charles had included a 12-page discursion on the change in his religious beliefs over the years from a literalist Christian in training for the ministry to a confirmed agnostic. It was this section that troubled his wife, Emma, a devout Christian. In order to protect Charles's reputation, she urged her son to remove the passages most directly critical of religion, as well as those suggesting that morality could be derived without reference to a god. The passages were removed for the 1887 edition but restored in 1958 (see Afterward).

KEEP IN MIND AS YOU READ

Darwin came to his agnosticism only gradually. He was deeply religious as a young man, having trained for the ministry. He described annoying his shipmates on the HMS *Beagle* with fundamentalist pronouncements. It was that five-year voyage of scientific discovery that led Darwin to thoroughly revise his opinions.

Emma Darwin's unease at allowing Charles's agnosticism and critiques of religion to be published was not without cause. In 1839, another widow, Mary Shelley, removed several strong religious critiques from a poem by her husband, Percy Shelley, when she edited his collected works. A publisher who restored the passages in 1841 was arrested and convicted of blasphemous libel.

Document: Charles Darwin, Autobiography (1887, 1958)

N.B. Bracketed and italicized text indicates passages omitted in the 1887 edition and restored in the 1958 edition.

During these two years[1] I was led to think much about religion. Whilst on board the *Beagle* I was quite orthodox, and I remember being heartily laughed at by several of the officers (although themselves orthodox) for quoting the Bible as an unanswerable authority on some point of morality. I suppose it was the novelty of the argument that amused them. *[But I had gradually come, by this time, to see that the Old Testament from its manifestly false history of the world, with the Tower of Babel, the rainbow as a sign, etc., etc., and from its attributing to God the feelings of a revengeful tyrant, was no more to be trusted than the sacred books of the Hindus, or the beliefs of any barbarian.]* The question then continually rose, before my mind and would not be banished,— is it credible that if God were now to make a revelation to the Hindus, he would permit it to be connected with the belief in Vishnu, Siva, etc., as Christianity is connected with the Old Testament? This appeared to me utterly incredible.

By further reflecting that the clearest evidence would be requisite to make any sane man believe in the miracles by which Christianity is supported,—and that the more we know of the fixed laws of nature the more incredible do miracles become,—that the men at that time were ignorant and credulous to a degree almost incomprehensible by us,—that the Gospels cannot be proved to have been written simultaneously with the events,—that they differ in many important details, far too important, as it seemed to me, to be admitted as the usual inaccuracies of eyewitnesses;—by such reflections as these, which I give not as having the least novelty or value, but as they influenced me, I gradually came to disbelieve in Christianity as a divine revelation. The fact that many false religions have spread over large portions of the earth like wild-fire had some weight with me. *[Beautiful as is the morality of the New Testament, it can be hardly denied that its perfection depends in part on the interpretation which we now put on metaphors and allegories.]*

But I was very unwilling to give up my belief; I feel sure of this, for I can well remember often and often inventing day-dreams of old letters between distinguished Romans, and manuscripts being discovered at Pompeii or elsewhere, which confirmed in the most striking manner all that was written in the Gospels. But I found it more and more difficult, with free scope given to my imagination, to invent evidence which would suffice to convince me. Thus disbelief crept over me at a very slow rate, but was at last complete. The rate was so slow that I felt no distress *[and have never since doubted for a single second that my conclusion was correct. I can indeed hardly see how anyone ought to wish Christianity to be true; for if so the plain language of the text seems to show that the men who do not believe, and this would include my Father, Brother and almost all of my friends, will be everlastingly punished. And this is a damnable doctrine.]*[2]

---

[1]October 1836–January 1839.

[2]"I should dislike the passage in brackets to be published," wrote Emma Darwin in the margin of the manuscript by this passage. "It seems to me raw. Nothing can be said too severe upon the doctrine of everlasting punishment for disbelief—but very few now wd. call that 'Christianity,' (tho' the words are there)."

Although I did not think much about the existence of a personal God until a considerably later period of my life, I will here give the vague conclusions to which I have been driven. The old argument from design in Nature, as given by **Paley**, which formerly seemed to me so conclusive, fails, now that the law of natural selection has been discovered. We can no longer argue that, for instance, the beautiful hinge of a bivalve shell must have been made by an intelligent being, like the hinge of a door by man. There seems to be no more design in the variability of organic beings, and in the action of natural selection, than in the course which the wind blows. *[Everything in nature is the result of fixed laws.]* But I have discussed this subject at the end of my book on the *Variations of Domesticated Animals and Plants*,[3] and the argument there given has never, as far as I can see, been answered.

> **Paley:** William Paley (1743–1805), British Christian philosopher and apologist, originator of the "watchmaker analogy" to support the existence of God (if you were to find a watch on the ground, you would not assume it had always been there, but would infer the existence of a watchmaker)

But passing over the endless beautiful adaptations which we everywhere meet with, it may be asked how can the generally beneficent arrangement of the world be accounted for? Some writers indeed are so much impressed with the amount of suffering in the world, that they doubt, if we look to all sentient beings, whether there is more of misery or of happiness; whether the world as a whole is a good or bad one. According to my judgment happiness decidedly prevails, though this would be very difficult to prove. If the truth of this conclusion be granted, it harmonizes well with the effects which we might expect from natural selection. If all the individuals of any species were habitually to suffer to an extreme degree, they would neglect to propagate their kind; but we have no reason to believe that this has ever, or at least often occurred. Some other considerations, moreover, lead to the belief that all sentient beings have been formed so as to enjoy, as a general rule, happiness.

Every one who believes, as I do, that all the corporeal and mental organs (excepting those which are neither advantageous nor disadvantageous to the possessor) of all beings have been developed through natural selection, or the survival of the fittest, together with use or habit, will admit that these organs have been formed so that their possessors may compete successfully with other beings, and thus increase in number. Now an animal may be led to pursue that course of action which is most beneficial to the species by suffering, such as pain, hunger, thirst, and fear; or by pleasure, as in eating and drinking, and in the propagation of the species, etc., or by both means combined, as in the search for food. But pain or suffering of any kind, if long continued, causes depression and lessens the power of action, yet is well adapted to make a creature guard itself against any great or sudden evil. Pleasurable sensations, on the other hand, may be long continued without any depressing effect; on the contrary, they stimulate the whole system to increased action. Hence it has come to pass that most or all

---

[3]Francis Darwin summarized the referenced passage in the first edition of the *Autobiography*: "My father asks whether we are to believe that the forms are preordained of the broken fragments of rock which are fitted together by man to build his houses. If not, why should we believe that the variations of domestic animals or plants are preordained for the sake of the breeder? But if we give up the principle in one case . . . no shadow of reason can be assigned for the belief that variations alike in nature and the result of the same general laws, which have been the groundwork through natural selection of the formation of the most perfectly adapted animals in the world, man included, were intentionally and specially guided." [N.B. The exact title of the book in question is *The Variation of Animals and Plants under Domestication* (1868).]

sentient beings have been developed in such a manner, through natural selection, that pleasurable sensations serve as their habitual guides. We see this in the pleasure from exertion, even occasionally from great exertion of the body or mind,— in the pleasure of our daily meals, and especially in the pleasure derived from sociability, and from loving our families. The sum of such pleasures as these, which are habitual or frequently recurrent, give, as I can hardly doubt, to most sentient beings an excess of happiness over misery, although many occasionally suffer much. Such suffering is quite compatible with the belief in Natural Selection, which is not perfect in its action, but tends only to render each species as successful as possible in the battle for life with other species, in wonderfully complex and changing circumstances.

That there is much suffering in the world no one disputes. Some have attempted to explain this with reference to man by imagining that it serves for his moral improvement. But the number of men in the world is as nothing compared with that of all other sentient beings, and they often suffer greatly without any moral improvement. *[A being so powerful and so full of knowledge as a God who could create the universe, is to our finite minds omnipotent and omniscient, and it revolts our understanding to suppose that his benevolence is not unbounded, for what advantage can there be in the suffering of millions of the lower animals throughout almost endless time?]* This very old argument from the existence of suffering against the existence of an intelligent First Cause seems to me a strong one; whereas, as just remarked, the presence of much suffering agrees well with the view that all organic beings have been developed through variation and natural selection.

At the present day the most usual argument for the existence of an intelligent God is drawn from the deep inward conviction and feelings which are experienced by most persons. *[But it cannot be doubted that Hindus, Mohammedans and others might argue in the same manner and with equal force in favour of the existence of one God, or of many Gods, or as with the Buddhists of no God. There are also many barbarian tribes who cannot be said with any truth to believe in what we call God: they believe indeed in spirits or ghosts, and it can be explained, as Tyler and Herbert Spencer have shown, how such a belief would be likely to arise.]*

Formerly I was led by feelings such as those just referred to (although I do not think that the religious sentiment was ever very strongly developed in me), to the firm conviction of the existence of God, and of the immortality of the soul. In my Journal I wrote that whilst standing in the midst of the grandeur of a Brazilian forest, "it is not possible to give an adequate idea of the higher feelings of wonder, admiration, and devotion, which fill and elevate the mind." I well remember my conviction that there is more in man than the mere breath of his body. But now the grandest scenes would not cause any such convictions and feelings to rise in my mind. It may be truly said that I am like a man who has become colour-blind, and the universal belief by men of the existence of redness makes my present loss of perception of not the least value as evidence. This argument would be a valid one if all men of all races had the same inward conviction of the existence of one God; but we know that this is very far from being the case. Therefore I cannot see that such inward convictions and feelings are of any weight as evidence of what really exists. The state of mind which grand scenes formerly excited in me, and which was intimately connected with a belief in God, did not essentially differ from that which is often called the sense of sublimity; and however difficult it may be to explain the genesis of this sense, it can hardly be advanced as an argument for the existence of God, any more than the powerful though vague and similar feelings excited by music.

With respect to immortality, nothing shows me how strong and almost instinctive a belief it is, as the consideration of the view now held by most physicists, namely, that the sun with all the planets will in time grow too cold for life, unless indeed some great body dashes into the sun, and thus gives it fresh life. Believing as I do that man in the distant future will be a far more perfect creature than he now is, it is an intolerable thought that he and all other sentient beings are doomed to complete annihilation after such long-continued slow progress. To those who fully admit the immortality of the human soul, the destruction of our world will not appear so dreadful.

Another source of conviction in the existence of God, connected with the reason, and not with the feelings, impresses me as having much more weight. This follows from the extreme difficulty or rather impossibility of conceiving this immense and wonderful universe, including man with his capacity of looking far backwards and far into futurity, as the result of blind chance or necessity. When thus reflecting I feel compelled to look to a First Cause having an intelligent mind in some degree analogous to that of man; and I deserve to be called a Theist. This conclusion was strong in my mind about the time, as far as I can remember, when I wrote the *Origin of Species*; and it is since that time that it has very gradually, with many fluctuations, become weaker. But then arises the doubt;—can the mind of man, which has, as I fully believe, been developed from a mind as low as that possessed by the lowest animals, be trusted when it draws such grand conclusions? *[May not these be the result of the connection between cause and effect which strikes us as a necessary one, but probably depends merely on inherited experience? Nor must we overlook the probability of the constant inculcation in a belief in God on the minds of children producing so strong and perhaps an inherited effect on their brains not fully developed, that it would be as difficult for them to throw off their belief in God, as for the monkey to throw off its instinctive fear and hatred of a snake.]*

I cannot pretend to throw the least light on such abstruse problems. The mystery of the beginning of all things is insoluble by us; and I for one must be content to remain an Agnostic.

[A man who has no assured and ever-present belief in the existence of a personal God or of future existence with retribution and reward, can have for his rule of life, as far as I can see, only to follow those impulses and instincts which are the strongest or which seem to him the best ones. A dog acts in this manner, but he does so blindly. A man, on the other hand, looks forwards and backwards, and compares his various feelings, desires and recollections. He then finds, in accordance with the verdict of all the wisest men that the highest satisfaction is derived from following certain impulses, namely the social instincts. If he acts for the good of others, he will receive the approbation of his fellow men and gain the love of those with whom he lives; and this latter gain undoubtedly is the highest pleasure on this earth. By degree it will become intolerable to him to obey his sensuous passions rather than his higher impulses, which when rendered habitual may be almost called instincts. His reason may occasionally tell him to act in opposition to the opinion of others, whose approbation he will then not receive; but he will still have the solid satisfaction of knowing that he has followed his innermost guide or conscience. As for myself I believe that I have acted rightly in steadily following and devoting my life to science. I feel no remorse from having committed any great sin, but have often and often regretted that I have not done more direct good to my fellow

creatures. My sole and poor excuse is much ill-health and my mental constitution, which makes it extremely difficult for me to turn from one subject or occupation to another. I can imagine with high satisfaction giving up my whole life to philanthropy, but not a portion of it; though this would have been a far better line of conduct.

Nothing is more remarkable than the spread of skepticism or rationalism during the latter half of my life. Before I was engaged to be married, my father advised me to conceal carefully my doubts, for he said he had known extreme misery thus created with married persons. Things went on pretty well until the wife or husband became out of health, and then some women suffered miserably by doubting upon the salvation of their husbands, thus making them likewise to suffer. My father added that he had known during his whole long life only three women who were sceptics; and it should be remembered that he knew well a multitude of persons and possessed extraordinary power of winning confidence. When I asked him who the three women were, he had to own with respect to one of them, his sister-in-law Kitty Wedgwood, that he had no good evidence, only the vaguest hints, aided by the conviction that so clear-sighted a woman could not be a believer. At the present time, with my small acquaintance, I know (or have known) several married ladies, who believe very little more than their husbands. My father used to quote an unanswerable argument, by which an old lady, a Mrs. Barlow, who suspected him of unorthodoxy, hoped to convert him:—"Doctor, I know that sugar is sweet in my mouth, and I know that my Redeemer Liveth."]

Source: Expurgated text from Darwin, Charles. *The Autobiography of Charles Darwin.* London: John Murray, 1887. Restored passages from Darwin, Charles. *The Autobiography of Charles Darwin, with Original Omissions Restored.* Edited by Nora Barlow. New York: Harcourt, Brace, 1958, 85–96.

THE LADY HOPE STORY

Deathbed recantations of religious unbelief or heresy constitute a large subgenre of modern religious folklore. A rumor among Catholics in 16th-century Europe suggested that Protestant reformer Martin Luther had recanted and returned to Catholicism as he lay dying in 1546, a claim for which no evidence exists. Rumors about last-minute conversions to religious orthodoxy also spread rapidly after the deaths of Thomas Paine, Abraham Lincoln, Thomas Edison, Jean-Paul Sartre, John Lennon, and scores of other prominent figures whose opinions, to varying degrees, lay outside of traditional religious orthodoxy.

A particularly bold attempt was made by Elizabeth Reid, Lady Hope (1842–1922), a British evangelist who claimed, in an American Baptist newspaper in 1915, to have heard Darwin renounce evolution and accept Christ on his deathbed. "I was a young man with unformed ideas," she quoted him as saying. "I threw out queries, suggestions, wondering all the time over everything, and to my astonishment, the ideas took like wildfire. People made a religion of them." She claimed that Darwin then spoke of the "holiness of God" and asked her to speak of "Christ Jesus and his salvation."

Darwin's entire remaining family, regardless of their own religious beliefs, uniformly denounced the Lady Hope story as a complete fabrication. "Lady Hope's account of my father's views on religion is quite untrue," wrote his son Francis in 1918. "I have publicly accused her of falsehood, but have not seen any reply."

Four years later, Darwin's daughter Henrietta Litchfield said, "I was present at his deathbed, Lady Hope was not present during his last illness, or any illness. I believe he never even saw her, but in any case she had no influence over him in any department of thought or belief. He never recanted any of his scientific views, either then or earlier."

AFTERWARD

In the five years between Darwin's death and the first publication of his *Autobiography*, his family argued fiercely over what should appear and not appear in the book, coming at one point to the brink of an intrafamilial lawsuit. In the end, Francis removed the passages his mother had requested. The resulting text gives only a vague impression of Darwin's doubts.

Francis offered some editorial notes on the question: "In his published works [Charles] was reticent on the matter of religion, and what he has left on the subject was not written with the view to publication . . . I believe that his reticence arose from several causes. He felt strongly that a man's religion is essentially a private matter, and one concerning himself alone. This is indicated by the following extract from a letter of 1879: 'What my own views may be is a question of no consequence to any one but myself. But, as you ask, I may state that my judgment often fluctuates . . . In my most extreme fluctuations I have never been an Atheist in the sense of denying the existence of a God. I think that generally (and more and more as I grow older), but not always, that an Agnostic would be the more correct description of my state of mind.'"

Seventy-one years later in 1958, after all the principals in the original fight had died, Nora Barlow, niece of Francis and granddaughter of Charles, restored the omitted passages, giving a fuller picture of the development of Charles's religious opinions than had previously been available. It is from the 1958 unabridged edition that the excerpts above are taken.

ASK YOURSELF

1. Given Charles's statement that he wrote the memoir because it "would amuse me, and might possibly interest my children or their children," do you think he intended it to be published to a wider audience?
2. If you had been Emma or Francis, would you have been as concerned about the possible repercussions of publishing his true opinions on religion?

TOPICS AND ACTIVITIES TO CONSIDER

Choose an audience—your family, perhaps, or friends, or the general public—and write a brief essay detailing the development of your own religious opinions for that audience. How does your choice of audience affect your approach, your tone, and the details you include?

Further Information

Darwin, Charles. *The Autobiography of Charles Darwin, with Original Omissions Restored*. Edited by Nora Barlow. New York: Harcourt, Brace, 1958.

Web Sites

Darwin Correspondence Project: http://www.darwinproject.ac.uk.
Darwin on religion: http://darwiniana.org/religion.htm.

19. An Atheist in Parliament—Charles Bradlaugh's "Humanity's Gain from Unbelief" (1889)

INTRODUCTION

Charles Bradlaugh (1833–1891) was the best-known British atheist of the 19th century. A journalist, political activist, and eventual member of Parliament, Bradlaugh founded the National Secular Society in 1866, which remains one of Britain's premier nontheistic associations. In 1880, after being elected a member of Parliament for Northampton, Bradlaugh claimed the right to affirm rather than swear a religious oath upon taking office. This right was denied. He finally took his seat after a six-year delay (see The Bradlaugh Affair in England sidebar).

While many atheist and agnostic writings argue that religious unbelief is not the force for evil it is often presumed to be, Bradlaugh's "Humanity's Gain from Unbelief" goes a step beyond, arguing that unbelief has been the driving force behind several examples of moral and intellectual progress in human history, including knowledge of our physical world, the rejection of harmful superstitions, the abolition of slavery, the advance of medicine, and free expression. The excerpt below focuses solely on Bradlaugh's argument regarding the place of unbelief and unbelievers in the dismantlement of slavery in the West.

KEEP IN MIND AS YOU READ

Though Bradlaugh was the first openly nontheistic member of Parliament, he was hardly alone in Victorian society. Though the Victorian era in the United Kingdom (1837–1901) often brings to mind conservative moral and social attitudes, it was also a time of great intellectual ferment and growth. Many public figures, including philosophers (John Stuart Mill, Jeremy Bentham, Herbert Spencer), poets (George Eliot, Algernon Swinburne, Thomas Hardy), social reformers (Beatrice Webb, Ernestine Rose, Annie Besant), and scientists (Sir James Hall, Thomas Huxley), were openly agnostic or atheist during the Victorian era.

Since the end of the Second World War, the United Kingdom has experienced an extraordinary secularization. Though Bradlaugh's overt rejection of religion was shocking in the Parliament of 1880, by 2011 over 100 members of Parliament were self-identified as nontheistic by their membership in the All Party Parliamentary Humanist Group.

Document: Charles Bradlaugh, "Humanity's Gain from Unbelief" (1889)

Scepticism: U.K. spelling of *skepticism*: doubt concerning the truth of a given claim or system of belief
juste milieu: the middle or moderate path

As an unbeliever, I ask leave to plead that humanity has been the real gainer from **scepticism**, and that the gradual and growing rejection of Christianity—like the rejection of the faiths which preceded it—has in fact added, and will add, to man's happiness and well being. I maintain that in physics science is the outcome of scepticism, and that general progress is impossible without scepticism on matters of religion. I mean by religion every form of belief which accepts or asserts the supernatural. I write as a Monist, and use the word "nature" as meaning all phenomena, every phenomenon, all that is necessary for the happening of any and every phenomenon. Every religion is constantly changing, and at any given time is the measure of the civilisation attained by what Guizot described as the *juste milieu* of those who profess it. Each religion is slowly but certainly modified in its dogma and practice by the gradual development of the peoples amongst whom it is professed . . .

Take one clear gain to humanity consequent on unbelief, i.e. in the abolition of slavery in some countries, in the abolition of the slave trade in most civilised countries, and in the tendency to its total abolition. I am unaware of any religion in the world which in the past forbade slavery. The professors of Christianity for ages supported it; the Old Testament repeatedly sanctioned [i.e. supported] it by special laws; the New Testament has no repealing declaration. Though we are at the close of the nineteenth century of the Christian era, it is only during the past three-quarters of a century that the battle for freedom has been gradually won. It is scarcely a quarter of a century since the famous emancipation amendment was carried to the United States Constitution. And it is impossible for any well-informed Christian to deny that the abolition movement in North America was most steadily and bitterly opposed by the religious bodies in the various States. Henry Wilson, in his "Rise and Fall of the Slave Power in America"; Samuel J. May, in his "Recollections of the Anti-Slavery Conflict"; and J. Greenleaf Whittier, in his poems, alike are witnesses that the Bible and pulpit, the Church and its great influence, were used against abolition and in favor of the slaveowner.

I know that Christians in the present day often declare that Christianity had a large share in bringing about the abolition of slavery, and this because men professing Christianity were abolitionists. I plead that these so-called Christian abolitionists were men and women whose humanity, recognising freedom for all, was in this in direct conflict with Christianity. It is not yet fifty years since the European Christian powers jointly agreed to abolish the slave trade.

What of the effect of Christianity on these powers in the centuries which had preceded? The heretic Condorcet pleaded powerfully for freedom whilst Christian France was still slave-holding. For many centuries Christian Spain and Christian Portugal held slaves. Porto Rico [sic] freedom is not of long date; and Cuban emancipation is even yet newer. It was a Christian King, Charles V, and a Christian friar, who founded in Spanish America the slave trade between the Old World and the New. For some 1800 years, almost, Christians kept slaves, bought slaves, sold slaves, bred slaves, stole slaves. Pious Bristol and godly Liverpool less than 100 years ago openly grew rich on the traffic. During the ninth century Greek Christians sold slaves to the Saracens. In the eleventh century prostitutes were publicly sold as slaves in Rome, and the profit went to the Church . . .

When William Lloyd Garrison, the pure-minded and most earnest abolitionist, delivered his first anti-slavery address in Boston, Massachusetts, the only building he could obtain, in which to speak, was the infidel hall owned by Abner Kneeland, the "infidel" editor of the *Boston Investigatory* who had been sent to jail for blasphemy. Every Christian sect had in turn refused Mr. Lloyd Garrison the use of the buildings they severally controlled. Lloyd Garrison told me himself how honored deacons of a Christian Church joined in an actual attempt to hang him.

When abolition was advocated in the United States in 1790, the representative from South Carolina was able to plead that the Southern clergy "did not condemn either slavery or the slave trade"; and Mr. Jackson, the representative from Georgia, pleaded that "from Genesis to Revelation" the current was favorable to slavery. **Elias Hicks**, the brave Abolitionist Quaker, was denounced as an Atheist, and less than twenty years ago a Hicksite Quaker was expelled from one of the Southern American Legislatures, because of the reputed irreligion of these abolitionist "Friends".

When the **Fugitive Slave Law** was under discussion in North America, large numbers of clergymen of nearly every denomination were found ready to defend this infamous law. Samuel James May, the famous abolitionist, was driven from the pulpit as irreligious, solely because of his attacks on slave-holding. Northern clergymen tried to induce "silver tongued" **Wendell Phillips** to abandon his advocacy of abolition. Southern pulpits rang with praises for the murderous attack on Charles Sumner. The slayers of **Elijah Lovejoy** were highly reputed Christian men.

Guizot, notwithstanding that he tries to claim that the Church exerted its influence to restrain slavery, says ("European Civilisation", vol. i., p. 110):

"It has often been repeated that the abolition of slavery among modern people is entirely due to Christians. That, I think, is saying too much. Slavery existed for a long period in the heart of Christian society, without its being particularly astonished or irritated. A multitude of causes, and a great development in other ideas and principles of civilisation, were necessary for the abolition of this iniquity of all iniquities."

Source: Bradlaugh, Charles. "Humanity's Gain from Unbelief." Originally appeared in *The North American Review*, March 1889. Available online at Project Gutenberg: http://www.gutenberg.org/ebooks/30206.

Elias Hicks (1748–1830): Quaker preacher who taught that God is a matter of individual experience, and that no person can tell another what to believe

Fugitive Slave Law: a series of U.S. laws passed between 1793 and 1850 providing for the return of slaves who escaped into another state or territory

Wendell Phillips (1811–1884): Abolitionist, advocate for Native American rights, renowned orator

Elijah Lovejoy (1802–1837): Presbyterian minister murdered by a mob in Alton, Illinois, for printing and distributing literature calling for an end to slavery. Has been called "the first casualty of the Civil War"

François Pierre Guillaume Guizot (1787–1874): French historian and orator

THE BRADLAUGH AFFAIR IN ENGLAND

In 1880, as he was preparing to be sworn in as a newly elected member of the British Parliament from Northampton, British atheist Charles Bradlaugh asked that he be allowed to affirm the oath of allegiance to the Crown instead of swearing the traditional religious oath of allegiance. When his request was denied, Bradlaugh agreed to take the religious oath as a "matter of form," a request that was rejected by the leadership of the House of Commons as insincere.

Bradlaugh attempted to take his seat without being sworn and was arrested and imprisoned for a short time. Four successive attempts were then made to elect a replacement, all of which were won by Bradlaugh. Supporters of Bradlaugh's right to be seated included Prime Minister William Gladstone and playwright George Bernard Shaw. Opponents included the leadership of the Conservative Party, the Catholic Church, and the Church of England.

After years of debate, Bradlaugh was finally permitted to take his seat in 1886, though a new Oaths Act officially allowing the choice of affirmation instead of a religious oath both in Parliament and in courts of law was not passed until 1888—an effort that was led by Bradlaugh.

AFTERWARD

Bradlaugh continued his secular activism unabated during his 11 years in Parliament, including the publication of "Humanity's Gain from Unbelief." His most lasting achievement was his leadership in securing the Oaths Act of 1888, which confirmed the right of members of Parliament, as well as witnesses in civil and criminal trials, to affirm rather than swear a religious oath. He died at age 56 in 1891.

RELIGION IS "OPIUM," GOD IS "DEAD"

Several prominent atheist philosophers of the 19th century, including Friedrich Nietzsche, Karl Marx, and Arthur Schopenhauer, made powerful statements about religion, many of which have been later misunderstood. Nietzsche's famous declaration that "God is dead . . . and we have killed him" was intended not as a literal statement that God once existed and had been killed, but that the concept of God, long believed, was being ever more completely rejected by the human mind.

Marx's declaration that religion is "the opium of the people" was part of a more nuanced and complex passage than is usually realized. "Religion is the sigh of the oppressed creature, the heart of a heartless world, and the soul of soulless conditions," he wrote. "It is the opium of the people." So long as the human condition is characterized by oppression and suffering, says Marx, religion will blunt the pain, as medicinal opium did at the time. But he goes on to make his position on religion crystal clear—it is a hallucinatory happiness that keeps humanity from seeking the genuine good: "The abolition of religion as the illusory happiness of the people is the demand for their real happiness. To call on them to give up their illusions about their condition is to call on them to give up a condition that requires illusions. The criticism of religion is, therefore, in embryo, the criticism of that vale of tears of which religion is the halo."

ASK YOURSELF

1. Was Bradlaugh's stand worth taking?
2. If his views had not been widely known, should he have simply taken the religious oath without first asking to be allowed a secular affirmation?

TOPICS AND ACTIVITIES TO CONSIDER

~ Build a case for and against the requirement of specifically religious oaths in a political body or a courtroom. Why might advocates of the religious oath have felt a secular one inadequate? Do you agree?

Further Information

Wilson, A. N. *God's Funeral: The Decline of Faith in Western Civilization*. New York: Norton, 1999.

Web Site

Writings of Bradlaugh: http://www.infidels.org/library/historical/charles_bradlaugh/.

THE 20TH CENTURY

20. Unbelief in the Heartland—Letters to the *Blue Grass Blade* (1903)

INTRODUCTION

Recent campaigns by atheist and humanist organizations in the United States and the UK have urged "closeted" atheists—those whose atheism is not known to those around them—to make their opinions known. The intention of such campaigns is to dispel the popular misconception that atheism is a rare position held only by ill-defined "others," showing instead that many of those closest to us are also complete skeptics of religion.

Though resurgent in recent years, such campaigns are not new. One such attempt was made in 1903 by Charles Chilton Moore (1837–1906), founding editor of the *Blue Grass Blade*, the first newspaper in the United States published by atheists for the primary purpose of promoting religious unbelief.

After a brief career as a minister, Moore's confidence in the Christian church began to diminish as a result of the endorsements of slavery heard both in scripture and in the pulpit. He then engaged in an extended conversation with an atheist friend and came to doubt the Bible further, becoming first a deist, then an agnostic, before finally calling himself an atheist. He started the *Blue Grass Blade* in Lexington, Kentucky, in 1884.

In 1903, Moore put out a call to his readership for letters on the topic "Why I Am an Atheist." Responses poured in from around the country, including many traditionally conservative localities. A few of the responses are included below, including some who preferred to answer instead why they were agnostics, infidels, or freethinkers.

KEEP IN MIND AS YOU READ

Moore's opinions drew shock and outrage in his relatively conservative time and place, resulting in several threats to his life and two brief imprisonments, including a two-month stint in 1894 for declaring, "If there is a devil, Bourbon County [Kentucky] is nearer and dearer to his heart than any place of its size on earth."

By identifying themselves as atheists in the *Blade*, the correspondents below also risked being ostracized or worse by those around them. For this reason, many of the correspondents signed their letters with partial names or initials.

Document: "Why I Am an Atheist"—Letters from Readers of the Blue Grass Blade (1903)

WHY I AM AN ATHEIST

I read the New Testament through in my twelfth year. I was greatly grieved and shocked at the way the chief priests treated Christ, and asked my mother why Christ did not strike his enemies dead or paralyze them. She told me that Christ had to be crucified; that nobody could be saved unless Christ shed His blood for the sins of the whole world.

Well, right there I took up the notion that there was something unjust and cruel about the whole business, and that God was not a just God if he would crucify His own innocent Son to save a wicked world. I am an old man now and I see no just cause why my judgment at twelve years should be set aside.

I have always tried to be truthful and honest, and I can now say with a clear conscience that I have never known God to do anything whatever, not even to answer a prayer. I am aware of a power above me, but I am perfectly satisfied that this power is not a person with a brain and thought that a man may talk to and understand.

The power that causes this earth to turn on its axis once in twenty-four hours, and to go around the sun in a little over 365 days, is not an individual with brain and thought.

I find that faith or belief is not an involuntary thing, but is entirely dependent on evidence; hence to believe or be damned would not be in accordance with an all-wise being. If there were a personal God, according to the Scriptures, He certainly could have everything exactly the way He wanted it. Otherwise, He would not be supreme. I would like to say something about the foolishness of the six days of creation and the talk the gods had about the tower of Babel, but I'll stop right here.

J. N. BROWN
Bronston, Kentucky

WHY I AM AN ATHEIST

Why am I an Atheist? Because I am honest. Because I do not think there is a God. Why do I not think there is a God? Because I think there is no personality great enough to comprehend the illimitable details of the vastness of the universe. When we think of the great empire of space studied with planets innumerable, all obeying the impulse imparted to them by Nature and following their individual orbit courses endlessly, while man lives scarcely long enough to learn more than to eat and sleep before he is deprived of existence.

Can we expect man to learn anything of the creation of that which he does not understand? The man of one generation begins his knowledge where the man of the last generation left off. All the knowledge the world has gained permits the honest man to admit that he does not know.

As the existence of God is not yet demonstrated, I claim the right to disbelieve in such existence. Therefore, I am an Atheist. Do I feel the need of a God? No. I can get through this life, or any other life, without a God. Does this life end my being? I believe so. Do I regret not being immortal? No, I am satisfied with one life. Man is wearied out with one life.

Nature is under no obligation to furnish man with perpetual life. It takes all of joy, grief, concord, and discord to make life replete. Man experiences it all and his voyage ends. With Nature's system of birth, the world would be overpopulated if death did not ensue; hence death is a necessity. I have my turn at life's game, and must make room for the next player. It behooves me to play my point well, or else I do not advance but retard the gradual elevation of mankind.

I must take life as I find it. I cannot change its mode or extend the tenure. I must live and let live. In youth we hope, in age we see. A life well spent is all the recompense I desire. I have judged the Christian by his fruit as he advises. I like him not. His character is as unloving as selfishness can make it. God, in shining through the Christian character, sheds a bad light, a pseudo virtue.

A man plus God, who does wrong, is bad. A man minus God, who does well, is good. A man who does right of his own volition is noble. A man who needs God to enable him to do right is not complete. He is undeveloped.

JOHN F. CLARKE
Arlington, Maryland

WHY I AM AN ATHEIST

I am an Atheist because the more I read, and the more I think, I see that religion is made up of superstition. I do not believe in being good for fear of being forever damned, but I believe in being good and doing good because it is right to do good. This world is all I wish to worry about.

MARGARET COPPOCK
Indianapolis, Indiana

WHY I AM AN ATHEIST

My reason for being an Atheist is that I used reason with a fearless determination to know the true or false position of religion when I first began to investigate the subject. Through the kindness of an Atheist friend, with whom I became acquainted, and to whom I shall always feel grateful for the interest he took in me to get me to see things in their natural and proper light. I soon dispelled the clouds of superstition by studying nature and its laws, adhering closely to the material side and rejecting everything that would not bear the light of reason.

Having been raised a Catholic, the doctrine and belief in a hell and purgatory was a torture to my mind, to think of a human being suffering endless torment; but by the study of the law of gravitation, and the changing of matter by combustion, I soon succeeded in running out of fuel and could see no way of keeping up the supply.

Now everything is perfectly natural, and I feel in perfect harmony with myself and nature, with no fears of an angry God, but knowing that to live in accordance or violation of nature's laws we are rewarded or punished, mentally or physically, in this life and not in an imaginary existence of a hereafter.

A. M. BRUNSWICK
Los Angeles, California

WHY I AM AN AGNOSTIC

I am an Agnostic because it is a principle that stands for truth and honor, because it is a principle that is devoid of hypocrisy, deceit, and superstition, because it is a principle that would maintain an open court of investigation. I am an Agnostic because it is a principle that spurns faith and courts facts, and stands for every virtue, liberty, fraternity, equality, and humanity, and for the further reason because it is a principle that stands shoulder to shoulder with the Atheist and the materialist.

J. E. ARNOLD
Nebraska, Indiana

WHY I AM AN ATHEIST

Because no Supreme being has ever demonstrated His existence; because every carnivorous animal is a cannibal; because nature lives by destroying life; because there exists an infamous book called the Holy Bible that is a disgrace to intelligence and reason, claimed to be His word, which is false in its chronology, false in its astronomy, false in its geology, false in its geography, and most damnably false in its so-called inspiration.

Because Canada thistles, and every useless and injurious vegetation, grows without effort, while toil and sweat and continuous labor is necessary to support existence; because the human world is full of ignorance, disease, suffering; and the material world is stuffed with poisonous malaria, venomous reptiles, storms, hurricanes, simoons, daily wrecks of appalling horror by land and ocean, sea, and river.

Because every intelligent thought secured by humanity has been earned by the slow process of mental toil; because no Supreme being ever gave a thought to assist the mental toil of research. Like priests, he delights in ignorance, dogmatics, and usurpation of power and revenue, and He is simply the bastard spawn of those clerical, prating liars, existing only in the imagination of bigoted monomania or hypocritical lust and greed.

Because the history of this "moral monstrosity" called God is so abhorrent, revolting, disgusting, cruel, savage, vindictive, malicious, murderous, bloodthirsty, petulant, jealous, childish, ignorant, and degrading as to excite nothing but contempt and disgust.

GEORGE H. BOYD
Sandusky, Ohio

WHY I AM AN ATHEIST

I am an Atheist because from a business standpoint and by reasoning from cause to effect, I find no evidence or intellectual reasoning to convince me that I should think otherwise.

NOAH COLER
Dayton, Ohio

WHY I AM AN ATHEIST

I am an Atheist for several reasons. The main reason why I am an Atheist is because I do not believe in a God; and again, I have no particular use for a God.

I have learned to rely upon my own efforts, and I find that I get along in life fully as well as those who are always on their knees before some **Joss** asking for help.

In my estimation, it is just as honorable to be a hobo begging handouts at back doors as to be continually coaxing, begging, and praying to an imaginary being beyond the clouds.

Joss: a god, especially a household god. A European readoption of a Chinese corruption of the Portuguese word "deus"

Yet, the question of whether or not there is a God should not vex the minds of our noble men and women as much as the question of how to put an end to insanity and crime.

If there is a God, who was powerful enough to call into existence this universe of worlds, he certainly cannot be so small and mean as to get mad if some of us poor mortals have the temerity to doubt his existence.

I have arrived at my conclusions from observation. I have observed that when the lighting frost comes it blights the bud and blossom and the green corn of those who entreat and pray as well as the bud and blossom and corn of those who do not.

So I conclude that if there is a God he is deaf and dumb and blind to the prayers and entreaties of man.

When the thunders roll and the lightnings flash, churches and temples that have been built by man, dedicated to God, and turned over to his protecting care, are as remorselessly destroyed as in the worst saloon or the lowest gambling hell [sic] that ever disgraced the earth.

If there is a designer back of nature, and the being called God is the designer, it looks to one who has been born only once as if this God was either a fool or a bungler. If there is a God who has any use for churches or temples, this God, having control of the elements of nature, would protect his own property.

CHARLES EVANS
Lima, Ohio

WHY I AM AN INFIDEL

I am almost afraid to make the start to tell. Why? for fear I will take up too much space. But I became tired of so much deceit, hypocrisy, and fraud; tired of being a slave to I did not know what. I wanted to do what was right. I had been raised in the M.E. [Methodist Episcopal] Church, and I had tried to keep my faith in the church, but I could not.

I was in a sea of trouble; had the same old burdens to bear that all fool Christians fear and call it the cross of Christ. But I broke away from the church. Threw the old cross away and began to think for myself.

Then the light began to dawn. Then I got Thomas Paine's *Age of Reason*, and next, dear old Robert Ingersoll's *Liberty of Man, Woman, Child*. Then I was on the true road to happiness. Then I got C. C. Moore's *Blue Grass Blade* and got more light. I was free, and could see what a great mistake I had made in trying to find happiness in prayers and tears and kissing the lids of that old book of lies and fables they call the holy word. Then I married an Infidel, and that completed my happiness.

MRS. NELLIE EVANS
Lima, Ohio

WHY I AM AN ATHEIST

I am an Atheist, and neither ashamed nor proud of the fact—simply satisfied.

My feelings may be compared to those of a person who, after wandering until discouraged and exhausted in a trackless forest, suddenly and unexpectedly emerges into surroundings, which, though seen for the first time, afford unmistakable evidence of human habitation.

My life, from earliest childhood to manhood, was spent in the gloomy forest of Christian superstition, but when suddenly and unexpectedly I was brought face to face with Ingersoll and Paine, I recognized, not faces I had seen before, but thoughts that had been dimly shadowed in my own mind but which found not the courage for expression.

When Nature's cause was presented I became her advocate. The theological structure that had been so patiently and persistently cobbled up in my mind by Christian junk-collectors became suspiciously rickety, so I abandoned it for a home of my own construction, aided by those whose workmanship inspired my confidence.

Who can conceive the beginning of time? Who can conceive the end? Who can think of a limit to space? Who can limit matter?

The Bible professes a knowledge of each of these unthinkable limits, but offers no proof that science does not make too ridiculous for a second mention.

No intelligent person who is free from early, superstitious teachings believes the Bible inspired.

I am an Atheist because reason has supplanted credulity.

L. C. KIMBERLY
Circleville, Ohio

WHY I AM AN AGNOSTIC

I will tell you. I was raised a Baptist. I was not allowed to laugh on Sunday; went to church every Sunday twice, and to Sunday school. The sermons were two hours long. I used to get so weary, would nearly die, had to sit up straight and bow when they prayed. I continued, and when I was 14 years old I went to a Methodist revival. He gave us hellfire and broke up a couple of chairs, knocked the stove down, hammered the desk with his fists, jumped up nearly three feet, scared the very life out of me.

> **mourner's bench:** a bench for mourners and repentant sinners found at the front of a southern U.S. religious revival meeting

I went to the **mourner's bench**; was told I had God in my heart. I tried to realize it, but was not satisfied in my mind, as I felt as I always used to before. The deaconess of the Baptist church said to me that I would feel all right after I was baptized. I was baptized in a fount in the Baptist church at Ann Arbor, Michigan by Elder Cornelius. He was then 80 years old. After I came up out of the water, I stood on a grate so the water would not soil the carpet. The deaconess came to me with consoling words and said to me: "Well, sister, how do you feel now?"

I answered: "I feel ashamed."

Mrs. Royce said: "Don't say that."

I answered: "Well, it is a fact; I do feel ashamed."

After I went to remove my baptismal robe, which was all wet, Mrs. Royce (the deaconess) and Ma said: "Now, your sins are all washed away, a new life you will follow, you are born again; now do you feel the presence of the Lord in your heart?"

I answered that I felt ashamed.

Ma said, "Don't say that."

Mrs. Royce said, "Don't tell all you think; keep such to yourself."

I said it's so. I thought I must be a very bad sinner. I would try and pray, and read the Bible all the spare time I had.

I read the Bible through before I was 14 years old. It was all we could read on Sunday. My mother said to me, "You are just like your father; he was so skeptical, no one could talk such things into his head."

My father died before I was 19. The best friend, and may I say the only one I ever had. Time went on. I finished school, married, moved west to Illinois. Was a **steady attendant**.

My husband, who was a physician and surgeon, was one of Col. R. G. Ingersoll's brightest lights. He would go to hear his lectures and buy all of his writings. He would often say to me, "What do you go to that hypocritical church for?"

> **steady attendant:** a regular churchgoer

I would answer and say, "Doctor, I am trying to find out what Christianity is, and I can't." I read all the Freethought literature I could get, and gradually came to think Christ and all was humbug.

A presiding Elder, by the name of Adams, was the last screw in the orthodox coffin for me. I called at his house one day. His wife had gone to her people [relatives], and he, Adams, was alone. I rang. He came to the door. I enquired for Mrs. Adams. He said, "Come right in, sister. Mrs. Adams is at her people; come in the parlor and let us have a good, quiet visit. I always admired you. You are on my mind night and day. When you come in church and sit in the audience I see only you. I can't preach. My sermon goes out of my head. I can't stand it any longer. You are the only one in the church. I am crazy to have you close to me. Come in the parlor and we'll have a good, enjoyable time."

I answered, "No, Mr. Adams, I can't." I started out.

He said, "Don't for heaven's sake go; come back."

I went and I thought: is that religion; is there no sincerity in this world but licentiousness; and to think a preacher, presiding Elder, a man God had called to be a mediator between earth and heaven.

I never saw him again. I went home, and the thoughts! You can imagine!

I never told anyone. If I had, my husband would have murdered him in cold blood. Mr. Adams resigned the next Sunday. The Deacon McGrew and his wife said to me, "What in this world do you suppose Elder Adams resigned for? We held a church meeting, and we couldn't get a word out of him. He said: 'I think I will go South.'"

If I told anyone, they would have disgraced me.

After that, I didn't try to find any mercy or grace in the religion of Jesus Christ. I began to think for myself, and I do what I see proper and right. I am now a thorough Agnostic in belief. Ingersoll is my Bible. He never made a mistake. There are no cunning lies in his works. All are wise and good. I mourn his loss. It is sad for such a human machine to die. If I have written too much, it is the truth to the hilt.

ESTHER VAN RIPER, M.D.
Circleville, Ohio

Source: Moore, Charles Chilton. "Why I Am an Atheist." Letters from readers. *Blue Grass Blade*, 1903.

AFTERWARD

The *Blue Grass Blade* continued to be written and distributed by Moore's publisher, James Edward Hughes, until 1910, four years after Moore's death. Moore's court cases helped to establish key precedents related to religious freedom and freedom of the press.

ASK YOURSELF

1. Like Moore, many of the most prominent and outspoken atheist activists today are former ministers. What might account for this?
2. Why do members of "invisible" minority groups, such as gays/lesbians or atheists, consider it important to become visible through campaigns such as these?

TOPICS AND ACTIVITIES TO CONSIDER

- Write a letter to a newspaper (real or imagined) explaining why you hold the worldview you do.
- Prepare a research project comparing "out" campaigns in the gay and lesbian community with those in the atheist and agnostic community.

Further Information

Lawson, Thomas. *Letters from an Atheist Nation.* Kindle edition. Amazon Digital Services, 2011.

Sparks, John. *Kentucky's Most Hated Man: Charles Chilton Moore and the Bluegrass Blade.* Nicholasville, KY: Wind Publications, 2009.

Web Site

Digitized images of the *Blue Grass Blade* at the "Chronicling America" project of the National Endowment for the Humanities and the U.S. Library of Congress: http://chroniclingamerica.loc.gov/lccn/sn86069867/issues/.

21. The "Most Hated Woman in America"— Emma Goldman and "The Philosophy of Atheism" (1916)

INTRODUCTION

Emma Goldman (1869–1940) was an anarchist and radical political and social reformer. In addition to advocating atheism, Goldman (a.k.a. "Red Emma") spoke, wrote, and rallied for prison reform, freedom of speech, free love, and gay rights and against militarism and capitalism. First appearing in *Mother Earth*, an anarchist journal she had cofounded, "The Philosophy of Atheism" was the most detailed and explicit description of Goldman's atheism published in her lifetime.

KEEP IN MIND AS YOU READ

Journalists and cultural commentators have often conferred the title of "Most Hated Woman (or Man) in America" on controversial figures. Some of the recipients of this moniker have been criminals, but just as often the designation has gone to someone who held strong opinions outside of accepted norms. Madalyn Murray O'Hair was called the "Most Hated Woman in America" in 1961 after she brought a successful lawsuit to ban organized Bible readings in public schools. Likewise, Emma Goldman's outspoken atheist and communist views, including the article below, earned her the epithet during her lifetime.

Document: Emma Goldman, "The Philosophy of Atheism" (1916)

God, today, no longer represents the same forces as in the beginning of His existence; neither does He direct human destiny with the same iron hand as of yore. Rather does the God idea express a sort of spiritualistic stimulus to satisfy the fads and fancies of every shade of human weakness. In the course of human development, the God idea has been forced to adapt itself to every phase of human affairs, which is perfectly consistent with the origin of the idea itself.

The conception of gods originated in fear and curiosity. Primitive man, unable to understand the phenomena of nature and harassed by them, saw in every terrifying manifestation some sinister force expressly directed against him;

and as ignorance and fear are the parents of all superstition, the troubled fancy of primitive man wove the God idea . . .

Already there are indications that theism, which is the theory of speculation, is being replaced by Atheism, the science of demonstration; the one hangs in the metaphysical clouds of the Beyond, while the other has its roots firmly in the soil. It is the earth, not heaven, which man must rescue if he is truly to be saved.

The decline of theism is a most interesting spectacle, especially as manifested in the anxiety of the theists, whatever their particular brand. They realize, much to their distress, that the masses are growing daily more atheistic, more anti-religious; that they are quite willing to leave the Great Beyond and its heavenly domain to the angels and sparrows; because more and more the masses are becoming engrossed in the problems of their immediate existence . . .

The philosophy of Atheism expresses the expansion and growth of the human mind. The philosophy of theism, if we can call it philosophy, is static and fixed. Even the mere attempt to pierce these mysteries represents, from the theistic point of view, non-belief in the all-embracing omnipotence, and even a denial of the wisdom of the divine powers outside of man. Fortunately, however, the human mind never was, and never can be, bound by fixities. Hence it is forging ahead in its restless march towards knowledge and life. The human mind is realizing "that the universe is not the result of a creative fiat by some divine intelligence, out of nothing, producing a masterpiece chaotic in perfect operation," but that it is the product of chaotic forces operating through aeons of time, of clashes and cataclysms, of repulsion and attraction crystallizing through the prin-

> **Joseph McCabe (1867–1955):** British Catholic priest who became an atheist activist and strong critic of Catholicism later in life

ciple of selection into what the theists call, "the universe guided into order and beauty." As **Joseph McCabe** well points out in his *Existence of God*: "a law of nature is not a formula drawn up by a legislator, but a mere summary of the observed facts—a 'bundle of facts.' Things do not act in a particular way because there is a law, but we state the 'law' because they act in that way."

The philosophy of Atheism represents a concept of life without any metaphysical Beyond or Divine Regulator. It is the concept of an actual, real world with its liberating, expanding and beautifying possibilities, as against an unreal world, which, with its spirits, oracles, and mean contentment has kept humanity in helpless degradation.

It may seem a wild paradox, and yet it is pathetically true, that this real, visible world and our life should have been so long under the influence of metaphysical speculation, rather than of physical demonstrable forces. Under the lash of the theistic idea, this earth has served no other purpose than as a temporary station to test man's capacity for immolation to the will of God. But the moment man attempted to ascertain the nature of that will, he was told that it was utterly futile for "finite human intelligence" to get beyond the all-powerful infinite will. Under the terrific weight of this omnipotence, man has been bowed into the dust—a will-less creature, broken and sweating in the dark. The triumph of the philosophy of Atheism is to free man from the nightmare of gods; it means the dissolution of the phantoms of the beyond. Again and again the light of reason has dispelled the theistic nightmare, but poverty, misery and fear have recreated the phantoms—though whether old or new, whatever their external form, they differed little in their essence. Atheism, on the other hand, in its philosophic aspect refuses allegiance not merely to a definite concept of God, but it refuses all servitude to the God idea, and opposes the theistic principle as such. Gods in their individual function are not half as pernicious as the principle of theism which represents the belief in a supernatural, or even omnipotent, power to rule the earth and man upon it. It is the absolutism of theism, its pernicious influence upon humanity, its paralyzing effect upon thought and action, which Atheism is fighting with all its power.

The philosophy of Atheism has its root in the earth, in this life; its aim is the emancipation of the human race from all God-heads, be they Judaic, Christian, **Mohammedan**, Buddhistic, **Brahministic**, or what not. Mankind has been punished long and heavily for having created its gods; nothing but pain and persecution have been man's lot since gods began. There is but one way out of this blunder: Man must break his fetters which have chained him to the gates of heaven and hell, so that he can begin to fashion out of his reawakened and illumined consciousness a new world upon earth.

> **Mohammedan:** a now outdated synonym for "Islamic"
> **Brahministic:** a now outdated term for "Hinduistic"

Only after the triumph of the Atheistic philosophy in the minds and hearts of man will freedom and beauty be realized. Beauty as a gift from heaven has proved useless. It will, however, become the essence and impetus of life when man learns to see in the earth the only heaven fit for man. Atheism is already helping to free man from his dependence upon punishment and reward as the heavenly bargain-counter for the poor in spirit.

Do not all theists insist that there can be no morality, no justice, honesty or fidelity without the belief in a Divine Power? Based upon fear and hope, such morality has always been a vile product, imbued partly with self-righteousness, partly with hypocrisy. As to truth, justice, and fidelity, who have been their brave exponents and daring proclaimers? Nearly always the godless ones: the Atheists; they lived, fought, and died for them. They knew that justice, truth, and fidelity are not conditioned in heaven, but that they are related to and interwoven with the tremendous changes going on in the social and material life of the human race; not fixed and eternal, but fluctuating, even as life itself. To what heights the philosophy of Atheism may yet attain, no one can prophesy. But this much can already be predicted: only by its regenerating fire will human relations be purged from the horrors of the past.

Thoughtful people are beginning to realize that moral precepts, imposed upon humanity through religious terror, have become stereotyped and have therefore lost all vitality. A glance at life today, at its disintegrating character, its conflicting interests with their hatreds, crimes, and greed, suffices to prove the sterility of theistic morality.

Man must get back to himself before he can learn his relation to his fellows. Prometheus chained to the Rock of Ages is doomed to remain the prey of the vultures of darkness. Unbind Prometheus, and you dispel the night and its horrors.

Atheism in its negation of gods is at the same time the strongest affirmation of man, and through man, the eternal yea to life, purpose, and beauty.

Source: Goldman, Emma. "The Philosophy of Atheism." *Mother Earth*, 1916.

AFTERWARD

Like Ernestine Rose, Goldman wrote and spoke in a time of war and was frequently accused of treasonous activity. Goldman's work more directly criticized the government and its policies. Her criticism of the war increased as the conflict wore on, and she was arrested in 1917 for opposing the military draft. It was shortly after the war, as fear of Soviet communism grew into the Red Scare of 1919–1920, that Goldman was called "the most hated woman in America." Goldman and her lifelong companion, Alexander Berkman, were called "two of the most dangerous anarchists in this country" by future FBI director J. Edgar Hoover and deported to Russia. She lived the remainder of her life in several countries and continued her activism, up to and including opposition to the approaching Second World War. She died in Toronto, Canada, in 1940.

ASK YOURSELF

Goldman is one of several atheists and agnostics in this collection specifically associated with social reform. Religious reformers often point to their creed as a motivating factor. What reason might an atheist like Emma Goldman give for devoting herself to the improvement of the human condition?

TOPICS AND ACTIVITIES TO CONSIDER

Anarchy ("an" = without; "archia" = ruler) is the advocacy of human society without government. Advocates of anarchism vary on the models they propose instead of government systems, but none advocate what is the usual popular conception of anarchy —violent mobs roaming the streets unchallenged. Read Goldman's essay "Anarchism: What It Really Stands For" (link below), then prepare brief arguments in support of and in opposition to her position.

Further Information
Goldman, Emma. *Living My Life*. New York: Knopf, 1931.

Web Sites
"Anarchism: What It Really Stands For" (1917), by Emma Goldman: http://sunsite.berkeley.edu/goldman/Writings/Anarchism/anarchism.html.
Emma Goldman Papers at University of California, Berkeley: http://sunsite.berkeley.edu/Goldman/.
Works by Emma Goldman at Project Gutenberg: http://www.gutenberg.org/browse/authors/g#a840.

22. A New Meaning for "God"—John Dewey's *A Common Faith* (1934)

INTRODUCTION

American philosopher and education reformer John Dewey (1859–1952) was among the 20th-century thinkers who exerted the greatest influence on American education. Though an atheist and humanist, he rarely addressed religious topics. One exception was the Terry Lectures, given at Yale in 1933, in which Dewey described a "crisis in religion" brought on by the rapidly increasing difficulty of reconciling traditional supernatural beliefs with our growing scientific knowledge.

Unlike many atheist commentators, Dewey saw value and integrity in the religious impulse but felt that rescuing those valuable elements—including community, piety, and a striving for the ideal—required setting aside unworkable supernatural concepts in favor of a natural, humanistic form of religion.

Perhaps most controversial of all was Dewey's suggestion that the word "God" itself could be retained, denoting not a divine being but "the unity of all ideal ends arousing us to desire and actions." He saw such redefinitions as part of the mandate of humanism. "What Humanism means to me is *an expansion, not a contraction, of human life*," he wrote in 1930, "*an expansion in which nature and the science of nature are made the willing servants of human good.*"

Yale University Press published the content of Dewey's Terry Lectures the following year under the title *A Common Faith*.

KEEP IN MIND AS YOU READ

The Dwight Terry Lectureship at Yale University was endowed in 1905 for "the assimilation and interpretation of that which has been or shall be hereafter discovered, and its application to human welfare, especially by the building of the truths of science and philosophy into the structure of a broadened and purified religion," with the ultimate goal that "the Christian spirit may be nurtured in the fullest light of the world's knowledge and that mankind may be helped to attain its highest possible welfare and happiness upon this earth." In this way, the Terry Series is similar to the Gifford Lectures in Scotland (see document "The God Hypothesis," Carl Sagan).

Document: John Dewey, A Common Faith *(1934)*

Never before in history has mankind been so much of two minds, so divided into two camps, as it is today. Religions have traditionally been allied with ideas of the supernatural, and often have been based upon explicit beliefs about it. Today there are many who hold that nothing worthy of being called religious is possible apart from the supernatural. Those who hold this belief differ in many respects. They range from those who accept the dogmas and sacraments of the Greek and Roman Catholic Church as the only sure means of access to the supernatural to the theist or mild deist. Between them are the many Protestant denominations who think the Scriptures, aided by a pure conscience, are adequate avenues to supernatural truth and power. But they agree on one point: the necessity for a Supernatural Being and for an immortality that is beyond the powers of nature.

The opposed group consists of those who think the advance of culture and science has completely discredited the supernatural and with it all religions that were allied with belief in it. But they go beyond this point. The extremists of this group believe that with the elimination of the supernatural not only must historic religions be dismissed but with them everything of a religious nature. When historical knowledge has discredited the claims made for the supernatural character of the persons said to have founded historic religions; when the supernatural inspiration attributed to literatures held sacred has been riddled, and when anthropological and psychological knowledge has disclosed the all-too-human source from which religious beliefs and practices have sprung, everything religious must, they say, also go.

There is one idea held in common by these two opposite groups: identification of the religious with the supernatural. The questions I shall raise concern the ground and the consequences of this identification: its reasons and its value. I develop another conception of the nature of the religious phase of experience, one that separates it from the supernatural and the things that have grown up about it. I shall try to show that these derivations are encumbrances and that what is genuinely religious will undergo an emancipation when it is relieved from them; that then, for the first time, the religious aspect of experience will be free to develop freely on its own account. . . .

Are the ideals that move us genuinely ideal, or are they ideal only in contrast with our present estate?

The import of the question extends far. It determines the meaning given to the word "God." On one score, the word can mean only a particular Being. On the other score, it denotes the unity of all ideal ends arousing us to desire and actions. Does the unification have a claim upon our attitude and conduct because it is already, apart from us, in realized existence, or because of its own inherent meaning and value? Suppose for the moment that the word "God" means the ideal ends that at a given time and place one acknowledges as having authority over his volition and emotion. The values to which one is supremely devoted, as far as these ends, through imagination, take on unity. If we make this supposition, the issue will stand out clearly in contrast with the doctrine of religions that "God" designates some kind of Being having prior and therefore non-ideal existence. . . .

One reason why personally I think it fitting to use the word "God" to denote that uniting of the ideal and actual which has been spoken of, lies in the fact that aggressive atheism seems to me to have something in common with traditional supernaturalism. I do not mean merely that the former is mainly so negative that it fails to give positive direction to thought, though that fact is pertinent. What I have in mind especially is the exclusive preoccupation of both militant atheism and supernaturalism with humanity in isolation. For in spite of supernaturalism's reference to something beyond nature, it conceived of this earth as the moral center of the universe and of human beings as the apex of the whole scheme of things. It regards the drama of sin and redemption enacted within the isolated and lonely soul as the one thing of ultimate importance. Apart from humanity, nature is held either accursed or negligible. Militant atheism is also affected by lack of natural piety. The ties binding us to nature that poets have always celebrated are passed over lightly. The attitude taken is often that of our living in an indifferent and hostile world and issuing blasts of defiance. . . .

Were the naturalistic foundations and bearings of religion grasped, the religious element in life would emerge from the throes of the crisis in religion. Religion would then be found to have its natural place in every aspect of human experience that is concerned with an estimate of possibilities, with emotional stir by possibilities as yet unrealized, and with all action in behalf of their realization. All that is significant in human experience falls within this frame.

The things in civilization we most prize are not of ourselves. They exist by grace of the doings and sufferings of the continuous human community in which we are a link. Ours is the responsibility of conserving, transmitting, rectifying and expanding the heritage of values we received that those who come after us may receive it more solid and secure, more widely accessible and more generously shared than we have received it. Here are all the elements for a religious faith that shall not be confined to sect, class, or race. Such a faith has always been implicitly the common faith of humanity. It remains to make it explicit and militant.

Source: Dewey, John. *A Common Faith*. New Haven, CT: Yale University Press, 1934, 1–2, 42, 52, 57, 87. Copyright © 1934 by Yale University Press. Copyright renewed 1962 by Roberta L. Dewey. All rights reserved. Reprinted with permission.

AFTERWARD

In addition to his profound contributions to education, Dewey became more deeply engaged in humanism in the last decades years of his life, including membership in the advisory board of the First Humanist Society of New York and signing the first Humanist Manifesto in 1933.

ASK YOURSELF

1. Many atheists and theists alike have protested Dewey's idea to retain the word "God" while stripping it of all supernatural associations. Regardless of your position, how do you feel about this idea? How might Dewey respond to your position?

2. What do you think of Dewey's larger idea that religion can and should continue to exist without the idea of a supernatural God?

TOPICS AND ACTIVITIES TO CONSIDER

- Read Dewey's "What Humanism Means to Me" for a fuller description of his own post-theistic vision. Available online or in *John Dewey, the Later Works (1925–1952)*, vol. 5, Southern Illinois University Press (1984).
- Using the documents from Dewey and Lamont as sources, write an essay describing humanism in the 20th century.

Further Information

Dewey, John. *A Common Faith*. New Haven: Yale University Press, 1934.

Dewey, John. *John Dewey, the Later Works (1925–1952)*. Carbondale: Southern Illinois University Press, 1984.

Web Site

Center for Dewey Studies at Southern Illinois University, Carbondale: http://www.siuc.edu/~deweyctr/.

23. An Atheist in the Halls
of Power—Jawaharlal Nehru (1936)

INTRODUCTION

Jawaharlal Nehru (1889–1964) wrote his autobiography *Toward Freedom* during one of several imprisonments for civil disobedience against the British occupation in the years prior to Indian independence. Nehru wrote the book in part to explain how he had come to be imprisoned, beginning with the flight of his ancestors from Kashmir and culminating in his own activism in the Indian independence movement of the 1930s.

In addition to many other topics important to Nehru, the book contains a detailed exploration of his thoughts on religion, which he called "an empty form devoid of real content . . . And even where something of value still remains," he wrote, "it is enveloped by other and harmful contents."

Though an admirer and strong supporter of Mohandas Gandhi, particularly his focus on nonviolent action as a means to political and social progress, Nehru criticized Gandhi's use of religion as a framework for Indian identity and for the movement toward independence. "Religion, in India and elsewhere has filled me with horror," Nehru wrote, "and I have frequently condemned it and wished to make a clean sweep of it." He expressed particular concern that Gandhi's intense religiosity encouraged the people to do too little and think too little. "Was the way of faith the right way to train a nation?" he wondered. "It might pay for a short while, but in the long run?"

KEEP IN MIND AS YOU READ

Even at the time of his imprisonment, Nehru was a man with high political aspirations. In many other cultures, this would have made a public pronouncement of atheism and a strong critique of religion unthinkable. But the long history of religious and cultural pluralism in India, including atheistic religious traditions such as Jainism, created a very different set of expectations. Some historians have noted that his lack of alignment with any religious identity paradoxically made him the ideal candidate for the first prime minister of a country in which multiple religions share both cultural and physical space. "The only alternative to coexistence," he said, "is codestruction."

The passage below begins with Nehru reflecting on whether a fast by Gandhi a few years earlier had represented the best approach to the problems of India and the Indian people.

Document: "What Is Religion?," from Toward Freedom by Jawaharlal Nehru (1936)

I watched the emotional upheaval of the country during the fast,[1] and I wondered more and more if this was the right method in politics. It seemed to be sheer revivalism, and clear thinking had not a ghost of a chance against it. All India, or most of it, stared reverently at the Mahatma and expected him to perform miracle after miracle and put an end to untouchability and get *Swaraj* [self-governance] and so on—and did precious little itself! And **Gandhiji** did not encourage others to think; his insistence was only on purity and sacrifice. I felt that I was drifting further and further away from him mentally, in spite of my strong emotional attachment to him. Often enough he was guided in his political activities by an unerring instinct. He had the flair for action, but was the way of faith the right way to train a nation? It might pay for a short while, but in the long run?

> **Gandhiji:** "ji" is a suffix appended to a name in Hindi or Urdu as a sign of special respect

And I could not understand how he could accept, as he seemed to do, the present social order, which was based on violence and conflict. Within me also conflict raged, and I was torn between rival loyalties. I knew that there was trouble ahead for me, when the enforced protection of jail was removed. I felt lonely and homeless; and India, to whom I had given my love and for whom I had labored, seemed a strange and bewildering land to me. Was it my fault that I could not enter into the spirit and ways of thinking of my countrymen? Even with my closest associates I felt that an invisible barrier came between us, and, unhappy at being unable to overcome it, I shrank back into my shell. The old world seemed to envelop them, the old world of past ideologies, hopes, and desires. The new world was yet far distant.

> Wandering between two worlds, one dead,
> The other powerless to be born,
> With nowhere yet to rest his head[2]

> **Sikh:** an adherent of Sikhism, a religion that originated in 15th-century India and is practiced today by over 30 million people

India is supposed to be a religious country above everything else. Hindu, Moslem, **Sikh**, and others take pride in their faiths and testify to their truth by breaking heads. The spectacle of what is called religion, or at any rate organized religion, in India and elsewhere has filled me with horror, and I have frequently condemned it and wished to make a clean sweep of it. Almost always it seems to stand for blind belief and reaction, dogma and bigotry, superstition and exploitation and the preservation of vested interests. And yet I knew well that there was something else in it, something which supplied a deep inner craving of human beings. How else could it have been the tremendous power it has been and brought

---

[1] A 21-day self-purification fast by Mohandas Gandhi in May 1933 in support of the Harijan movement. Harijan, or "Children of God," was Gandhi's term for the lowest caste (social level) in the old Indian caste system. The Harijan were also called "untouchables" or Dalits ("broken people").

[2] From the Matthew Arnold (1822–1888) poem "Stanzas from the Grande Chartreuse."

peace and comfort to innumerable tortured souls? Was that peace merely the shelter of blind belief and absence of questioning, the calm that comes from being safe in harbor, protected from the storms of the open sea, or was it something more? In some cases certainly it was something more.

But organized religion, whatever its past may have been, today is very largely an empty form devoid of real content. It has been filled up with some totally different substance. And, even where something of value still remains, it is enveloped by other and harmful contents. . . .

Protestantism tried to adapt itself to new conditions and wanted to have the best of both worlds. It succeeded remarkably so far as this world is concerned, but from the religious point of view it fell, as an organized religion, between two stools, and religion gradually gave place to sentimentality and big business. Roman Catholicism escaped this fate, as it stuck on to the old stool, and, so long as that stool holds, it will flourish. Today it seems to be the only living religion, in the restricted sense of the word, in the West. A Roman Catholic friend sent me in prison many books on Catholicism and papal encyclicals, and I read them with interest. Studying them, I realized the hold it had on such large numbers of people. It offered, as Islam and popular Hinduism offer, a safe anchorage from doubt and mental conflict, an assurance of a future life which will make up for the deficiencies of this life.

I am afraid it is impossible for me to seek harborage in this way. I prefer the open sea, with all its storms and tempests. Nor am I greatly interested in the afterlife, in what happens after death. I find the problems of this life sufficiently absorbing to fill my mind. The traditional Chinese outlook, fundamentally ethical and yet irreligious or tinged with religious skepticism, has an appeal for me, though in its application to life I may not agree. It is the *Tao*, the path to be followed and the way of life, that interests me; how to understand life, not to reject it but to accept it, to conform to it, and to improve it. But the usual religious outlook does not concern itself with this world. It seems to me to be the

> **Tao (pronounced "dhow" or "dow"):** literally "the path," Tao is an ancient Eastern concept of right living and thought found in several religious and philosophical traditions

enemy of clear thought, for it is based not only on the acceptance without demur of certain fixed and unalterable theories and dogmas, but also on sentiment and emotion and passion. It is far removed from what I consider spirituality and things of the spirit, and it deliberately or unconsciously shuts its eyes to reality lest reality may not fit in with preconceived notions. It is narrow and intolerant of other opinions and ideas; it is self-centered and egotistic; and it often allows itself to be exploited by self-seekers and opportunists.

This does not mean that men of religion have not been and are not still often of the highest moral and spiritual type. But it does mean that the religious outlook does not help, and even hinders, the moral and spiritual progress of a people, if morality and spirituality are to be judged by this world's standards, and not by the hereafter.

"No man can live without religion," Gandhiji has written some where. "There are some who in the egotism of their reason declare that they have nothing to do with religion. But that is like a man saying that he breathes, but that he has no nose." Again he says: "My devotion to truth has drawn me into the field of politics; and I can say without the slightest hesitation, and yet in all humility, that those who say that religion has nothing to do with politics do not know what religion means." Perhaps it would have been more correct if he had said that most of these people who want to exclude religion from life and politics mean by that word "religion" something very different from what he means. It is obvious that he is using it in a sense probably moral and ethical more than any other different from that of the critics of religion.

Source: Nehru, Jawaharlal. *Toward Freedom.* London: The Bodley Head, 1936.

AFTERWARD

Nehru continued to work for Indian independence, which was achieved in August 1947. He was elected the first president of the new nation, a post he held until his death in 1964, and advocated strongly for the creation of a secular government and freedom of religion.

ASK YOURSELF

1. What advantage might Nehru's atheism have given him as the first prime minister of India?
2. How might his challenges and opportunities have differed if he had identified as Hindu, Muslim, or Sikh?

TOPICS AND ACTIVITIES TO CONSIDER

Imagine you are in charge of developing policy for a new nation. What would your religious policy be? Would there be a state religion? Would individuals have freedom of religious belief and practice? If so, would there be any limits on those freedoms?

Further Information

Luce, Edward. *In Spite of the Gods: The Rise of Modern India.* New York: Anchor Books, 2007.
Nehru, Jawaharlal. *The Discovery of India.* Oxford: Oxford University Press, 1946.

24. "Am I an Atheist or an Agnostic?"— Bertrand Russell (1947)

INTRODUCTION

British philosopher Bertrand Russell (1872–1970) is among the towering figures of modern philosophy. In addition to major contributions in several branches of philosophy and mathematics, he was an active supporter of pacifism and opponent of militarism and an advocate of social reform.

Russell's father was John Russell, Viscount Amberly, an atheist social reformer who wished for his children to be raised without religion. When he and his wife, Katherine, died in their early 30s, his wishes were countermanded by the Court of Chancery, and Bertrand was placed in a course of Christian education. "I think perhaps the Court of Chancery might have regretted that since," Russell joked years later. "It does not seem to have done as much good as they hoped."

As a result of his strong engagement with social and political issues, Russell's life and career were marked by constant activity and frequent conflict, especially his strong opposition to the United Kingdom's entry into World War I. These included the loss of college teaching positions, bans on travel, and imprisonment.

In a 1947 speech to the Rationalist Press Association titled "Am I an Atheist or an Agnostic?," Russell addresses the common misconception that the two terms are mutually exclusive.

KEEP IN MIND AS YOU READ

Russell is speaking to a sympathetic audience of self-described Rationalists. Consider as you read how his arguments and presentation might be modified for an audience less inclined to religious skepticism.

Document: Bertrand Russell, "Am I an Atheist or an Agnostic? A Plea for Tolerance in the Face of New Dogmas" (1947)

I speak as one who was intended by my father to be brought up as a Rationalist. He was quite as much of a Rationalist as I am, but he died when I was three years old, and the Court of Chancery decided that I was to have the benefits of a Christian education.

I think perhaps the Court of Chancery might have regretted that since. It does not seem to have done as much good as they hoped. Perhaps you may say that it would be rather a pity if Christian education were to cease, because you would then get no more Rationalists.

They arise chiefly out of reaction to a system of education which considers it quite right that a father should decree that his son should be brought up as a Muggletonian, we will say, or brought up on any other kind of nonsense, but he must on no account be brought up to think rationally. When I was young that was considered to be illegal.

Sin And The Bishops

Since I became a Rationalist I have found that there is still considerable scope in the world for the practical importance of a rationalist outlook, not only in matters of geology, but in all sorts of practical matters, such as divorce and birth control, and a question which has come up quite recently, artificial insemination, where bishops tell us that something is gravely sinful, but it is only gravely sinful because there is some text in the Bible about it. It is not gravely sinful because it does anybody harm, and that is not the argument. As long as you can say, and as long as you can persuade Parliament to go on saying, that a thing must not be done solely because there is some text in the Bible about it, so long obviously there is great need of Rationalism in practice.

As you may know, I got into great trouble in the United States solely because, on some practical issues, I considered that the ethical advice given in the Bible was not conclusive, and that on some points one should act differently from what the Bible says. On this ground it was decreed by a Law Court that I was not a fit person to teach in any university in the United States, so that I have some practical ground for preferring Rationalism to other outlooks.

Don't Be Too Certain!

The question of how to define Rationalism is not altogether an easy one. I do not think that you could define it by rejection of this or that Christian dogma. It would be perfectly possible to be a complete and absolute Rationalist in the true sense of the term and yet accept this or that dogma.

The question is how to arrive at your opinions and not what your opinions are. The thing in which we believe is the supremacy of reason. If reason should lead you to orthodox conclusions, well and good; you are still a Rationalist. To my mind the essential thing is that one should base one's arguments upon the kind of grounds that are accepted in science, and one should not regard anything that one accepts as quite certain, but only as probable in a greater or a less degree. Not to be absolutely certain is, I think, one of the essential things in rationality.

Proof of God

Here there comes a practical question which has often troubled me. Whenever I go into a foreign country or a prison or any similar place, they always ask me what is my religion.

I never know whether I should say "Agnostic" or whether I should say "Atheist". It is a very difficult question and I daresay that some of you have been troubled by it. As a philosopher, if I were speaking to a purely philosophic audience I should say that I ought to describe myself as an Agnostic, because I do not think that there is a conclusive argument by which one prove that there is not a God.

On the other hand, if I am to convey the right impression to the ordinary man in the street I think I ought to say that I am an Atheist, because when I say that I cannot prove that there is not a God, I ought to add equally that I cannot prove that there are not the Homeric gods.

None of us would seriously consider the possibility that all the gods of Homer really exist, and yet if you were to set to work to give a logical demonstration that Zeus, Hera, Poseidon, and the rest of them did not exist you would find it an awful job. You could not get such proof.

Therefore, in regard to the Olympic gods, speaking to a purely philosophical audience, I would say that I am an Agnostic. But speaking popularly, I think that all of us would say in regard to those gods that we were Atheists. In regard to the Christian God, I should, I think, take exactly the same line.

Skepticism

There is exactly the same degree of possibility and likelihood of the existence of the Christian God as there is of the existence of the Homeric gods. I cannot prove that either the Christian God or the Homeric gods do not exist, but I do not think that their existence is an alternative that is sufficiently probable to be worth serious consideration. Therefore, I suppose that that on these documents that they submit to me on these occasions I ought to say "Atheist", although it has been a very difficult problem, and sometimes I have said one and sometimes the other without any clear principle by which to go.

When one admits that nothing is certain one must, I think, also admit that some things are much more nearly certain than others. It is much more nearly certain that we are assembled here tonight than it is that this or that political party is in the right. Certainly there are degrees of certainty, and one should be very careful to emphasize that fact, because otherwise one is landed in an utter skepticism, and complete skepticism would, of course, be totally barren and completely useless.

Persecution

One must remember that some things are very much more probable than others and may be so probable that it is not worth while to remember in practice that they are not wholly certain, except when it comes to questions of persecution.

If it comes to burning somebody at the stake for not believing it, then it is worthwhile to remember that after all he may be right, and it is not worth while to persecute him.

In general, if a man says, for instance, that the earth is flat, I am quite willing that he should propagate his opinion as hard as he likes. He may, of course, be right but I do not think he is. In practice you will, I think, do better to assume that the earth is round, although, of course, you may be mistaken. Therefore,

I do not think we should go in for complete skepticism, but for a doctrine of degrees of probability.

I think that, on the whole, that is the kind of doctrine that the world needs. The world has become very full of new dogmas. The old dogmas have perhaps decayed, but new dogmas have arisen and, on the whole, I think that a dogma is harmful in proportion to its novelty. New dogmas are much worse than old ones.

Source: Russell, Bertrand. "Am I An Atheist or an Agnostic? A Plea for Tolerance in the Face of New Dogmas." A transcribed speech by Russell to the Rationalist Press Association, later printed in *The Literary Guide and Rationalist Review* 64, no. 7 (July 1949). Used with permission of the Rationalist Press Association, http://www.newhumanist.org.uk.

AFTERWARD

In 1958, Russell created a useful analogy known as "Russell's teapot" to explain the agnostic position further: "I ought to call myself an agnostic; but, for all practical purposes, I am an atheist. I do not think the existence of the Christian God any more probable than the existence of the Gods of Olympus or Valhalla. To take another illustration: nobody can prove that there is not between the Earth and Mars a china teapot revolving in an elliptical orbit, but nobody thinks this sufficiently likely to be taken into account in practice. I think the Christian God just as unlikely."

Russell received the Nobel Prize for Literature in 1950.

ASK YOURSELF

1. Do you agree with Russell's assertion that "new dogmas are much worse than old ones"? Can you give examples of each?
2. Is his suggestion that we must all consider ourselves agnostic regarding the Homeric gods a valid point? Why or why not?

TOPICS AND ACTIVITIES TO CONSIDER

Take up Russell's challenge by writing a compelling proof that the gods of ancient Greece do not exist.

Further Information

Russell, Bertrand. *The Autobiography of Bertrand Russell.* 1st American ed. New York: Little, Brown, 1967.

Russell, Bertrand. *Unpopular Essays.* London: George Allen & Unwin, 1950.

Russell, Bertrand. *Why I Am Not a Christian.* London: Watts, 1927.

Web Site

The Bertrand Russell Archives at McMaster University: http://www.mcmaster.ca/russdocs/russell.htm.

25. "The Unholy Mrs. Knight"—Margaret Knight's "Morals without Religion" (1955)

INTRODUCTION

British psychologist Margaret Knight (1903–1983) was in her third year as a student at Cambridge when, under the influence of philosophers including Bertrand Russell, she found what she called the "moral courage" to give up her religious beliefs. She later wrote that it was as if "a fresh, cleansing wind swept through the stuffy room that contained the relics of my religious beliefs. I let them go with a profound sense of relief, and ever since I have lived happily without them."

In the years immediately following the Second World War, immigration from Eastern Europe and from Commonwealth countries including India led to a rapid increase in racial, ethnic, and religious diversity. In the early 1950s, the British Broadcasting Corporation (BBC) announced its intention to permit the broadcasting of a wider variety of belief perspectives, including unbelief. In 1953, Margaret Knight submitted a draft of proposed remarks, which she later wrote was "rather forcibly rejected" by a Catholic BBC executive. She persisted, and in 1955 delivered two brief radio addresses on the BBC Home Service under the title "Morals without Religion."

KEEP IN MIND AS YOU READ

In addition to increased ethnic and religious diversity, the UK has undergone a rapid and somewhat unanticipated secularization. Polls show both churchgoing and religious belief in the UK in rapid decline throughout the last half of the 20th century. A Eurobarometer poll in 2005 showed only 38 percent of the population expressing a belief in a God.

Margaret Knight's broadcasts, which took place a full decade into this trend, may have been met with particular alarm because they seemed to confirm the suspicion that religion in the United Kingdom was "under attack" and on the decline.

Document: Margaret Knight, Excerpt from the Radio Address "Morals without Religion" (1955)

If [a child] is brought up in the orthodox way, he will accept what he is told happily enough to begin with. But if he is normally intelligent, he is almost bound to get the impression that there is something odd about religious statements. If he is taken to church, for example, he hears that death is the gateway to eternal life, and should be welcomed rather than shunned; yet outside he sees death regarded as the greatest of all evils, and everything possible done to postpone it. In church he hears precepts like "resist not evil," and "Take no thought for the morrow"; but he soon realizes that these are not really meant to be practiced outside. If he asks questions, he gets embarrassed, evasive answers: "Well, dear, you're not quite old enough to understand yet, but some of these things are true in a deeper sense"; and so on. The child soon gets the idea that there are two kinds of truth—the ordinary kind, and another, rather confusing and embarrassing kind, into which it is best not to inquire too closely.

Now all this is bad intellectual training. It tends to produce a certain intellectual timidity—a distrust of reason—a feeling that it is perhaps rather bad taste to pursue an argument to its logical conclusion, or to refuse to accept a belief on inadequate evidence. And that is not a desirable attitude in the citizens of a free democracy. However, it is the moral rather than the intellectual dangers that I am concerned with here; and they arise when the trustful child becomes a critical adolescent. He may then cast off all his religious beliefs; and, if his moral training has been closely tied up with religion, it is more than possible that the moral beliefs will go, too.

Source: Margaret Knight page, British Humanist Association. Available at http://www.humanism.org.uk/humanism/humanist-tradition/20century/margaret-knight.

AFTERWARD

Knight's broadcasts were met with an outraged response from media and public alike. The *Sunday Graphic* newspaper called her "The Unholy Mrs. Knight": "Don't let this woman fool you," said the article. "She looks—doesn't she—just like the typical housewife; cool, comfortable, harmless. But Mrs. Margaret Knight is a menace. A dangerous woman. Make no mistake about that."

Mrs. Knight later noted that she also received a good deal of supportive correspondence, including one letter from Germany that she found particularly moving:

Please accept the gratitude from an unknown man who has seen in your talk the sunrising of a new epoch based on the simple reflection; to do the good because it is good and not because you have to expect to be recompensed after your death. Being myself a victim of Nazi oppression I think that we all have to teach our children the supreme ethics based on facts and not on legends in the deepest interest for the future generations.

The lectures formed the basis of a book, published later that year under the same title. Knight was a lecturer in psychology at the University of Aberdeen until her retirement in 1970.

ASK YOURSELF

1. Do you think Knight's radio broadcast would have met with less outrage if it had been delivered by a man?
2. Would it meet with less outrage today?

TOPICS AND ACTIVITIES TO CONSIDER

Write a brief radio address on a topic about which you feel passionate. How does your approach change if you know the majority of your audience is hostile to your position?

Further Information

Gaylor, Annie Laurie, ed. *Women without Superstition: No Gods, No Masters*. Madison, WI: Freedom From Religion Foundation, 1997.

Knight, Margaret, ed. *The Humanist Anthology: From Confucius to Attenborough*. Revised by James Herrick. London: Barrie & Rockliff, 1995.

Knight, Margaret. *Morals without Religion*. London: Dobson Books, 1955.

Web Site

The Margaret Knight page of the British Humanist Association Web site, including full text of the radio addresses: http://www.humanism.org.uk/humanism/humanist-tradition/20century/margaret-knight.

26. "You May Call Me an Agnostic"— Interviews and Correspondence of Albert Einstein on Religion (1930–1950s)

INTRODUCTION

As a result of his unprecedented scientific accomplishments, Albert Einstein (1879–1955) quickly entered the public consciousness as a paragon of the human intellect. Champions of religion and atheism alike have attempted to claim Einstein as one of their own. Below are presented excerpts from Einstein's personal correspondence in which he endeavors to make his agnostic position clear.

KEEP IN MIND AS YOU READ

Many of Einstein's own statements, often in paraphrase ("God does not play dice with the Universe," "God is subtle but he is not malicious," "I believe in Spinoza's God"), seemed to point to a conventional religious view. Many others ("I have repeatedly said that in my opinion the idea of a personal God is a childlike one") seemed to many observers—especially atheists—to suggest atheism.

   As Einstein became aware of such attempts to co-opt and characterize his religious opinions, he began to clarify his position. "You may call me an agnostic," he said to one correspondent, refuting both traditional theism and atheism in the same breath. Einstein becomes just the latest agnostic voice in this collection (see also Huxley, Wright, and Russell) to struggle against the common desire to force nuanced thoughts and opinions into predetermined polar categories.

Document: Excerpts from Interviews and Personal Correspondence of Albert Einstein (1930–1950s)

I have repeatedly said that in my opinion the idea of a personal God is a childlike one. You may call me an agnostic, but I do not share the crusading spirit of the professional atheist whose fervor is mostly due to a painful act of liberation from the fetters of religious indoctrination received in youth. I prefer an attitude of humility corresponding to the weakness of our intellectual understanding of nature and of our own being.

—Letter to Guy H. Raner Jr. (28 September 1949)

Source: Letter from Albert Einstein to Guy H. Raner Jr. September 28, 1949. Albert Einstein Archives, 57–289.

My position concerning God is that of an agnostic. I am convinced that a vivid consciousness of the primary importance of moral principles for the betterment and ennoblement of life does not need the idea of a law-giver, especially a law-giver who works on the basis of reward and punishment.

—Letter to M. Berkowitz, Oct. 25, 1950

Source: Letter from Albert Einstein to Morton Berkowitz, October 25, 1950. Albert Einstein Archives, 59–215.

It was, of course, a lie what you read about my religious convictions, a lie which is being systematically repeated. I do not believe in a personal God and I have never denied this but have expressed it clearly. If something is in me which can be called religious then it is the unbounded admiration for the structure of the world so far as our science can reveal it.

—Letter of March 24, 1954 to a correspondent asking him to clarify his religious views.

Source: Dukas, Helen, and Banesh Hoffman, eds. *Albert Einstein: The Human Side.* Princeton, NJ: Princeton University Press, 1981, 43.

I'm absolutely not an atheist. I don't think I can call myself a **pantheist**. The problem involved is too vast for our limited minds. We are in the position of a little child entering a huge library filled with books in many languages. The child knows someone must have written those books. It does not know how. It does not understand the languages in which they are written. The child dimly suspects a mysterious order in the arrangement of the books but doesn't know what it is. That, it seems to me, is the attitude of even the most intelligent human being toward God. We see the universe marvelously arranged and obeying certain laws but only dimly understand these laws. Our limited minds grasp the mysterious force that moves the constellations. I am fascinated by Spinoza's pantheism, but admire even more his contribution to modern thought because he is the first philosopher to deal with the soul and body as one, and not two separate things.

—From a 1930 interview with poet, writer, and later Nazi propagandist G. S. Viereck

> **Pantheist:** a person holding the view that the universe and God are one and the same. Rejects conceptions of a personal creator God who interacts with, or is even aware of, humanity

Source: Frankenberry, Nancy K. *The Faith of Scientists: In Their Own Words.* Princeton, NJ: Princeton University Press, 2008, 153.

The word God is for me nothing more than the expression and product of human weaknesses, the Bible a collection of honorable but still primitive legends

ADOLF HITLER AND RELIGION

Advocates of religious belief and religious unbelief, each anxious to claim the pre-eminent genius of Albert Einstein, have been even more eager to dissociate themselves from the genocidal dictator Adolf Hitler (1889–1945).

In the course of a lifetime of public and private statements, Hitler praised and criticized Christianity with equal fervor but to different audiences. Many historians have argued that regardless of his own convictions, he used religious imagery and identity as political tools to consolidate and retain his power over a German population that identified strongly with the Christian church. But Hitler's lifelong criticism of atheism, which he associated with the communist enemies of Germany, never waned. "We have therefore undertaken the fight against the atheistic movement," he said in a Berlin speech in November 1933, "[and] we have stamped it out."

Historians of the Second World War including Richard Overy have suggested that Hitler, especially in his later years, was not a Christian but a theistic believer in what he referred to as "the Lawgiver" or "Providence," a supernatural force that guided the struggle between races of humanity and that would ultimately ensure the victory of the Aryan people. Though he never denied the existence of a God, this perspective also places him outside of mainstream Christian identity in his later years.

which are nevertheless pretty childish. No interpretation no matter how subtle can (for me) change this. These subtilized interpretations are highly manifold according to their nature and have almost nothing to do with the original text. For me the Jewish religion, like all other religions, is an incarnation of the most childish superstitions. And the Jewish people to whom I gladly belong and with whose mentality I have a deep affinity have no different quality for me than all other people. As far as my experience goes, they are also no better than other human groups, although they are protected from the worst cancers by a lack of power. Otherwise I cannot see anything 'chosen' about them.

In general I find it painful that you claim a privileged position and try to defend it by two walls of pride, an external one as a man and an internal one as a Jew. As a man you claim, so to speak, a dispensation from causality otherwise accepted, as a Jew the privilege of monotheism . . . With such walls we can only attain a certain self-deception, but our moral efforts are not furthered by them. On the contrary.
With friendly thanks and best wishes
Yours, A. Einstein
    —Letter from Einstein to author Eric Gutkind, January 1954, in response to
        receiving Gutkind's book *Choose Life: The Biblical Call to Revolt.*

Source: "Einstein's Letter Makes View of Religion Relatively Clear." *The Guardian*,
    May 13, 2008.

AFTERWARD

Later in life, Einstein became a particular supporter of Ethical Culture, a humanistic, creedless philosophical movement founded by social reformer Felix Adler, and served on the advisory board of the First Humanist Society of New York. Though he identified with Judaism culturally, Einstein asked not to be buried in the Jewish tradition.

ASK YOURSELF

1. How much credence should be given to the opinions of great thinkers in areas outside of their primary expertise?
2. Does intelligence or accomplishment in one field automatically guarantee credibility in another?
3. If not, does it lend *any* weight to a person's convictions in unrelated fields?

TOPICS AND ACTIVITIES TO CONSIDER

Can you recall a time when someone you admired greatly differed from you on a topic close to your heart? Did the discovery change your opinion about the person, the topic, or neither?

Further Information

Jammer, Max. *Einstein and Religion*. Princeton NJ: Princeton University Press, 2002.

Web Site

A collection of Einstein's writings on religion: http://einsteinandreligion.com/.

27. "An Atheist with Gandhi"—Gora (1951)

INTRODUCTION

Goparaju Ramachandra Rao (1902–1975), better known as Gora, was an atheist activist, educator, and social reformer in India. In 1930, Gora wrote to Mohandas Gandhi, whose Salt March had just brought him and his principles of nonviolent resistance to national attention. His letter was brief: *"You use the word god,"* he said. *"May I know its meaning and how far the meaning is consistent with the practice of life?"* Gandhi replied with a single sentence: *"God is beyond human comprehension."*

Ten years later, Gora founded the Atheist Centre in Krishna district on the Indian Ocean coast and began seeking opportunities to interact more closely with Gandhi about atheism and its usefulness in social reform. "An Atheist with Gandhi" is a short booklet detailing those interactions.

KEEP IN MIND AS YOU READ

Gandhi only agreed to meet with Gora after many attempts by Gora to gain an invitation. Gora joined Gandhi's ashram (spiritual retreat), laboring and meditating until Gandhi would agree to speak. At last he was granted a series of interviews, of which excerpts follow.

Document: *Gora,* An Atheist with Gandhi *(1951)*

Chapter IV My First Interview with Gandhiji

On the appointed evening I waited outside Gandhiji's hut. Just at 5:30 p.m. Gandhiji came out of his hut for the usual walk. I was introduced to him. He greeted me with a broad smile and the first question, "What shall I talk to a godless man?"

We both laughed heartily and I replied, "Bapuji, I am not a godless man, I am an atheist." Then the conversation continued as we walked together.

Gandhiji: How do you differentiate between godlessness and atheism?

I: Godlessness is negative. It merely denies the existence of god. Atheism is positive. It asserts the condition that results from the denial of god.

G: You say that atheism is positive?

I: Yes. In positive terms atheism means self-confidence and free will. Atheism is not negative in meaning though it is negative in form. Look at the words: *non-co-operation, non-violence, ahimsa.* They have positive connotations, though they are negative in form. To express an idea that is unfamiliar, we often use the negative of a negative. For instance 'fearlessness' for 'courage'.

G: You are talking of words.

I: Atheism bears a positive significance in the practice of life. Belief in god implies subordination of man to the divine will. In Hindu thought man's life is subordinated to *karma* or fate. In general, theism is the manifestation of the feeling of slavishness in man. Conversely, atheism is the manifestation of the feeling of freedom in man. Thus theism and atheism are opposite and they represent the opposite feelings, namely, dependence and independence respectively.

G: You are too theoretical. I am not so intellectual. Go to professors and discuss.

The remark pulled me up. I realized that Gandhiji's bent of mind was primarily practical. So I adjusted myself and said:

I: If atheism were only theoretical, I would not have cared for it, nor wasted your time. We have practical programmes based upon the atheistic outlook.

G: Ah, ah, I know that, so I am talking to you. Tell me what you are doing among the villagers.

I: We conduct **cosmopolitan dinners** regularly on every full-moon night. We have selected the full-moon day for the dinner because we get moonlight and there is no need of lamplights. For the dinner the invitation is open to all who pay one **anna** towards the cost of their fare. One anna per head is sufficient in a village, because, the menu is very simple, we get fuel and vegetables free and we collect buttermilk from the villagers. At the cosmopolitan dinners we care more for eating together than for eating full or well. The venue of the dinner is changed every time, a common place in the *Harijanwada* or a friend's house in the village. Normally forty to fifty guests drawn from different castes partake in the dinner. A host is selected every time and the guests pay him their annas at least a day in advance of the full-moon. The host holds himself responsible for the arrangements in connection with that dinner. The balance of money, if any, is credited to the next month.

Some of us do not attend public functions and wedding celebrations unless they include cosmopolitan dinners. Besides cosmopolitan dinners, we hold night literacy classes in *Harijanwadas* and adult education classes for the general public of the village. The adult education mainly consists of newspaper reading, map pointing and explanation. Everywhere we encourage cosmopolitan habits. Social mixing is not an easy affair especially in the villages now. It becomes more difficult when **Harijans** are brought into the picture.

G: Yes, I know that. But you could carry on this programme without atheism.

> **Cosmopolitan dinner:** a dinner in which guests are invited to take part without regard to caste or creed
>
> **Anna:** a former currency unit of India, equal to one-sixteenth rupee (approx. one-eighth U.S. penny)

> **Harijanwada:** a place of residence (wada) for members of the lowest social caste (**Harijans**)

I: My method is atheism. I find that the atheistic outlook provides a favourable background for cosmopolitan practices. Acceptance of atheism at once pulls down caste and religious barriers between man and man. There is no longer a Hindu, a Muslim or a Christian. All are human beings. Further, the atheistic outlook puts man on his legs. There is neither divine will nor fate to control his actions. The release of free will awakens Harijans and the depressed classes from the stupor of inferiority into which they were pressed all these ages when they were made to believe that they were fated to be untouchables. So I find the atheistic outlook helpful for my work. After all it is man that created god to make society moral and to silence restless inquisitiveness about the how and the why of natural phenomena. Of course god was useful though a falsehood. But like all falsehoods, belief in god also gave rise to many evils in course of time and today it is not only useless but harmful to human progress. So I take to the propagation of atheism as an aid to my work. The results justify my choice.

Bapuji listened to me patiently and in the end said stiffly, "I should fast even because atheism is spreading."

I: I will fast against your fast. (I answered at once.)

G: You will fast? (Gandhiji said looking straight into my face.)

I: Yes, Bapuji; but why should you fast? Tell me how atheism is wrong and I will change.

G: I see, your conviction in atheism is deep. (Gandhiji said slowly.) I bowed.

G: The present conduct of people is giving room for the spread of atheism. (Gandhiji said reflectively.)

By then we had walked and conversed together for about twenty minutes. Gandhiji looked at me thoughtfully. There was a pause. . . . He smiled and said that he would fix up for me another interview with him very soon.

Chapter VII A Long Interview

Bapuji lay stretched full length on his low bed in the open air beside his cottage. I greeted him. He beckoned me to sit by his bed. I did. The situation was encouraging. I felt like sitting by the side of my father to consult him closely on a domestic affair.

"Now, you tell me, why do you want atheism?" Bapuji asked me in a calm and affectionate voice.

I was struck by the tone as well as by the nature of the question. It was not the usual question: What is atheism? or what is the use of atheism? Such questions call forth only academic answers. "Why do you want atheism?" had something remarkably human and practical about it. It was Bapu-like. To my recollection, in all my numerous discussions on atheism, no one had put the question to me in that form. But, instead of taking me by surprise on account of its singularity, the question touched my heart and I poured out my heart.

I began: "I was in Calcutta last year. I saw the famine-stricken destitutes walking heavily on the pavements. Here and there some of them dropped dead in the streets. They died beside the marts and stalls which exhibited their sweets and fruits for sale. Suppose there was a hungry dog or a bull in the same situation. Would he die of hunger? No. Beat him, scold him, he would persist in his attempts to pounce upon the shop, somehow eat the sweets and fruits and satisfy his hunger. Why did not the destitute do the same? I do not think they were afraid of the policeman. The destitutes were there in hundreds and thousands. No concerted action was required of them. If a fraction of their number had fallen upon the shops, all the policemen in Calcutta put together could not have stopped them. Even confinement in a gaol with its poor diet would have been preferable to death due to starvation. Why, then, the destitutes did not feel desperate and loot the shops? Were all the destitutes abject cowards without exception? Or had all of them such a high sense of civic responsibility as to be unwilling to disturb law and order? No. They were all simple, normal folk with no knowledge of civic rights and duties. Had they known their civic rights and duties in the least, there would have been no Bengal famine at all.

"Looking at the other side, were all the shop-keepers so cruel as to allow their fellow-men to die of dire hunger before their own eyes? No. On the other hand they shed tears of pity and contributed liberally and ran the gruel kitchens for the destitutes. They recited hymns of ethics every day.

"If the destitute is not cowardly and if the shopman is not cruel, why did so many people die of hunger? I think the reason is their philosophy of life.

"Both the destitute and the shop-keeper are votaries of the same philosophy of life. Each one said to himself: 'It is my fate, that is his fate; God made me like this, God made him like that.' On account of the commonness of their philosophy, there was no change in their relationship, though some ate their fill and many starved to death. The destitute's faith in that philosophy made his behaviour different from the animals.

"What I have said with regard to the Bengal famine applies also to the relationship between the untouchables and the caste Hindus, between the dark-skinned and the white-skinned. The same philosophy rules all these relationships.

"What is the result of following that philosophy of life? Man has become worse than the animal. Instead of living well, he is dying ill. His strength to resist evil is very much weakened. The pleasures of the few are built upon the bones of the many. This is really the unhappy fact in spite of our moral professions and pious wishes for the happiness of all humanity. This philosophy of life based upon belief in God and fate—this theistic philosophy—I hold responsible for defeating our efforts at ethical life and idealism. It cannot securely preserve the balance of unequal social relations any longer, because the pains of the flesh have begun to revolt against that philosophy. Hate and war are already replacing love and peace.

"I want ethics to rule and idealism to grow. That can be achieved only when belief in god and fate is done away with and consequently the theistic philosophy of life is changed. In positive terms, I want atheism, so that man shall cease to depend on god and stand firmly on his own legs. In such a man a healthy social outlook will grow, because atheism finds no justification for the economic and social inequalities between man and man. The inequalities have been kept so far by the acquiescence of the mass of theists rather than by any force of arms. When the belief in god goes and when man begins to stand on his own legs, all humanity becomes one and equal, because not only do men resemble much more than they differ but fellow-feeling smoothens the differences.

"I cannot remove god, if god were the truth. But it is not so. God is a falsehood conceived by man. Like many falsehoods, it was, in the past, useful to some extent. But like all falsehoods, it polluted life in the long run. So belief in god can go and it must go now in order to wash off corruption and to increase morality in mankind.

"I want atheism to make man self-confident and to establish social and economic equalities non-violently. Tell me, Bapu, where am I wrong?"

Bapuji listened to my long explanation patiently. Then he sat up in the bed and said slowly, "Yes, I see an ideal in your talk. I can neither say that my theism is right nor your atheism is wrong. We are seekers after truth. We change whenever we find ourselves in the wrong. I changed like that many times in my life. I see you are a worker. You are not a fanatic. You will change whenever you find yourself in the wrong. There is no harm as long as you are not fanatical. Whether you are in the right or I am in the right, results will prove. Then I may go your way or you may come my way; or both of us may go a third way. So go ahead with your work. I will help you, though your method is against mine."

Source: Rao, Goparaju Ramachandra. *An Atheist with Gandhi*. Ahmedabad, India: Navijan Trust, 1951. Reprinted with permission.

AFTERWARD

Gora spent the remainder of his life working for an improvement in the social and political conditions of the harijan and the advancement of the atheist perspective in India and beyond.

ASK YOURSELF

1. Given India's history of religious pluralism, how might Gora's task have differed from that of Ernestine Rose, Charles Bradlaugh, and others in this collection?
2. Do you think the strong presence of diverse religious traditions would make a difference in how atheism is received?

TOPICS AND ACTIVITIES TO CONSIDER

Pair up with a classmate whose religious perspective differs significantly from your own. Engage in conversation modeled on the Gora/Gandhi dialogues. Is one of you in a culturally more dominant position? What might the purpose and direction of the conversation be?

Further Information

Hiorth, Finngeir. *Atheism in India*. Mumbai: Indian Secular Society, 1998.
Rao, Goparaju Ramachandra. *An Atheist with Gandhi*. Ahmedabad, India: Navijan Trust, 1951.

Web Site

The Atheist Centre, founded by Gora: http://www.atheistcentre.in/.

28. AN ATHEIST IN AUSCHWITZ— PRIMO LEVI (1959)

INTRODUCTION

Among the common assumptions about atheism is that it will be quickly abandoned in favor of the consolations of religion under severe duress. The aphorism "There are no atheists in foxholes" captures this concept. Primo Levi (1919–1987) challenged this idea in memoirs of his year in the Auschwitz death camp during the Second World War. "I too entered the Lager [Auschwitz] as a nonbeliever, and as a nonbeliever I was liberated and have lived to this day," he wrote years later.

Though atheistic in belief, he was ethnically Jewish at the time of his arrest and transportation to the camp in 1943.

KEEP IN MIND AS YOU READ

Prior to his internment, Levi was not a writer but a chemist. It was the experience of the camps that led him to a new career, documenting the atrocities of the Nazi era while drawing broad and compelling conclusions about the implications and lessons for humanity.

Document: Primo Levi, Excerpts from If This Is a Man (1959) and The Drowned and the Saved (1986)

Silence slowly prevails and then, from my bunk on the top row, I see and hear old Kuhn praying aloud, with his beret on his head, swaying backwards and forwards violently. Kuhn is thanking God because he has not been chosen. Kuhn is out of his senses. Does he not see Beppo the Greek in the bunk next to him, Beppo who is twenty years old and is going to the gas-chamber the day after tomorrow and knows it and lies there looking fixedly at the light without saying anything and without even thinking anymore? Can Kuhn fail to realize that next time it will be his turn? Does Kuhn not understand that what has happened today is an abomination, which no propitiatory prayer, no pardon, no expiation by the guilty, which nothing at all in the power of man can ever clean again?

If I was God, I would spit at Kuhn's prayer.

Source: Levi, Primo. *If This Is a Man*. London: Orion Press, 1959. Quoted in Christopher Hitchens, *The Portable Atheist*. Cambridge, MA: Da Capo Press, 2007.

I too entered the Lager [Auschwitz] as a nonbeliever, and as a nonbeliever I was liberated and have lived to this day. Actually, the experience of the Lager with its frightful iniquity confirmed me in my nonbelief. It has prevented me, and still prevents me, from conceiving of any form of providence or transcendent justice . . . I must nevertheless admit that I experienced (and again only once) the temptation to yield, to seek refuge in prayer. This happened in October 1944, in the one moment in which I lucidly perceived the imminence of death . . . naked and compressed among my naked companions with my personal index card in hand, I was waiting to file past the "commission" that with one glance would decide whether I should go immediately into the gas chamber or was instead strong enough to go on working. For one instance I felt the need to ask for help and asylum; then, despite my anguish, equanimity prevailed: one does not change the rules of the game at the end of the match, nor when you are losing. A prayer under these conditions would have been not only absurd (what rights could I claim? and from whom?) but blasphemous, obscene, laden with the greatest impiety of which a nonbeliever is capable. I rejected the temptation: I knew that otherwise were I to survive, I would have to be ashamed of it.

Source: Levi, Primo. *The Drowned and the Saved*. New York: Vintage, 1989. Quoted in Christopher Hitchens, *The Portable Atheist*. Cambridge, MA: Da Capo Press, 2007.

AFTERWARD

Levi remained a professional chemist after the war but devoted an increasing amount of time and effort to documenting his experiences. During the last years of his life, he became a significant literary figure in Italy and one of the most influential voices among survivors of the Nazi concentration camps, winning literary awards including the Premio Campiello, Strega, Bagutta, and Viareggio Prizes.

Levi died in 1987 after falling from the railing of his third-floor apartment in Turin. Though Levi had suffered from depression throughout his life and his death was officially ruled a suicide, some Levi scholars including Diego Gambetta have argued that the evidence suggests an accidental fall.

Levi's book *The Truce*, an account of his return to Turin from Auschwitz, is now required reading in Italian schools.

ASK YOURSELF

1. Why does Levi say, "If I was God, I would spit at Kuhn's prayer"?
2. Why does he resist the momentary urge to pray for deliverance in his most desperate moment?

TOPICS AND ACTIVITIES TO CONSIDER

Levi was momentarily tempted to pray, then recoiled from this impulse. Think of one or more times in your life when you felt deeply vulnerable and afraid. Did this frame of mind change your willingness to violate your own values or beliefs? How did you respond?

Further Information

Levi, Primo. *The Drowned and the Saved.* New York: Vintage, 1989.

Levi, Primo. *If This Is a Man.* London: Orion Press, 1959. Published in the United States as *Survival in Auschwitz* by Touchstone, 1995.

Thomson, Ian. *Primo Levi: A Life.* London: Picador, 2004.

Web Site

The Primo Levi Center: http://www.primolevicenter.org/Home.html.

29. RELIGION WITHOUT GOD—SHERWIN WINE'S *HUMANISTIC JUDAISM* (1978)

INTRODUCTION

Though all of the major world religions include strong connections to specific cultures and ethnicities, Judaism arguably represents the most tightly interwoven fabric of religious, cultural, and ethnic identity. As a result, being Jewish has always had significance well beyond shared theological beliefs.

In 1963, Sherwin Wine took the dramatic step of announcing to his congregation in Windsor, Ontario, that he did not believe in the existence of God and had not for some time. "It is beneath my dignity to say things that I do not believe," he said, and invited those who wished to do so to follow him in creating a nontheistic Jewish congregation. Wine founded Birmingham Temple in suburban Detroit that September with eight families. It was the birth of Humanistic Judaism, a movement that attempts to retain the valued cultural and ethical elements of Jewish identity without supernatural beliefs.

KEEP IN MIND AS YOU READ

At the time this excerpt was written, Humanistic Judaism was still a relatively new concept, and many in the Jewish community were dismissive of or hostile to the idea of Judaism without belief in God. Wine was writing to both those convinced and those unconvinced of the movement's validity.

Document: Excerpt from Humanistic Judaism

The most interesting Jews of the last one hundred years never joined a synagogue.

They never prayed.

They were disinterested in God.

They paid no attention to the Torah lifestyle.

Reform: a movement within Judaism advocating the modernizing of Jewish practices and increased compatibility with surrounding non-Jewish culture

Orthodoxy: Orthodox Judaism, the more traditional and conservative of the major movements within Judaism

Conservatism: Conservative Judaism, a branch of Judaism more moderate in practice and belief than Orthodox but more traditional than Reform Judaism

Barmitsvah: a Jewish coming-of-age ceremony

Yahrzeit: a Jewish observance marking the anniversary of a person's death

They found bourgeois **Reform** as parochial as traditional **Orthodoxy**.

They preferred writing new books to worrying about the meaning of old books.

They had names like Albert Einstein, Sigmund Freud, and Theodore Herzl.

They were the stars of the contemporary Jewish world. No rabbi or theologian had their power or relevance.

Although they were not aware of the label, they represented the boldness and excitement of a new kind of Judaism. They were the non-deliberate prophets of Humanistic Judaism.

Humanistic Judaism is less well known than Orthodoxy, **Conservatism**, or Reform. But, on a behavioral level, it represents many more American Jews than any of these official ideologies.

Humanistic Judaism is the philosophy of life which motivates the actions of the vast majority of contemporary Jewry. Most Humanistic Jews do not know that they are what they are. They have never confronted their behavior. They have never bothered to articulate the real beliefs that lie behind their lifestyle—because to do so would force them to deal with the discrepancy between what they say they believe and what they actually do believe. . . .

The first need of American Jewry is *not* survival; it is honesty. Before we can plan what we should be, we have to know what we are. Before we can discuss the conditions of group endurance, we have to confront the reality that endures. Pious statements of non-existent belief will do us no good. It is ludicrous to praise bibles we do not read and gods we do not worship. It is futile to announce commitments we have long since abandoned and attachments we have clearly discarded. Self-deception is a common human art, which finds its most comfortable home in modern religious institutions. . . .

As for the life of prayer and worship, it exists as a very dim memory in the psyche of the suburban Jew. While it is periodically indulged at **Barmitsvahs** and **Yahrzeits**, it is a somewhat vicarious experience, in which the rabbi, cantor, or choir perform for a passive audience. The reason for this laxity is clear. To the skeptical, analytic, and sophisticated mind, worship is difficult; and to the devotee who has redefined God as a natural, impersonal force, prayer is silly. Without the imagined presence of an awesome, all-powerful father figure, the whole structure of Jewish worship collapses. The recent Reform revision of the Union Prayer Book seems a bit anachronistic. Why bother to improve prayers for people who don't want to pray? Perhaps more drastic alternatives are needed.

Source: Wine, Sherwin. *Humanistic Judaism.* Amherst, NY: Prometheus Books, 1978, 1–2, 5, 9.

UNBELIEF IN SCANDINAVIA

Norway, Sweden, and Denmark have long been among the nations with the lowest measures of religious identity and belief. Repeated surveys over the course of several decades show less than one-third of the population in each country reporting belief in God.

Despite the insistence by many religious commentators that societies without belief in God and an afterlife would be amoral, selfish, violent, and evil, the Scandinavian countries are, as sociologist Phil Zuckerman notes, "a markedly irreligious society that is, above all, moral, stable, humane and deeply good."

In every major international assessment of quality of life, the nations of Scandinavia rank at or near the top in child welfare, education, economic equality, standard of living, low incidence of crime and poverty, and generosity in international aid. A 2005 op-ed in the *Guardian* (UK) called the Scandinavian countries "the most successful societies the world has ever known."

Seeming contradictions in belief and practice are common. While 71.3 percent of the population of Sweden belongs to the Lutheran Church of Sweden, the Eurobarometer Poll of 2005 indicated that only 23 percent of Swedes self-report believing in a god.

Far from expressing anger or irritation toward religion, Zuckerman notes that for most Scandinavians, religion is a "nonissue." And in 2006, the Lutheran Church of Norway, for nearly 500 years the official state church, voted to disestablish itself as the national church, a step already taken by the Church of Sweden in 2000.

AFTERWARD

Humanistic Judaism has spread to include congregations worldwide and is now recognized as one of the five main branches of Judaism. The Society for Humanistic Judaism, founded by Wine, currently has over 40,000 members.

Sherwin Wine was named Humanist of the Year by the American Humanist Association in 2003. He died in an automobile accident in Morocco in 2007.

ASK YOURSELF

1. Before reading the excerpt, would the concept of being both nontheistic and Jewish have made sense to you? Does it seem more sensible after reading the excerpt?
2. What does Wine mean by a "non-deliberate prophet"?

TOPICS AND ACTIVITIES TO CONSIDER

Imagine that you are a member of the clergy—an Episcopal minister, a Catholic priest, or a Muslim imam, for example—who has decided to form a new secular congregation while retaining the cultural identity, ethics, and some of the traditions of your denomination. Write a brief sermon divulging your decision to your congregation as Sherwin Wine did in 1963. What would you include? What considerations are important regarding your tone and presentation? What do you think the reactions would be, and how would you respond effectively?

Further Information

Seid, Judith. *God-Optional Judaism.* New York: Citadel Books, 2001.
Wine, Sherwin. *Humanistic Judaism.* Amherst, NY: Prometheus Books, 1978.
Wine, Sherwin. *Judaism Beyond God: A Radical New Way to Be Jewish.* Detroit: Society for Humanistic Judaism, 1985.

Web Site

Society for Humanistic Judaism: http://www.shj.org/.

30. "The God Hypothesis"—Carl Sagan (1985)

INTRODUCTION

Carl Sagan (1934–1996) was an American astronomer and astrophysicist whose ability to render complex ideas comprehensible to the lay public made him one of the great popularizers of science in the 20th century.

In 1985, the agnostic scientist was invited to deliver a series of addresses for the centennial celebration of the Gifford Lectures at the University of Glasgow. The Gifford Lectures are an ongoing series established in the late 19th century to "promote and diffuse the study of Natural Theology in the widest sense of the term—in other words, the knowledge of God."

Echoing William James's classic text *The Varieties of Religious Experience*, Sagan chose as his title *The Varieties of Scientific Experience: A Personal View of the Search for God*, suggesting that the idea of God should be subjected to the same scrutiny as any other hypothesis—and concluding ultimately that the hypothesis has failed to stand up to that scrutiny.

Sagan's Gifford Lectures remained unpublished until 2006, the 10th anniversary of his death, when Sagan's widow, Ann Druyan, published the series in book form.

KEEP IN MIND AS YOU READ

The Gifford Lectures are dedicated to the exploration of natural theology, which the series defines as "the attempt to prove the existence of God and divine purpose through observation of nature and the use of human reason." This stands opposed to revealed theology, which assumes that God is not accessible to human understanding.

Given this distinction, Sagan's challenging, evidence-based approach was well suited to the stated purpose and vision of the Gifford Lectures.

Document: Carl Sagan, "The God Hypothesis," from the Gifford Lectures (1985)

Imagine that there is a set of holy books in all cultures in which there are a few enigmatic phrases that God or the gods tell our ancestors are to be passed on to

Babylonian exile: the period of forced detention of Jews in Babylon following Babylon's conquest of Judah in the sixth century BCE

the future with no change. Very important to get it exactly right. Now, so far that's not very different from the actual circumstances of alleged holy books. But suppose that the phrases in question were phrases that we would recognize today that could not have been recognized then. Simple example: The Sun is a star. Now, nobody knew that, let's say, in the sixth century B.C., when the Jews were in the **Babylonian exile** and picked up the Babylonian cosmology from the principal astronomers of the time. Ancient Babylonian science is the cosmology that is still enshrined in the book of Genesis. Suppose instead the story was "Don't forget, the Sun is a star." Or "Don't forget, Mars is a rusty place with volcanoes. Mars, you know, that red star? That's a world. It has volcanoes, it's rusty, there are clouds, there used to be rivers. There aren't anymore. You'll understand this later. Trust me. Right now, don't forget."

Or, "A body in motion tends to remain in motion. Don't think that bodies have to be moved to keep going. It's just the opposite, really. So later on you'll understand that if you didn't have friction, a moving object would just keep moving." Now, we can imagine the patriarchs scratching their heads in bewilderment, but after all it's God telling them. So they would copy it down dutifully, and this would be one of the many mysteries in holy books that would then go on to the future until we could recognize the truth, realize that no one back then could possibly have figured it out, and therefore deduce the existence of God. . . .

This business of proofs of God, had God wished to give us some, need not be restricted to this somewhat questionable method of making enigmatic statements to ancient sages and hoping they would survive. God could have engraved the Ten Commandments on the Moon. Large. Ten kilometers across per commandment. And nobody could see it from the Earth but then one day large telescopes would be invented or spacecraft would approach the Moon, and there it would be, engraved on the lunar surface. People would say, "How could that have gotten there?" And then there would be various hypotheses, most of which would be extremely interesting. . . .

Put another way, why should God be so clear in the Bible and so obscure in the world?

Source: Sagan, Carl. *The Varieties of Scientific Experience.* Edited by Ann Druyan. New York: Penguin Press, 2006, 165–68.

AFTERWARD

Sagan published over 20 books and several hundred scientific papers in his lifetime, winning honors including the Pulitzer Prize for *Dragons of Eden* and a Peabody Award for his breakthrough television series *Cosmos.* He taught a course in critical thinking at Cornell University during the last years of his life. In 1996, he died from complications related to myelodysplastic syndrome.

ASK YOURSELF

1. Sagan declared himself an agnostic rather than an atheist, saying "An atheist has to know a lot more than I know. An atheist is someone who knows there is no god."

Richard Dawkins, Bertrand Russell and others have disputed this definition of atheism, noting that a strong conviction is not the same as absolute certainty, and that few atheists speak in terms of "knowing" God does not exist. Reread the Afterward section for Russell's "Am I an Atheist or an Agnostic?" How might Sagan's agnosticism be described in Russell's terms?

2. What is the implication of Sagan's title, "The God Hypothesis"? How does "hypothesis" suggest a different way of seeing the question of God's existence? Do you agree with this way of seeing the question?

TOPICS AND ACTIVITIES TO CONSIDER

Provide one or more answers to Sagan's question, "Why should God be so clear in the Bible and so obscure in the world?"

Further Information

Sagan, Carl. *The Demon-Haunted World: Science as a Candle in the Dark*. New York: Random House, 1995.

Sagan, Carl. *The Varieties of Scientific Experience*. Edited by Ann Druyan. New York: Penguin Press, 2006.

Web Sites

The Carl Sagan Portal: http://www.carlsagan.com.

Video excerpt from Carl Sagan's *Cosmos*, on gods and religion: http://www.youtube.com/watch?v=8FQZlc4S268.

31. A Minister's Farewell to Faith—Dan Barker (1984)

INTRODUCTION

On January 16, 1984, Rev. Dan Barker mailed a letter to 50 colleagues, friends, and family members. After 19 years in Christian ministry, Barker had decided he no longer believed in the claims and tenets of Christianity and had in fact concluded that God did not exist. The letter, simple and straightforward, was intended to let those closest to him know about his change of mind and is presented in full below.

Barker was deeply involved in Christian ministry, belief, and practice. He received what he describes as a "call to the ministry" at age 15 during a series of Charismatic revival meetings near his Southern California home. "There was no time to waste since the world could end at any moment," recalls Barker. "I started carrying my bible to school, talking to friends about Jesus." He took part in short missionary trips to Mexico, founded a Christian student group, then attended a local Bible college where he studied religion. He subsequently spent time as an assistant pastor for three churches and as a composer of Christian musicals before study and thought led him to atheism in 1984.

KEEP IN MIND AS YOU READ

Barker's audience made for a complex task. Included among his readers were family members who considered their shared faith central to their relationship with him, fellow evangelists and missionaries, even people who Barker himself had led to faith. As a former believer himself, he would have been well aware that an announcement of this kind was likely to bring reactions ranging from sadness to anger to betrayal—including from those he was closest to.

Document: Dan Barker, Personal Letter to Friends and Family (1984)

Dear friend,

You probably already know that I have gone through some significant changes regarding spiritual things. The past five or six years have been a time of deep re-evaluation for me, and during the last couple of years I have decided that I can no longer honestly call myself a Christian. You can probably imagine that it has been an agonizing process for me. I was raised in a good Christian home, served in missions and evangelism, went to a Christian college, became ordained and ministered in three churches as Assistant Pastor. During these years I was 100 percent convinced of my faith, and now I am just about 100 percent unconvinced.

The purpose of this letter is not to present my case. Yet, I will point out that my studies have brought me through many important areas, most notably: the authenticity of the Bible, faith vs. reason, church history—and a bunch of other fun subjects like evolution, physics, psychology, self-esteem, philosophy, para-psychology, pseudo-science, mathematics, etc.

I'm not sure what the purpose of this letter is, except to serve as a point of information to a friend or relative whom I consider to be important in my life, and with whom I could not bear to be dishonest. I have not thrown the baby out with the bath water. I still basically maintain the same Christian values of kindness, love, giving, temperance and respect that I was raised with. Christianity has much good. Yet I feel I can demonstrate an alternate, rational basis for those values outside of a system of faith and authority. Of course, I admit, those values cannot save me from the fires of hell—but it is irrational to hold a fear of something which is non-existent, and to allow that fear to dominate one's philosophy and way of life.

If the Bible is true I will run to it willingly. If there is a God, I would be silly to deny Him. In fact, the little child in me still sometimes wishes to regain the comforts and reassurances of my former beliefs. I am a human being with the same fears and feelings we all share. The Bible says those who seek will find. You know me. I am constantly seeking. And I have not found. Right now I am somewhere between the agnostic and the atheist, although I spend a great deal of time in both camps.

There is much more to say, and I would greatly appreciate any input you can offer. I would suggest, though, that before we attempt any meaningful dialogue, we should understand as much as possible about each other's thoughts. If you wish, I will send you any of various papers I am preparing, including: The Bible, Faith vs. Reason, . . .

Finally, I am not your enemy. Our enemy is the one who doesn't care about these subjects—who thinks that you and I are silly to be concerned with life and values. I intend no disrespect to you, or anyone who is genuinely interested in religion and philosophy. It is the non-thinker who bothers me and with whom meaningful interaction is impossible.
Dan Barker

Source: Barker, Dan. *Losing Faith in Faith: From Preacher to Atheist.* Madison, WI: Freedom From Religion Foundation, 1992.

AFTERWARD

Barker received a wide range of responses to his letter. "Sorry to hear about your recent commitment to be uncommitted to the Lamb of God," wrote a fellow pastor and co-missionary.

"Meaningful interaction you want?" wrote the pastor's wife. "There is nothing meaningful about the beliefs you have chosen . . . Humble yourself in the sight of the Lord." Others were more accepting. "I totally support your sincere desire to seek out the truth in love," wrote another pastor's wife and friend. "Thank you for letting us know the status of your life change," wrote a former teacher. "Rest assured that the pureness and clarity of your communication is being accepted in a spirit of love and consideration."

Barker went on to become an atheist activist, first as public relations director for the Freedom from Religion Foundation from 1987 to 2004, then as copresident with his wife, Annie Laurie Gaylor.

ASK YOURSELF

1. What would have happened if Jean Meslier (see document *Memoir of the Thoughts and Sentiments of Jean Meslier*, Jean Meslier), instead of writing a book to be revealed upon his death, had written a letter of this kind during his life? What accounts for the difference in reception between the 1720s and the 1980s? Do you think acceptance of nontheistic conclusions will improve further in the future?
2. What rhetorical and persuasive techniques did Barker use to temper the probable impact of his announcement?

TOPICS AND ACTIVITIES TO CONSIDER

Write a letter to friends and family announcing something about you that is not widely known and might not be well received. What considerations guide your language, your tone, and your overall approach? Whether to send the letter (as Barker did) or to keep it for yourself (as Meslier did during his lifetime) is up to you.

Further Information

Barker, Dan. *Godless: How an Evangelical Preacher Became One of America's Leading Atheists.* Berkeley, CA: Ulysses Press, 2008.

Barker, Dan. *Losing Faith in Faith: From Preacher to Atheist.* Madison, WI: Freedom From Religion Foundation, 1992.

Web Site

Freedom From Religion Foundation: http://ffrf.org.

32. Imagining a Humanist Civilization—Corliss Lamont (1992)

INTRODUCTION

Though American philosopher Corliss Lamont (1902–1995) taught philosophy at Harvard, Columbia, Cornell, and the New School for Social Research during his long, productive career, he was best known for several legal battles with the U.S. government over civil liberties. Court victories that Lamont initiated set the stage for later advances in personal privacy and rights of association.

From 1946 to 1959, Lamont taught a course at Columbia called "The Philosophy of Naturalistic Humanism," the content of which he published in 1949 as *Humanism as a Philosophy*. Later renamed *The Philosophy of Humanism*, the book has been called the definitive study of humanism.

KEEP IN MIND AS YOU READ

The excerpt that follows is drawn from "A Humanist Civilization," the final chapter of the book. This chapter represents one of the first extended attempts to envision and describe a post-theistic society.

Document: Corliss Lamont, "A Humanist Civilization," from The Philosophy of Humanism (1992)

A Humanist civilization is one in which the principles of the Humanist philosophy are dominant and find practical embodiment in laws, institutions, economics, culture, and indeed all the more significant aspects of individual and social life. This requires, as the eighth proposition of Humanism phrases it, "a far-reaching social program that stands for the establishment throughout the world of democracy and peace on the foundations of a flourishing and cooperative economic order, both national and international."

Humanism's thorough democratization of education and culture will result, I am convinced, in a cultural flowering comparable in achievement to the outstanding epochs of the past and going far beyond them in breadth of impact. A Humanist society will invest in education and general cultural activity sums proportionate to what present-day governments allocate to armaments and war. Particularly will schools and colleges, universities and research institutes, with their perennial budget difficulties benefit from vastly enlarged financial resources. At long last educational institutions will be able to construct adequate physical plants and employ full teaching staffs at generous salaries. Thus current overcrowding will be done away with and the advantages of individual attention for all types of students realized to the full. It is generally recognized that the current crisis in American education is principally due to a tidal wave of students, the result of an all-time high birth rate, inundating already inadequate schools, colleges, and universities.

Humanist education naturally accents social rather than individualistic aims. This implies both more attention to social studies, such as economics, politics (including civil liberties), and sociology, and inclusion in the curriculum of courses on ethics in order to train the youth of a nation in the broad Humanist attitudes of loyalty to the social group and to humanity. Humanism would also greatly extend the teaching of science and scientific method, putting emphasis on the student's learning to think straight, but not neglecting the inculcation of basic facts. There need be no opposition between science and the Humanities, from both of which the Humanist draws inspiration, and no concentration upon one of them to the exclusion of the other.

The Humanist educational program will be a large factor in spreading a fundamental awareness of literature and art among all of the people. This does not mean any letdown in standards; on the contrary the effects will be just the opposite, by raising to unprecedented levels the average cultural understanding and by widening to an unprecedented extent the range of true artistic accomplishment on the part of both amateurs and professionals.

The Humanist stress on complete cultural democracy and freedom of expression means that artists and writers should have the widest latitude in what they produce and say. A free art and a free literature are absolute essentials for a free culture. A Humanist civilization will contain many different and contradictory currents of thought, including non-Humanist and anti-Humanist tendencies. It certainly will not bring pressure on art and literature to conform to any official philosophy; or seek to force the novel, the theater, and the motion picture to deal with Humanist themes. Those who so wish will criticize and satirize to their hearts' content; and will be at entire liberty to present unconventional ideas that shock and stir the Humanist orthodox.

Narrowly moralistic restraints on artists and writers have ever been a bane in the history of the West; and those restraints have frequently stemmed from the supernaturalist's suspicion of earthly pleasures. As Professor **Irwin Edman** explains: "The traditional quarrel between the artist and the puritan has been the quarrel between those who were frankly interested in the sensuous appearances and surfaces of things and those to whom any involvement or excitement of the senses was a corruption of the spirit or a deflection of some ordered harmony of reason. The history of censorship in the fine arts, if it could be told in full, would be found to revolve in no small measure around the assumed peril of corruption of the spirit by the incitements of the flesh through beautiful things."

Irwin Edman (1896–1954): influential American professor of philosophy

One of the challenges to Humanist writers and artists will be to embody in artistic and literary work the general point of view for which Humanism stands; to express that sense of the beauty and glory of life which Michelangelo, for instance, so superbly portrayed in the Sistine Chapel through the medium of a subject matter centered upon the supernatural. There is nothing in the nature of art, literature, or poetry that makes treatment of the Christian myth lead to great creative accomplishment and that prevents a similar result in the representation of the humanistic and naturalistic worldview. Genius is not confined to the delineation of any one philosophic position concerning the universe and humanity.

Santayana enlarges upon our point. "The naturalistic poet," he writes, "abandons fairy land, because he has discovered nature, history, the actual passions of man. His imagination has reached maturity. . . . Throw open to the young poet the infinity of nature; let him feel the precariousness of life, the variety of purposes, civilizations, and religions even upon this little planet; let him trace the triumphs and follies of art and philosophy, and their perpetual resurrections—like that of the downcast Faust. If, under the stimulus of such a scene, he does not some day compose a natural comedy as much surpassing Dante's divine comedy in sublimity and richness as it will surpass it in truth, the fault will not lie with the subject, which is inviting and magnificent, but with the halting genius that cannot render that subject worthily."

> **George Santayana (1863–1952):** Spanish-American philosopher and poet, agnostic

Great poets in the past have given expression to some particular philosophy or religion. In a general sense we can call Homer the poet of Paganism, Lucretius the poet of Materialism, Dante the poet of Catholicism, Milton the poet of Protestantism, Goethe and Wordsworth, with differing emphases, the poets of Pantheism. As yet, however, no poet equal in rank to these just mentioned has put into enduring verse the basic themes of Humanism as a philosophy.

An essential function for artists and writers in a Humanist society will be to work out rituals and ceremonies that are consistent with the central tenets of Humanism. Such ceremonies should appeal to the emotions as well as the minds of the people, capturing their imagination and giving an outlet to their delight in pomp and pageantry. Present-day Humanists regard a festival like Christmas, which has already become secularized to a large extent in the United States, as a folk day symbolizing the joy of existence, the feeling of human kinship, and the ideal of democratic sharing. However, during the year's most intensive holiday season, many Humanists prefer to put their stress on New Year's Day rather than Christmas. Easter can be humanistically utilized to celebrate the re-birth of the vital forces of Nature and the renewal of our own human energies. In fact, according to the anthropologists, Easter probably originated in just such a way. Humanism will likewise naturally make much of the birthdays of outstanding leaders of the human race, and of other important anniversaries.

The average family in a Humanist civilization will also need wedding and funeral services based on a non-supernatural philosophy of life. It seems reasonable to suppose that even today millions of families in America and throughout the world would like to have available definitely Humanist rituals for the occasions of marriage and death. Since such families are not usually acquainted with services of dignity and beauty that are in harmony with their ideas regarding life and destiny, they tend to fall back on the traditional supernaturalist ceremonies.

One result of this has been that again and again rationalists, freethinkers, and Humanists are adjudged finally in the public eye as faithful supernaturalists because their funeral services are orthodox. A number of Humanist wedding and funeral services are already in use, such as those prepared by Ethical Culture and Humanist groups. . . .

Despite the appalling world wars and other ordeals through which humanity has passed during the twentieth century, despite the unrivaled menace of nuclear annihilation, Humanism takes the long view and remains hopeful of the decades to come. This philosophy, with its faith in human beings and in our ability to solve our problems through human intelligence and scientific techniques, holds to what might be called a reasoned optimism. It rejects the dead ends of despair as well as the daydreams of Utopia. I believe firmly that human beings, who have shown themselves to be a very resourceful species, have the best part of their career still before them. And there is at least the possibility that by the close of this century, "the Humanist breakthrough," in **Sir Julian Huxley**'s phrase, will spread throughout the globe to create a higher civilization of world dimensions.

> **Sir Julian Huxley (1887–1975):** evolutionary biologist and humanist; grandson of Thomas Henry Huxley

In the meaningful perspectives of the Humanist philosophy, humankind, although no longer the darling of the universe or even of this earth, stands out far more heroically than in any of the supernaturalist creeds, old or new. We have become truly Promethean in our almost infinite powers and potentialities. For our great achievements, which were attained utilizing the resources and the laws of Nature, yet without Divine aid, we can take full credit. Similarly, for our shortcomings we must take full responsibility. Humanism assigns to us nothing less than the task of being our own savior and redeemer.

Source: Lamont, Corliss. *The Philosophy of Humanism*. Washington, DC: Humanist Press, 1992. Reprinted with permission from Beth Lamont.

AFTERWARD

After the publication of his landmark book, Lamont continued his civil liberties work. Among his most important efforts was the unanimous decision in his favor by the U.S. Supreme Court in 1965's *Lamont v. Postmaster General*—the first time the Supreme Court had struck down a congressional law because it violated the First Amendment.

Lamont was active in the American Humanist Association from the time of its founding in 1941 and was later named its president emeritus, and in 1997, its Humanist of the Year. A copy of *The Philosophy of Humanism* is now given to each new member of the AHA.

ASK YOURSELF

1. Like several other authors in this collection, Lamont chooses to capitalize the word "Humanist." Kurt Vonnegut, who was also a president emeritus of the American Humanist Association, called humanism "a handy synonym for good citizenship and common decency . . . an ideal so Earthbound and unmajestic that I never capitalize it." How does the effect of the word change depending on this choice?

2. Lamont sees a Humanist civilization as the answer to problems ranging from public education to human rights to artistic freedom? How does he support this claim? Do you agree with it? Why or why not?
3. Do you find the Humanistic civilization Lamont describes appealing?
4. Do you think it is a credible or likely future?

TOPICS AND ACTIVITIES TO CONSIDER

Imagine that a worldview or philosophy of your own choosing has become a guiding principle of civilization, such as radical individualism, unfettered free speech, communism, libertarianism, modernism, Christian socialism, or animal liberation. Write an essay of your own describing the resulting civilization as Lamont has done with Humanism.

Further Information

Lamont, Corliss. *The Philosophy of Humanism*. Washington, DC: Humanist Press, 1992.

Web Site

The Corliss Lamont site: http://www.corliss-lamont.org/.

33. Religion and Race in the American South—Alice Walker (1997)

INTRODUCTION

Humanist, novelist, and poet Alice Walker (b. 1944) received the 1983 Pulitzer Prize and the American Book Award for her novel *The Color Purple*, a depiction of the lives of African American women in Depression-era Georgia.

"The Only Reason You Want to Go to Heaven" is adapted from a speech given by Walker to the Auburn Theological Seminary in 1995. Combining reflections on religion, poverty, class, and race, it is considered by many to be among the most powerful personal humanist reflections of the 20th century.

KEEP IN MIND AS YOU READ

Like Sikivu Hutchinson (see "This Far by Faith"), Walker's identification as an unbeliever puts her at odds with one of the defining features of African American community—the Christian church. In separating herself from religious community, Walker pays particular attention to those elements that continue to connect her to other women, to other African Americans, and to humanity as a whole. As you read, think about the ways in which Walker's task is more complicated than it might be for someone who is not African American—or, as Hutchinson argues, who is not a woman.

Document: Alice Walker, "The Only Reason You Want to Go to Heaven Is That You Have Been Driven Out of Your Mind (Off Your Land and Out of Your Lover's Arms") (1995)

There has never been anyone who amazed and delighted me as consistently as my mother did when I was a child. Part of her magic was her calm, no-nonsense manner. If it could be done, she could probably do it, was her attitude. She enjoyed being strong and capable. Anything she didn't know how to do, she could learn. I was thrilled to be her apprentice.

My father and brother cleared the cemetery of brush and cut the grass around the church while we were inside. By the time we were finished, everything sparkled. We stood back and admired our work.

Sister Walker, my mother, was thanked for making the church so beautiful, but this wise woman, who knew so many things about life and the mysteries of the heart, the spirit, and the soul, was never asked to speak to the congregation. If she and other "mothers" and "sisters" of the church had been asked to speak, if it had been taken for granted that they had vision and insight to match their labor and their love, would the church be alive today?

And what would the women have said? Would they have protested that the Eve of the Bible did not represent them? That they had never been that curious? But of course they had been just as curious. If a tree had appeared in their midst with an attractive fruit on it, and furthermore one that they were informed would make them wise, they would have nibbled it.

And what could be so wrong about that? Anyway, God had told Adam about the forbidden fruit; He hadn't said a word directly to Eve. And what kind of God would be so cruel as to curse women and men forever for eating a piece of fruit, no matter how forbidden? Would they have said that Adam was a weak man who evaded personal responsibility for his actions? Would they have pointed out how quickly and obsequiously he turned in his wife to God, as if she had forced him to eat the fruit, rather than simply offered him a bite? Would they have said Adam's behavior reminded them of a man who got a woman pregnant, and then blamed the woman for tempting him to have intercourse, thereby placing all the blame on her? Would they have said that God was unfair? Well, he was white, His son was white, and it truly was a white man's world, as far as they could see.

Would they have spoken of the God they had found, not in the Bible, but in life, as they wrestled death while delivering babies, or as they worked almost beyond, and sometimes beyond, capacity in the white man's fields? I remember my mother telling me of a time when she was hugely pregnant and had an enormous field of cotton, 25 or 30 acres, to weed and thin. Her older children were in school, from which she refused to take them; her youngest trailed behind her and fell asleep in the furrows. My father, who was laborer, dairyman and chauffeur, had driven the boss lady to town. As my mother looked out over the immense acreage still to be covered, she felt so ill she could barely lift the hoe. Never had she felt so alone. Coming to the end of a row, she lay down under a tree and asked to die. Instead, she fell into a deep sleep, and when she awakened she was fully restored. In fact, she felt wonderful, as if a healing breeze had touched her soul. She picked up the hoe and continued her work.

What God rescued my mother? Was it the God who said women deserve to suffer and were evil anyway, or was it the God of nonjudgmental Nature, calming and soothing her with the green coolness of the tree she slept under and the warm earth she lay upon? I try to imagine my mother and the other women calling on God as they gave birth, and I shudder at the image of Him they must have conjured. He was someone, for all we knew, who actually had said black people were cursed to be drawers of water and hewers of wood. That some people enslaved and abused others was taken for granted by Him. He ordered the killing of women and children, by the hundreds of thousands, if they were not of his chosen tribe. The women would have had to know how little they and their newborns really mattered, because they were female, poor, and black, like the accursed children of Hagar and Ham; and they would have had to promise to be extra good, obedient, trusting, and so forth, to make up for it.

Life was so hard for my parents' generation that the subject of heaven was never distant from their thoughts. The preacher would gleefully, or so it seemed to me, run down all the trials and tribulations of an existence that ground us into dust, only to pull heaven out of the biblical hat at the last minute. I was intrigued. Where is heaven? I asked my parents. Who is going to be there? What about accommodations, and food? I was told what they sincerely believed: that heaven was in the sky, in space, as we would later describe it; that only the best people on earth would go there when they died. We'd all have couches to lounge on, great food to eat. Wonderful music, because all the angels played harp. It would be grand. Would there be any white people? Probably. Oh.

There was not one white person in the county that any black person felt comfortable with. And though there was a rumor that a good white woman, or man, had been observed sometime, somewhere, no one seemed to know this for a fact.

Now that there's been so much space travel and men have been on the moon, I wonder if preachers still preach about going to heaven, and whether it's the same place.

The truth was, we already lived in paradise but were worked too hard by the land-grabbers to enjoy it. This is what my mother, and perhaps the other women knew, and this was one reason why they were not permitted to speak. They might have demanded that the men of the church notice Earth. Which always leads to revolution. In fact, everyone has known this for a very long time. For the other, more immediate and basic reason my mother and the other women were not permitted to speak in church was that the Bible forbade it. And it is forbidden in the Bible because, in the Bible, men alone are sanctioned to own property, in this case, Earth itself. And woman herself is property, along with the asses, the oxen, and the sheep.

I can imagine some latter day Jezebel in our community (Jezebel apparently practiced a Goddess-centered, pagan religion, one of those the God of the Old Testament is always trying to wipe out) having the nerve to speak up about being silenced. And the smugness with which our uninspiring and indifferently trained minister, Reverend Whisby, might have directed her to a passage from the New Testament that is attributed to Saint Paul: "Let women keep silence in the churches." He would run his pudgy finger underneath the sentence, and she would read it and feel thoroughly put down. For God wrote the Bible, she would have been persuaded; and every word, even every word about murdering the suckling babies of your enemies and stealing all their worldly goods, was Truth.

I remember going with my mother to get water from the spring. What is a spring? Many will ask, just as I did. It is a place in the earth where water just bubbles up, pure and sweet. You don't ask for it, you don't put it there. It simply appears. There was one down the hill from our house, in a quiet grove of trees. Someone years before had put a piece of a terra-cotta culvert around it, with a notch in the lip for overflow. We'd dip our battered aluminum buckets in the shallow well, always careful to spot where the crawfish might be hiding, and perhaps sit for a minute before trudging back up the hill. How on earth did the crawfish get in there? I'd ask. They are always in healthy springs, was the answer. Yes, but why? I don't know, that's just the way it is.

But why is that the way it is? Where did they come from? There were no other crawfish for miles around. I never saw them in the creek, for instance, where my brothers and I waded. This was a mystery that was not explained by my mother's final exasperated "God brought them."

I was happier with my father's explanation: "Well you see, these crawfishes used to live over 'round Buckhead, but it just got too goldarn hot on account of all them fires the lumber company makes cleaning up the slag . . . so they held a crawfish convention, kinda like our revivals, and they resolved to move East. So they traveled and they traveled and one day they came to this place where there was this pretty little girl sitting looking down in the water. And you know crawfish love to be looked at, so . . ." In fact, neither of my parents knew how the crawfish got into the spring.

On the one hand I could strain to imagine a large white man in a white robe—unfortunately real-life white men in robes belonged to the Ku Klux Klan—lovingly carrying two tiny crawfish down the hill to place them in our spring, or I could fantasize about the stouthearted crawfish pioneers leaving Buckhead with their Sears Roebuck Catalog, crawfish-size, suitcases.

Because of the criminal exploitation inherent in the sharecropping system—in which the landowner controlled land, seeds, and tools, as well as records of account—sharecroppers were often worse off than slaves, which was the point. Sharecropping was the former slave owners' revenge against black people for having attained their freedom. It is no wonder that under such complete subjugation and outright terrorism that included rape, beatings, burnings, and being thrown off the land, along with the entrenched Southern custom of lynching, people like my parents sought succor from any God they were forced to have. The idea that as descendants of Africans and Native Americans and Europeans Scottish and Irish on both my mother's and my father's side, they might have had their own ancient Gods, or that as free human beings they might choose a God uniquely perceived by themselves, never entered their minds, except negatively. The "heathen" from whom they were descended knew nothing of salvation, they were warned in church, and any God except the one in the Bible was just another illusion produced by Satan, designed to keep them out of heaven. Satan: always described as evil, in color, black or red. African or Native American? Never admitted to be also a son of God, made also in the image of his creator, just the shadow side of him. And yet everyone in our family and in our church understood instinctively who Satan was. He was the other side of "the son of God" we always saw in the white people around us. Never did we see "Jesus" among those who insisted we worship him. Only Judas, and every day.

"Pagan" means "of the land, country dweller, peasant," all of which my family was. It also means a person whose primary spiritual relationship is with Nature and the Earth. And this, I could see, day to day, was true not only of me but of my parents; but there was no way to ritually express the magical intimacy we felt with Creation without being accused of, and ridiculed for, indulging in heathenism, that other word for paganism. And Christianity, we were informed, had fought long and hard to deliver us from *that*. In fact, millions of people were broken, physically and spiritually, literally destroyed, for nearly two millennia, as the orthodox Christian Church "saved" them from their traditional worship of the Great Mystery they perceived in Nature.

In the Sixties, many of us scared our parents profoundly when we showed up dressed in our "African" or "Native American" or "Celtic" clothes. We shocked them by wearing our hair in its ancient naturalness. They saw us turning back to something they'd been taught to despise, and that by now they actively feared. Many of our parents had been taught that the world was only two or three thousand years old, and that spiritually civilized life began with the birth of Jesus Christ. Their only hope of enjoying a better existence, after a lifetime of crushing toil and persistent abuse, was to be as much like the longhaired rabbi from a small Jewish sect in a far-off desert, as possible: then, by the Grace of His father, who owned Heaven, they might be admitted there, after death. It would be segregated, of course. Who could imagine anything different? But perhaps Jesus Christ himself would be present, and would speak up on their behalf. After all, these were black people who were raised never to look a white person directly in the face.

I think now, and it hurts me to think it, of how tormented the true believers in our church must have been, wondering if, in heaven, Jesus Christ, a white man, the only good one besides Santa Claus and Abraham Lincoln they'd ever heard of, would deign to sit near them.

The water we collected had many uses. We drank it, we washed dishes, clothes, and ourselves with it. We watered our livestock and my mother's vegetable and flower gardens.

On Saturday night everyone in my family bathed from head to toe, even though this meant half a day spent carrying pails of water up a steep hill. The water was heated in the big black wash pot in the yard. On Sunday morning we rose, washed our faces, had a hearty breakfast, and went off to church. As the smallest, I was bathed by my mother, dressed by my mother, fed by my mother, and wedged into the front seat of our secondhand blue-and-cream Packard between my mother and father. They had worked hard all week for the landowner's benefit; this was their only time of pleasure, of rest, other than an occasional Saturday night film at the local picture show. We spent most of the day in church, listening to the minister, who stood on the carpeting my mother had laid and read from the Bible I had dusted. Sometimes there were wonderful stories: Daniel in the Lion's Den. The Three Wise Men. David and Goliath. The Life of Christ.

Everybody loved Jesus Christ. We recognized him as one of us, but a rebel and revolutionary, consistently speaking up for the poor, the sick, and the discriminated against, and going up against the bossmen: the orthodox Jewish religious leaders and rich men of his day. We knew that people who were really like Jesus were often lynched. I liked His gift for storytelling. I also loved that, after Moses and Joshua, he is the greatest magician in the Bible. He was also, I realized later, a fabulous masseur, healing by the power of touch and the laying on of hands. Much later still I learned he could dance! This quote from The Acts of John, from the Gnostic Gospels, is worth remembering: "To the Universe belongs the dancer. He who does not dance does not know what happens. Now if you follow my dance, see yourself in me."

But basically, according to the Scriptures: We had sinned. I did not know then that the root of the word "sin" means "to be." Woman was the cause. All of our life we must suffer just because we existed. Worthless, worthless us. Luckily enough, we would die, but even then only a very small number of us would get into heaven. There was hell, a pit of eternally burning fire, for the vast majority.

Where was hell? I wanted to know. Under the ground, I was informed. It was assumed most of the white people would be there, and therefore it would be more or less like here. Only fiery hot, hotter than the sun in the cotton field at midday. Nobody wanted to go there.

I had a problem with this doctrine at a very early age: I could not see how my parents had sinned. Each month my mother had suffered from what I would later recognize, because I unfortunately inherited it, as bad premenstrual syndrome. At those times her temper was terrible; the only safe thing was to stay out of her way. My father, slower to anger, was nonetheless a victim of sexist ideology learned from his father, the society and the church, which meant I battled with him throughout childhood, until I left home for good at 17. But I did not see that they were evil, that they should be cursed because they were black, because my mother was a woman. They were as innocent as trees, I felt. And, at heart, generous and sweet. I resented the minister and the book he read from that implied they could only be "saved" by confessing their sin and accepting suffering and degradation as their due, just because a very long time ago a snake had given a white woman an apple and she had eaten it and generously given a bite to her craven hearted husband. This was insulting to the most drowsy intelligence, I thought, noting that my exhausted father often napped while in church. But what could I do? I was three years old.

When I was in my 30s, I wrote this poem:

> SUNDAY SCHOOL, CIRCA 1950
> "Who made you?" was always
> The question,
> The answer was always "God."
> Well, there we stood
> Three feet high
> Heads bowed
> Leaning into
> Bosoms.
> Now I no longer recall
> The Catechism
> Or brood on the Genesis
> Of life
> No.
> I ponder the exchange
> Itself
> And salvage mostly
> The leaning.

It is ironic, to say the least, that the very woman out of whose body I came, whose pillowy arms still held me, willingly indoctrinated me away from herself and the earth from which both of us received sustenance, and toward a frightful, jealous, cruel, murderous "God" of another race and tribe of people, and expected me to forget the very breasts that had fed me and that I still leaned against. But such is the power of centuries-old indoctrination.

We know now with what absolute heartlessness the male leaders of the orthodox Christian church not unlike those of orthodox Judaism and Islam stamped out, generally after robbing them of their land and enslaving them, pagans and heathens, our ancestors and theirs, around the globe: a campaign of such unspeakable cruelty which has lasted for so long, and which still continues, that few have had the heart to encounter it in art, politics, literature, or consciousness until the present era. Thanks in large part to feminism and feminist scholarship, and to a resurgent belief in the sacredness of the feminine, which has been deliberately erased, demonized and disparaged in all major religions. But thanks also to indigenous peoples who, though a mere remnant of their former selves, before being invaded by conquerors professing Christianity, have risen up to speak in defense of the ancient Goddess/God of all pagans and heathens, Mother Earth. . . .

It is fatal to love a God who does not love you. A God specifically created to comfort, lead, advise, strengthen, and enlarge the tribal borders of someone else. We have been beggars at the table of a religion that sanctioned our destruction. Our own religions denied, forgotten; our own ancestral connections to All Creation something of which we are ashamed. I maintain that we are empty, lonely, without our pagan-heathen ancestors; that we must lively them up within ourselves, and begin to see them as whole and necessary and correct: their earth-Centered, Female-Reverencing religions, like their architecture, agriculture and music, suited perfectly to the lives they led. And lead, those who are left, today. I further maintain that the Jesus most of us have been brought up to adore must be expanded to include the "wizard" and the dancer, and that when this is done, it becomes clear that He coexists quite easily with pagan indigenous peoples. Indeed, it was because the teachings of Jesus were already familiar to many of our ancestors, especially in the New world they already practiced the love and sharing that he preached that the Christian Church was able to make as many genuine converts to the Christian religion as it did.

All people deserve to worship a God who also worships them. A God that made them, and likes them. That is why Nature, Mother Earth, is such a good choice. Never will Nature require that you cut off some part of your body to please her; Never will Mother Earth find anything wrong with your natural way. She made it, and she made it however it is so that you will be more comfortable as part of Her Creation, rather than less. Everyone deserves a God who adores our freedom: Nature would never advise us to do anything but be ourselves. Mother Earth will do all that she can to support our choices, whatever they are. For they are of Her, and inherent in our creation is Her Trust.

We are born knowing how to worship, just as we are born knowing how to laugh. . . .

And what is the result of decolonizing the spirit? . . . One begins to see the world from one's own point of view; to interact with it out of one's own conscience and heart. We begin to . . . [want] to survive, to be happy to enjoy one another and Life, and to laugh. We begin to distinguish between the need, singly, to throw rocks at whatever is oppressing us, and the creative joy that arises when we bring our collective stones of resistance against injustice together. We begin to see that we must be loved very much by whatever Creation is, to find ourselves on this wonderful Earth. We begin to recognize our sweet, generously appointed place in the makeup of the Cosmos. We begin to feel glad, and grateful that we are not in heaven, but that we are *here*.

Source: "The Only Reason You Want to Go to Heaven Is That You Have Been Driven Out of Your Mind (Off Your Land and Out of Your Lover's Arms)," from *Anything We Love Can Be Saved* by Alice Walker, copyright © 1997 by Alice Walker. Used by permission of Random House, Inc.

AFTERWARD

In the years since her Auburn speech, Walker has become increasingly involved in political activism, including antiwar protests during the Iraq War and opposition to the policies of Israel and the United States regarding the Palestinian people. She has continued to publish novels, poetry, and works of nonfiction, including *We Are the Ones We Have Been Waiting For*, *Hard Times Require Furious Dancing*, and *Why War Is Never a Good Idea*.

She was named Humanist of the Year by the American Humanist Association in 1997 and has received the Lillian Smith Award from the National Endowment for the Arts, the Rosenthal Award from the National Institute of Arts and Letters, and a Guggenheim Fellowship.

ASK YOURSELF

1. Why in Walker's opinion is the relationship of African Americans to God, Jesus, and Heaven complicated by issues of race?
2. What does Walker suggest in place of the worship of the Judeo-Christian God, and why?

TOPICS AND ACTIVITIES TO CONSIDER

Alice Walker denounces hypocrisy and bigotry in the guise of religion from outside the church doors. In "Letter from Birmingham Jail," Martin Luther King Jr. also denounces the hypocrisy and bigotry of church leaders but does so from the perspective of a Christian within the church. How are the two approaches similar and different? Is one more effective than the other in your view?

Further Information

Allen, Norm R., Jr., ed. *The Black Humanist Experience*. Amherst, NY: Prometheus Books, 2002.

Pinn, Anthony, ed. *By These Hands: A Documentary History of African American Humanism*. New York: New York University Press, 2001.

Walker, Alice. *The Color Purple*. San Diego: Harcourt Brace Jovanovich, 1982.

Walker, Alice. *We Are the Ones We Have Been Waiting For*. New York: The New Press, 2007.

Web Site

Official Web site of Alice Walker: http://www.alicewalkersgarden.com.

THE HUMORISTS

34. Twain Laughing, Twain Raging—*Thoughts of God* (1972) and the *Autobiography* (2010)

INTRODUCTION

Mark Twain (Samuel Clemens, 1835–1910) is one of several well-known and beloved figures in American history, including Thomas Edison, Susan B. Anthony, and Albert Einstein, whose atheism or agnosticism remains almost entirely unknown to the general public. Twain's own religious doubt was revealed only obliquely in works published during his lifetime. Though his late-life agnosticism was occasionally evident in his work ("If there is a God," he wrote in *Following the Equator*, "he is a malign thug"), it was only in works published posthumously, such as *Fables of Man* (1972) and his unabridged *Autobiography* (2010), that Twain's unbelief becomes clearly evident.

In the essay "Thoughts of God," Twain takes a scathingly satiric view of what today would be called "intelligent design theory"—the religious idea that every manifestation of life on Earth was created, and perfectly so, by God—by wondering aloud about a divine being that would create the fly. This excerpt is followed by a brief glimpse of Twain's newly-released *Autobiography*.

KEEP IN MIND AS YOU READ

Twain often employed satire as a means of leveling serious critiques at sensitive subjects, from race to social injustice to religion. As you read "Thoughts of God," note how each humorous statement draws a laugh *and* makes a point. If the satirist has succeeded, the reader will be not just entertained, but more convinced of the author's point of view by the end of the piece.

Document: Mark Twain, "Thoughts of God," from **Fables of Man**

How often we are moved to admit the intelligence exhibited in both the designing and the execution of some of His works. Take the fly, for instance. The planning of the fly was an application of pure intelligence, morals not being concerned. Not one of us could have planned the fly, not one of us could have constructed him; and no one would have considered it wise to try, except under an assumed name. It is believed by some that the fly was introduced to meet a long-felt want. In the course of ages, for some reason or other, there have been millions of these persons, but out of this vast multitude there has not been one who has been willing to explain what the want was. At least satisfactorily. A few have explained that there was need of a creature to remove disease-breeding garbage; but these being then asked to explain what long-felt want the disease-breeding garbage was introduced to supply, they have not been willing to undertake the contract.

There is much inconsistency concerning the fly. In all the ages he has not had a friend, there has never been a person in the earth who could have been persuaded to intervene between him and extermination; yet billions of persons have excused the Hand that made him—and this without a blush. Would they have excused a Man in the same circumstances, a man positively known to have invented the fly? On the contrary. For the credit of the race let us believe it would have been all day with that man. Would persons consider it just to **reprobate** in a child, with its undeveloped morals, a scandal which they would overlook in the Pope?

> **Reprobate:** used here as a verb meaning "to express or feel disapproval of"

When we reflect that the fly was not invented for pastime, but in the way of business; that he was not flung off in a heedless moment and with no object in view but to pass the time, but was the fruit of long and pains-taking labor and calculation, and with a definite and far-reaching, purpose in view; that his character and conduct were planned out with cold deliberation, that his career was foreseen and fore-ordered, and that there was no want which he could supply, we are hopelessly puzzled, we cannot understand the moral lapse that was able to render possible the conceiving and the consummation of this squalid and malevolent creature.

Let us try to think the unthinkable: let us try to imagine a Man of a sort willing to invent the fly; that is to say, a man destitute of feeling; a man willing to wantonly torture and harass and persecute myriads of creatures who had never done him any harm and could not if they wanted to, and—the majority of them—poor dumb things not even aware of his existence. In a word, let us try to imagine a man with so singular and so lumbering a code of morals as this: that it is fair and right to send afflictions upon the just—upon the unoffending as well as upon the offending, without discrimination.

If we can imagine such a man, that is the man that could invent the fly, and send him out on his mission and furnish him his orders: "Depart into the uttermost corners of the earth, and diligently do your appointed work. Persecute the sick child; settle upon its eyes, its face, its hands, and gnaw and pester and sting; worry and fret and madden the worn and tired mother who watches by the child, and who humbly prays for mercy and relief with the pathetic faith of the deceived and the unteachable. Settle upon the soldier's festering wounds in field and hospital and drive him frantic while he also prays, and betweentimes curses, with none to listen but you, Fly, who get all the petting and all the protection, without even praying for it. Harry and persecute the forlorn and forsaken wretch who is perishing of the plague, and in his terror and despair praying; bite, sting, feed upon his ulcers, dabble your feet in his rotten blood, gum them thick with plague-germs—feet cunningly designed and perfected for this function ages ago in the beginning—carry this freight to a hundred tables, among the just and the unjust. the high and the low, and walk over the food and gaum it with filth and death. Visit all; allow no man peace till he get it in the grave; visit and afflict the hard-worked and unoffending horse, mule, ox, ass, pester the patient cow, and all the kindly animals that labor without fair reward here and perish without hope of it hereafter; spare no creature, wild or tame; but wheresoever you find one, make his life a misery, treat him as the innocent deserve; and so please Me and increase My glory Who made the fly.

We hear much about His patience and forbearance and long-suffering; we hear nothing about our own, which much exceeds it. We hear much about His mercy and kindness and goodness—in words—the words of His Book and of His pulpit—and the meek multitude is content with this evidence, such as it is, seeking no further; but whoso searcheth after a concreted sample of it will in time acquire fatigue. There being no instances of it. For what are gilded as mercies are not in any recorded case more than mere common justices, and due—due without thanks or compliment. To rescue without personal risk a cripple from a burning house is not a mercy, it is a mere commonplace duty; anybody would do it that could. And not by proxy, either—delegating the work but confiscating the credit for it. If men neglected "God's poor" and "God's stricken and helpless ones" as He does, what would become of them? The answer is to be found in those dark lands where man follows His example and turns his indifferent back upon them: they get no help at all; they cry, and plead and pray in vain, they linger and suffer, and miserably die. If you will look at the matter rationally and without prejudice, the proper place to hunt for the facts of His mercy, is not where man does the mercies and He collects the praise, but in those regions where He has the field to Himself.

It is plain that there is one moral law for heaven and another for the earth. The pulpit assures us that wherever we see suffering and sorrow which we can relieve and do not do it, we sin, heavily. There was never yet a case of suffering or sorrow which God could not relieve. Does He sin, then? If He is the Source of Morals He does—certainly nothing can be plainer than that, you will admit. Surely the Source of law cannot violate law and stand unsmirched; surely the judge upon the bench cannot forbid crime and then revel in it himself unreproached. Nevertheless we have this curious spectacle: daily the trained parrot in the pulpit gravely delivers himself of these ironies, which he has acquired at second-hand and adopted without examination, to a trained congregation which accepts them without examination, and neither the speaker nor the hearer laughs at himself. It does seem as if we ought to be humble when we are at a **bench-show**, and not put on airs of intellectual superiority there.

> **Bench-show:** an exhibition of small dogs or other animals displayed for judging on small benches

Source: Clemens, Samuel. *Fables of Man*. Edited by John S. Tuckey, Kenneth M. Sanderson, Bernard L. Stein, and Frederick Anderson. Mark Twain Papers Series. Berkeley: University of California Press, 1972. Reprinted with permission.

Like many religious skeptics, Twain's opinions evolved considerably over his lifetime. In midcareer he called himself a Presbyterian. By the 1880s his views were essentially deistic, as Twain claimed to believe in a deity who was uninvolved in human life or

THE USE OF HUMOR TO CHALLENGE RELIGIOUS ORTHODOXY

It is easy and common to dismiss humor as mere entertainment. But as the examples in this chapter show, humorists throughout the centuries have wielded their pens to challenge the status quo, including the dominant religious assumptions of their times, often to profound effect. Though the critique of religion through humor is enjoying something of a renaissance in recent years, examples can be found throughout history—including in the *actual* Renaissance.

In 1509, Desiderius Erasmus (not an atheist—in fact, an Augustinian monk) wrote *The Praise of Folly*, a stinging satire in which the goddess Folly gives a speech in praise of all that the human race does to serve and promote her cause. After getting the reader chuckling at judges and tradesmen and fishwives for a hundred pages, Erasmus gradually turns to the church, taking long, relentless jabs at the avarice and hypocrisy of the Catholic clergy. Many historians believe only his personal friendship with Pope Julius II and his ability to hide in the skirts of satire stood between him and execution. A work of sober rational argument may have been his death warrant.

The Praise of Folly hit the continent like a firestorm. The book's subtext is a call for the return to simple Christian values. Many see it as one of the final nudges for the Reformation, which began eight years later. If true, that puts satire at the center of one of the most earthshaking challenges to the religious status quo in Western history.

the functioning of the universe, which he said "is governed by strict and immutable laws."

Still later in life, his criticism of religion and religious belief intensified and became sharper. The first of three volumes in the unabridged Autobiography of Mark Twain *was released in 2010, the centenary of the author's death. Though the passages said to contain Twain's most direct criticism of religious belief and practice are in volumes 2 and 3, still unreleased at this writing, one released passage hints at the tone and content to come:*

There is one notable thing about our Christianity: bad, bloody, merciless, money-grabbing and predatory as it is—in our country particularly, and in all other Christian countries in a somewhat modified degree—it is still a hundred times better than the Christianity of the Bible, with its prodigious crime—the invention of Hell. Measured by our Christianity of to-day, bad as it is, hypocritical as it is, empty and hollow as it is, neither the Deity nor His Son is a Christian, nor qualified for that moderately high place. Ours is a terrible religion. The fleets of the world could swim in spacious comfort in the innocent blood it has spilt.

Source: Twain, Mark. *The Autobiography of Mark Twain: The Complete and Authoritative Edition.* Edited by Harriet Elinor Smith et al. Berkeley: University of California Press, 2010.

AFTERWARD

Like Darwin's family a generation earlier, Twain's withheld publication of his harshest religious critiques. Twain himself was keen to avoid the fate of Thomas Paine, who was quickly demoted from national hero to villain in public opinion when his antireligious opinions became known. "I expose to the world only my trimmed and perfumed and carefully barbered public opinions," Twain wrote near the end of his life, "and conceal carefully, cautiously, wisely, my private ones." He asked that his *Autobiography* be released piecemeal in four to five editions, the full manuscript being released only 100 years after his death. His specific instructions, given in an introduction titled "Preface. As from the Grave":

> From the first, second, third and fourth editions all sound and sane expressions of opinion must be left out. There may be a market for that kind of wares a century from now. There is no hurry. Wait and see. . . . The editions should be issued twenty-five years apart. Many things that must be left out of the first will be proper for the second; many things that must be left out of both will be proper for the third; into the fourth or at least the fifth the whole Autobiography can go, unexpurgated.

Twain's *Autobiography* joins the *Testament* of Jean Meslier and *The Autobiography of Charles Darwin* as works censored, abridged, or withheld completely by their authors or those closest to them to prevent disclosure of the authors' strong criticisms of religious belief.

ASK YOURSELF

1. Was Twain's satirical approach in "Thoughts of God" effective as a means of convincing the reader that the idea of an intelligent designer is seriously flawed?
2. Why did Twain ask that his complete *Autobiography* be withheld for 100 years, rather than allowing the release upon his death?

TOPICS AND ACTIVITIES TO CONSIDER

Select a humorous passage from "Thoughts of God" that nonetheless makes a point. Rewrite the passage as a straightforward argument, without humor. Is the humorous passage more effective, or does the comedic approach distract from the message?

Further Information

Twain, Mark. *Autobiography of Mark Twain: The Complete and Authoritative Edition*. Vol. 1. Edited by Leslie Myrick. Berkeley: University of California Press, 2010.

Twain, Mark. *Letters from the Earth: Uncensored Writings*. Edited by Bernard DeVoto. New York: HarperCollins, 1962.

Twain, Mark. *Mark Twain's Fables of Man*. Edited by John S. Tuckey, Kenneth Sanderson, Bernard Stein, and Frederick Anderson. Mark Twain Papers Series. Berkeley: University of California Press, 1972.

Web Sites

Complete Letters of Mark Twain at Project Gutenberg: http://www.gutenberg.org/ebooks/3199.

List of Twain quotations challenging religion: http://www.positiveatheism.org/hist/quotes/twain.htm.

The Mark Twain Project at the University of California, Berkeley: http://www.marktwainproject.org/.

Twain stories and essays related to religion: http://www.positiveatheism.org/tochtwai.htm.

35. Douglas Adams on the Origin of Religion (1998)

INTRODUCTION

The following talk by science fiction novelist Douglas Adams (1952–2001) was delivered impromptu to Digital Biota 2, a conference of scientists studying the creation of synthetic organisms, in Cambridge, England, in 1998. In the course of the talk, Adams offered an analogy to the common human perception that the world was carefully designed for us, as opposed to humans being shaped by evolution to fit the world as it is. In the process, Adams created a compelling analogy (a world viewed from the perspective of a sentient puddle) to answer the primary arguments for "intelligent design," the idea that the universe is so complex and perfect that it must have been designed by a creative intelligence.

KEEP IN MIND AS YOU READ

Though speaking to a scientific audience, Adams approaches the question in a creative and humorous way. His science fiction works, including *The Hitchhiker's Guide to the Galaxy*, similarly used satire as a means to explore important philosophical and scientific questions.

Document: Douglas Adams, "Is There an Artificial God?," Speech to Digital Biota 2, Cambridge, UK (1998)

Where does the idea of God come from? Well, I think we have a very skewed point of view on an awful lot of things, but let's try and see where our point of view comes from. . . .

Early man has a moment to reflect and he thinks to himself, "Well, this is an interesting world that I find myself in," and then he asks himself a very treacherous question, a question which is totally meaningless and fallacious, but only comes about because of the nature of the sort of person he is, the sort of person he has evolved into and the sort of person who has thrived because he thinks this particular way. Man the maker looks at his world and says "So who made this then?" *Who made this?*—you can see why it's a treacherous question. Early man

199

thinks, "Well, because there's only one sort of being I know about who makes things, whoever made all this must therefore be a much bigger, much more powerful and necessarily invisible, one of me and because I tend to be the strong one who does all the stuff, he's probably male." And so we have the idea of a god. Then, because when we make things we do it with the intention of doing something with them, early man asks himself, "If he made it, what did he make it for?" Now the real trap springs, because early man is thinking, "This world fits me very well. Here are all these things that support me and feed me and look after me; yes, this world fits me nicely," and he reaches the inescapable conclusion that whoever made it, made it for him.

This is rather as if you imagine a puddle waking up one morning and thinking, "This is an interesting world I find myself in—an interesting hole I find myself in—fits me rather neatly, doesn't it? In fact it fits me staggeringly well, must have been made to have me in it!" This is such a powerful idea that as the sun rises in the sky and the air heats up and as, gradually, the puddle gets smaller and smaller, it's still frantically hanging on to the notion that everything's going to be all right, because this world was meant to have him in it, was built to have him in it; so the moment he disappears catches him rather by surprise. I think this may be something we need to be on the watch out for. . . .

There are some oddities in the perspective with which we see the world. The fact that we live at the bottom of a deep gravity well, on the surface of a gas covered planet going around a nuclear fireball 90 million miles away and think this to be normal is obviously some indication of how skewed our perspective tends to be.

Source: Adams, Douglas. Speech at Digital Biota 2, Cambridge, UK, September 1998. Accessed online at http://www.biota.org/people/douglasadams/.

AFTERWARD

Though Adams died unexpectedly from heart failure at 49, his body of work has continued to find an enthusiastic audience, including film and television adaptations and print collections of his fiction and nonfiction works.

ASK YOURSELF

Is Adams's puddle analogy effective? Do you think the analogy to human perspective is accurate and useful?

TOPICS AND ACTIVITIES TO CONSIDER

The Hitchhiker's Guide to the Galaxy begins with a human named Arthur Dent learning that the Earth is about to be destroyed by an alien race to make room for a hyperspace bypass. Some commentators have noted that such a scenario violates several assumptions from a traditional Christian religious perspective. Can you name them?

Further Information

Adams, Douglas. *The Salmon of Doubt: Hitchhiking the Galaxy One Last Time*. New York: Random House, 2002.

Web Site

Douglas Adams site: http://www.douglasadams.com/.

36. "Putting on the No-God Glasses"—Julia Sweeney's *Letting Go of God* (2004)

INTRODUCTION

After coming to national prominence as a member of the cast of *Saturday Night Live* in the early 1990s, comedian Julia Sweeney (b. 1959) has developed a career as an author and comic monologist, including a major portion focusing on her religious unbelief.

In contrast to the cerebral argumentation of scientists and philosophers, Sweeney gives voice to the accessible, everyday side of modern unbelief. Her one-woman show *Letting Go of God*, from which the passage below is excerpted, is a retelling of her own path from her childhood Catholicism through a number of religious experimentations to her arrival at last in outright unbelief. This excerpt, which takes place near the end of the monologue, describes her first halting attempts to see the world through entirely nontheistic eyes—and to deal with the astonishing implications.

KEEP IN MIND AS YOU READ

Sweeney frames her monologue in terms of personal experience rather than an attempt to convince or dictate conclusions to others. By doing so, and by using often self-deprecating comedy as a vehicle, she and other autobiographical humorists create a safe opportunity for others to engage in self-reflection without feeling defensive.

Document: Julia Sweeney, Letting Go of God *(2004)*

One day, as I was Cometing out my bathtub, I thought, "What if it's true? What if humans are here because of pure random chance? What if there is no guiding hand, no external regulation, no one watching? It is clearly possible that this may be true. In fact this is what our scientific evidence is pointing towards. But if it were true, what would that mean?"

I had spent so much time thinking about what God meant, that I hadn't really spent any time thinking about what not-God meant. A few days later, as I was walking from my office in my backyard into my house, I realized there was this little teeny-weenie voice whispering in my head. I'm not sure how long it had been there, but it suddenly got just one decibel louder. It whispered, "There is no God."

And I tried to ignore it. But it got a teeny bit louder. "There is no God. There is no God. *Oh my God, there is no God!*"

I sat down in my backyard under my barren apricot tree. (I didn't know trees were like people, they stop reproducing after they get old. Maybe that barren fig tree that Jesus condemned to death was just menopausal.) Anyway, I sat down and thought, "Okay. I admit it. I do not believe there is enough evidence to continue to believe in God. The world behaves exactly as you would expect it would, if there were no Supreme Being, no Supreme Consciousness, and no supernatural. My best judgment tells me that it's much more likely that we invented God, rather than God inventing us."

And I shuddered. I felt I was slipping off the raft.

And then I thought, "But I can't! I don't know if I CAN not believe in God! I need God. I mean we have a history together."

But then I thought, "Wait a minute. If you look over my life, every step of maturing for me, every single one, had the same common denominator. It was accepting what was true over what I wished were true. This was the case about guys, about my career, about my parents.

So how can I come up against this biggest question, the ultimate question, "Do I really believe in a personal God, and then turn away from the evidence? How can I believe, just because I want to? How will I have any respect for myself if I did that?

I thought of Pascal's Wager. Pascal argued that it's better to bet there is a God, because if you're wrong there's nothing to lose, but if there is, you win an eternity in heaven. But I can't force myself to believe, just in case it turns out to be true. The God I've been praying to knows what I think, he doesn't just make sure I show up for church. How could I possibly pretend to believe? I might convince other people, but surely not God.

And plus, if I lead my life according to my own deeply held moral principles, what difference did it make if I believed in God? Why would God care if I "believed" in him?

But then I thought, "But I don't know how to not believe in God. I don't know how you do it. How do you get up, how do you get through the day?"

I thought, "Okay, calm down. Let's just try on the not-believing-in-God glasses for a moment, just for a second. Just put on the no-God glasses and take a quick look around and then immediately throw them off."

So I put them on and I looked around.

I'm embarrassed to report that I initially felt dizzy. I actually had the thought, "Well, how does the Earth stay up in the sky? You mean, we're just hurtling through space? That's so vulnerable!" I wanted to run out and catch the earth as it fell out of space into my hands.

And then I thought, "Oh yeah, gravity and angular momentum is gonna keep us revolving around the sun for probably a really long time." Then I thought, "What's going to stop me from just, rushing out and murdering people?" And I had to walk myself through it, why are we ethical? Well, because we have to be. We're social animals. We're extremely complex social animals. We evolved a moral sense, like an aversion to wanton murder, in order for communities to exist. Because communities help us survive better in much bigger numbers. And eventually we codified these internal evolved ethics inside of us into laws against things like wanton murder. So . . . I guess that's why I won't be rushing out and murdering people!

And then suddenly I felt like I'd cheated on God somehow and I went into the house and prayed and asked God, "To please, help me have faith!" But already it felt slightly silly, and vacant and I felt like I was talking to myself.

I thought. "Okay, I'll just not believe in God for one hour a day and see how it goes." So, the next day, I tried it again.

Then I thought, "Wait a minute. Wait a minute. What about those people who are like . . . unjustifiably jailed somewhere horrible, and they are like . . . in solitary confinement and all they do is pray . . . this means that I . . . like, I think they're praying to nobody? Is that possible?" And then I thought, "We gotta do something to get those people outta jail!"

Because no one else is looking out for them but us, no God is hearing their pleas. And I guess that goes for really poor people too or really oppressed people, who I had this vague notion; they had God to comfort them. And an even vaguer idea, that God had orchestrated their lot, for some unknowable grand design.

I wandered around in a daze thinking, "No one is minding the store!" And I wondered how traffic worked, like how we weren't just in chaos all the time. And slowly, I began to see the world completely differently. I had to rethink what I thought about everything. It's like I had to go change the wallpaper of my mind.

Eventually I was able to say good-bye to God. And I imagined him as this old man, this old broken down man more like an older version of the God on the ceiling of the Sistine Chapel. And if you looked closely you could see the Jesus on my poster in my high school bedroom, but older, much older, with long gray and white hair and lots of lines on his face. An old hippie who still smoked. And at one time he seemed so all-powerful and all-knowing and all-protective, but now he just seemed a little stinky.

I could just see him sitting on his suitcases near the front door of my house. And I said to him, "I'm sorry God; it's not you. It's me. It's just, I don't think you exist. I mean, God, look at it this way: it's really because I take you so seriously that I can't bring myself to believe in you. If it's any consolation, it's sort of a sign of respect. So, you know, sit here as long as you want to, stay for a while, if you need to, there's no big hurry."

And slowly, over the course of several weeks, he disappeared.

Looking back on it, I think I just walked around in a daze for a few months. My mind became such a private place. I had shared my mind with a God my whole life and now I realized that my thoughts were completely my own. No one was monitoring them, no one was compassionately listening to them, my thoughts were my own private affair, and something no one but me knew about.

And I had so much thinking to do! One day I was walking along Larchmont Blvd., a busy shopping area near my house. I was lost in thought, thinking: "So, I don't think anything happens to us after we die. Consciousness fades and stops like every other organ. So people just die."

Then I thought, "Wait a minute, so Hitler, Hitler just . . . died? No one sat him down and said, 'You fucked up buddy! And now you're going to spend an eternity in HELL!' So Hitler just died." I thought, "We better make sure that doesn't happen again."

And my brother Mike. He just died. I always had this idea that Mike's death, while premature, was his divine destiny somehow. And that his spirit didn't really die, it lived on. Not just in the memory of those that knew him, but in a real tangible sense. And I realized that I now thought he died. He really died. And he was gone, forever.

And then I realized I had to go and basically kill off everyone I ever knew who died who I didn't think really died.

Then I thought, "Oh, I get it. So, I am going to die. I'm going to die." I sat down on a bench and watched people bustling by and thought, "Wow. Life is so cheap and so precious."

So, I guess I'm just another animal on Earth, just a type of primate, the third chimpanzee, better at using tools and able to talk. And then I'm going to die and there will be eons of more time when I will not exist, just like the eons of time before I did.

I'm in my forties, about halfway through life, I hope. At this moment, the sun and the Earth and I are all middle-aged. Just an animal on a planet in a solar system. Nothing special.

But then, I think about it in this way: The Earth is 4.5 billion years old. For a billion years there was no life at all, nothing. And then for three billion years, there were only algae and arche-bacteria. Dull green and brown primordial slime. For three billion years!

And then, just 500 million years ago, complex life came on the scene. Plants and animals, including us . . . who've been around for what? A few million years to a hundred thousand or so, depending on what you consider to be human?

If Genesis is a metaphor for creation, the metaphor is way off. God would not be creating man on the sixth day, but like, the six thousandth day. And all humanity would have been here for less than a second. Adam and Eve are blinking their eyes, just barely awake.

So, even if simple life exists all over the universe, it could be that any type of complex life is really rare. And then on top of that, when you think about how flying has evolved over and over again and how eyes have evolved over and over again, but how a species with a brain like ours, able to use language and tools the way we do, well, that's happened only once in 4 and a half billion years on Earth!

I mean it's not so improbable as to be impossible, given all the time involved and all the different species that have existed. But still, it's got to be pretty rare for animals like us to turn up. And in my DNA, is a history of this life on Earth. Not just back to the African Pliocene but even farther back from that, when we crawled out of the pond. And then even farther back from that when there were only single cell organisms. All told in the cells of my own body.

And to think that I live at a time when I can know and deeply understand that. It makes me feel so lucky.

Then I started thinking about all the little happenstances, all the little random moves, which resulted in me being alive, me in particular, at this very moment. Not just of my parents meeting, but even of the millions of sperm against the hundreds of possible eggs. I thought about this randomness multiplying, my parents, their parents: Marie meeting Tom in Yakima, Henrietta meeting Will on the cruise to Cuba, and then their parents, their parents, their parents. All the ways it could have gone one way, but it went the way it went. And all the possible people who could, just as easily, be here in my place.

Richard Dawkins wrote, "Certainly those unborn ghosts include poets greater than Keats, scientists greater than Newton. And in the teeth of these stupefying odds, it is you and I, in our ordinariness, that are here."

I suddenly felt very deeply that I was alive: Alive with my own particular thoughts, with my own particular story, in this itty-bitty splash of time. And in that splash of time, I get to think about things and do stuff and wonder about the world and love people, and drink my coffee if I want to. And then that's it.

I walked to my car and I had a ticket. My time had expired.

And I got in the car and I turned on the radio and there was that old Peggy Lee song. It used to be my Mom's favorite. I suddenly had this memory of us in the kitchen and that song coming on the radio. And my Mom was flipping hamburgers, dancing around the kitchen, taking care of all of her kids. "Is that all there is? If that's all there is my friends, then let's keep dancing."

Source: Sweeney, Julia. *Letting Go of God* (Audio CD). Los Angeles: Indefatigable, 2006. Reprinted with permission.

AFTERWARD

In 2006, Sweeney received the Richard Dawkins Award, given annually "to honor an outstanding atheist whose contributions raise public awareness of the nontheist life stance" and the American Humanist Association's Humanist Pioneer Award.

ASK YOURSELF

1. Works in which Sweeney describes her atheism have been described as "accessible" and "nonthreatening" while remaining extremely effective. What characteristics of this monologue can you give as examples of this combination?
2. What is your reaction to Sweeney's struggles with meaning, death, and justice in light of "Letting Go of God"? Does she describe consolations to counterbalance the difficulties?
3. What does she mean when she says, "Wow. Life is so cheap and so precious," and what triggered this observation?

TOPICS AND ACTIVITIES TO CONSIDER

Write and perform a brief personal monologue describing a life-changing realization of your own.

Further Information

Sweeney, Julia. *Letting Go of God* (Audio CD). Los Angeles: Indefatigable, 2006.

Web Site

Julia Sweeney site: http://www.JuliaSweeney.com.

37. Satire Responds to Pain and Outrage—Brian Keith Dalton's "Mr. Deity and the Planes" (2009)

INTRODUCTION

Religious satire is not limited to the printed page. Films such as *Life of Brian, Dogma, Religulous*, and *Saved!* have used visual media to satirize and critique religious ideas. After hearing religious commentators attempting to reconcile belief in a loving God with the deaths of 230,000 people in the 2004 Indian Ocean tsunami, film director Brian Keith Dalton penned a brief satire in which God works with his assistant, Larry, to determine what evil will be allowed in the new creation. Two years later, the skit became Episode 1 in the first season of *Mr. Deity*, a series of short comedy films exploring various aspects of Judeo-Christian religious belief and practice, with Dalton himself as Mr. Deity.

In a 2011 interview, Dalton noted that he has "a pretty extensive religious background . . . was raised Mormon, and really got into it in my teens and twenties," but rejected the empirical claims of Mormonism in 1993. This was followed by serious investigations of Catholicism and Judaism before Dalton self-identified as an atheist.[1]

KEEP IN MIND AS YOU READ

Like Richard Dawkins's article "Religion's Misguided Missiles," the text below was inspired by the terrorist attacks of September 11, 2001. Unlike Dawkins's text, which focuses on the pivotal role of afterlife belief in making the attacks possible, Dalton invites us to ask one of the oldest questions in religious thought, phrased by the philosopher Epicurus as follows: Either God wants to abolish evil, and cannot; or he can, but does not want to. If he wants to, but cannot, he is impotent. If he can, but does not want to, he is wicked. If God can abolish evil, and God really wants to do it, why is there evil in the world?

In Dalton's satiric vision, the Deity's assistant Larry grows increasingly upset and frustrated as September 11 approaches and the Deity offers weak and often revealing reasons for not intervening to prevent the tragedy.

---

[1] Interview with Brian Keith Dalton, Path of Reason Web site, http://aclamonica.blogspot.com/2011/03/interview-with-brian-keith-dalton.html.

Document: Brian Keith Dalton, "Mr. Deity and the Planes" (2009)

Season 3, Episode 6 of the "Mr. Deity" web video series

MR. DEITY'S assistant LARRY is on the telephone, disheveled and unshaven, a pure white background behind him and a silver laptop on the desk in front of him.

LARRY: So none of this can happen without his approval? (Looks exasperated.) Okay . . . thank you for trying.

Larry hangs up the phone. MR. DEITY enters, disheveled, in a bathrobe, rubbing his eyes, moaning.

MR. DEITY: Sweet Agamemnon's ghost, don't EVER let me sleep more than seventeen hours again. That was awful. I feel like I've missed the entire day.

LARRY: Well basically you have.

MR. DEITY: Oh look at you! You look worse than I do, thank you.

LARRY: Sir, I haven't slept for days. 'Kay?

MR. DEITY: You haven't slept . . . why haven't you slept . . . OMS, Larry, what is wrong with you?

LARRY: It's going down tomorrow.

MR. DEITY, *waving his hand dismissively:* Let it go. Let it go, bye bye . . .

LARRY: We could do something!

MR. DEITY: There's always something we could do!

LARRY: No, we could do something simple, okay? Something that doesn't break any of your "rules," free will, or natural law . . .

MR. DEITY: That completely misses the point.

> **Lucy:** short for Lucifer, Mr. Deity's on-again, off-again girlfriend. The Deity put her in charge of Hell after their first breakup because "he knew the kind of suffering she could dole out"

LARRY: No, I'll tell you what. We get **Lucy**, we get a couple of her pyros down there, right? And we could have them set that building on fire, and we could have it evacuated before the planes hit . . .

MR. DEITY: Yeah, first of all, that's way too obvious, and B, that doesn't save any of the people in the planes!

LARRY: I know, but . . .

MR. DEITY: So I'm supposed to save people in the buildings, but not in the planes.

LARRY: That's a lot of people! People with spouses and children . . .

MR. DEITY: Do you have any idea how arbitrary that makes me look? And who do you think these people are? I let millions die in genocide, all over the world—but Bob in Accounting, I've gotta save him, are you kidding me? Look up . . . uh . . . *(He points at LARRY'S laptop, which instead of Google shows "Godgle.")* Fulani Ngani on Godgle. Cute little African girl. You see her?

LARRY: Yeah.

MR. DEITY: Yeah? You get the point?

LARRY, *irritably:* Yeah, I get it!

MR. DEITY: She's gonna live four years, she's never gonna have a decent meal in her whole life, always feel hungry . . . she's gonna have pain and suffering her whole life! Okay, and plus, she's gonna have a fly land on her eyeball more than 50,000 times over the course of her life. Not the same fly, of course, but do you know how annoying that is? If I'm not saving her, I'm not saving anybody!

LARRY: So it's . . . all or nothing?

MR. DEITY: Yeah, because otherwise I have to pick and choose! You want me to be a respecter of persons? What if I saved some schmuck's daughter but I didn't save yours, huh, how would that make you feel?

LARRY: So we're just gonna take all of these people early.

MR. DEITY, *exasperated:* We're not taking *anyone*, the guys on the *plane* are taking them!

LARRY: So this isn't even part of your long-term plan that people don't understand?

MR. DEITY, *laughing:* Long term plan, Larry, do you . . . Oh, you're *serious.* Like, like what?

LARRY: I don't know, like . . . maybe if this mother's taken, you know, then this father has to step up to be the dad he was always supposed to be, you know, to his daughter. Or something like that.

MR. DEITY: That's sick, man. You don't kill somebody or let someone be killed so that someone else can learn a lesson, that's vile. Besides, do you have any idea the kind of logistics you're taking about, pulling something like that off for three thousand people? Can't be done.

LARRY: Okay, if . . . if you're not saving people, and you don't have a plan, where are you when this goes down?

MR. DEITY: Where am I, you mean . . . what, tomorrow specifically?

LARRY: No not . . . well yeah! Yeah, actually yeah, tomorrow! Where are you tomorrow?

MR. DEITY: I'm on the back nine at Augusta with Zeus, you know that, it's been on the iCal for three weeks, you gotta sync up, dude, why do you think I got the kilt pressed?

LARRY: People are gonna ask, where are you when this goes down?

MR. DEITY: People always ask that when the shiitake mushrooms hit the fan. But guess what, no matter how dark it gets, they're always able to find me, aren't they, *(in a mocking tone)* "It's a MIRACLE!" There's a guy tomorrow who is gonna break his shoelace when he's puttin' on his shoes, he's gonna have to stop, get a shoelace, because of that he's gonna be late, plane's gonna hit the building, he's not gonna be there, right where he sits, his floor . . .

LARRY: So we're gonna save this guy?

MR. DEITY: No we're not savin' this guy, he's a lucky bastard, just like this woman who for the first time in eighteen years has decided to take a vacation. She's on a plane right now to Paris.

LARRY: And you think you're gonna get credit for that.

MR. DEITY: Of course I'm gonna get the credit for that, who else would get it?

LARRY, *shrugs*: Fate?

MR. DEITY: Fate never gets the credit, why do you think she's always so ticked off at me?

LARRY: What about the firemen? Everybody loves a firefighter, right? Can't we save them?

MR. DEITY: Well, we'll never get **Rescue Me** launched, and you love that show as much as I do, so I'm gonna leave that in your hands.

> **Rescue Me**: a television drama centered on a New York City fire company living and working in the years following the 9/11 attacks. In a subtle reference to the Deity's omniscience, Mr. Deity and Larry "love that show," even though it premiered three years after the conversation depicted here

LARRY, *looks around sheepishly*: I do love that show. *(Serious again.)* I just feel so useless.

MR. DEITY: You *are* useless, Larry. But not to me, just to these people down there. You know what? You wanna be useful? I'm going up to shower. You got me another loofa, right?

LARRY: Yeah.

MR. DEITY: Don't take your allergy medication in the morning.

LARRY: Why?

MR. DEITY: Because I need you to caddy for me again.

LARRY: No, no, what about Peter?

MR. DEITY: He can't do it, he's got guard duty.

LARRY: So I've got to caddy, suffer an allergy attack, and mourn the loss of three thousand people?

MR. DEITY: I just need you to sneeze in his backswing.

Source: Transcription from online video at http://www.MrDeity.com. Reprinted with permission from Brian Dalton.

AFTERWARD

The Mr. Deity series has included 10 to 20 episodes per year, each exploring a different aspect of (usually Christian) religious belief. In addition to the Deity and his assistant, Larry, the cast includes Jesus (who Mr. Deity asks to do a "really big favor" by going to Earth, leading a sinless life, and dying in agony), Lucy (short for Lucifer, Mr. Deity's ex-girlfriend who is appointed to run Hell), and Timmy, God's technical adviser. Topics explored to date include prayer, the creation of light, commandments, war, meaning and purpose, the murder of Cain, gender in the Bible, gospel contradictions, the creation of Eve, and intelligent design.

ASK YOURSELF

1. Does the humorous presentation make it easier to think about these issues? Harder? Are valid points made, or is the value primarily one of entertainment?
2. What is the effect of the sudden change of topic to the next day's golf game at the end? Is this strictly for comedic effect, or is Dalton making a theological point?

TOPICS AND ACTIVITIES TO CONSIDER

Use Mr. Deity videos as the starting point for a conversation about the issues raised.

Web Site

Mr. Deity Web site, including all video episodes: http://www.mrdeity.com.

38. Parody as Protest—the Birth of Pastafarianism (2005)

INTRODUCTION

In 2005, the Kansas State Board of Education voted to amend the state science standards to introduce the teaching of the "intelligent design" (ID) hypothesis—the idea that some features of the universe, particularly life on Earth, are too complex to be explained without a supernatural creative force—into the curriculum. "Evolution has been proven false," said board member Kathy Martin as the hearings began. "ID is science-based and strong in facts," she said, and so deserves equal time in the classroom.

One of the more creative responses to the situation in Kansas was an open letter to the board by Bobby Henderson, then a 24-year-old graduate of the Oregon State University physics program. The letter pretends to agree with the board's decision to allow multiple points of view, then claims that another religious perspective, one based on the worship of a Flying Spaghetti Monster, also known as Pastafarianism, deserves equal time as well.

KEEP IN MIND AS YOU READ

Henderson uses the technique, time-honored both in rhetoric and in comedy, of pretending to agree with the opposition—in this case the idea that all hypotheses deserve equal time in the science classroom—in order to reveal their absurdities.

Document: Bobby Henderson, Open Letter to the Kansas School Board (2005)

I am writing you with much concern after having read of your hearing to decide whether the alternative theory of Intelligent Design should be taught along with the theory of Evolution. I think we can all agree that it is important for students to hear multiple viewpoints so they can choose for themselves the theory that makes the most sense to them. I am concerned, however, that students will only hear one theory of Intelligent Design.

Let us remember that there are multiple theories of Intelligent Design. I and many others around the world are of the strong belief that the universe was created by a Flying Spaghetti Monster. It was He who created all that we see and all that we feel. We feel strongly that the overwhelming scientific evidence pointing towards evolutionary processes is nothing but a coincidence, put in place by Him.

It is for this reason that I'm writing you today, to formally request that this alternative theory be taught in your schools, along with the other two theories. In fact, I will go so far as to say, if you do not agree to do this, we will be forced to proceed with legal action. I'm sure you see where we are coming from. If the Intelligent Design theory is not based on faith, but instead another scientific theory, as is claimed, then you must also allow our theory to be taught, as it is also based on science, not on faith.

Some find that hard to believe, so it may be helpful to tell you a little more about our beliefs. We have evidence that a Flying Spaghetti Monster created the universe. None of us, of course, were around to see it, but we have written accounts of it. We have several lengthy volumes explaining all details of His power. Also, you may be surprised to hear that there are over 10 million of us, and growing. We tend to be very secretive, as many people claim our beliefs are not substantiated by observable evidence.

What these people don't understand is that He built the world to make us think the earth is older than it really is. For example, a scientist may perform a carbon-dating process on an artifact. He finds that approximately 75% of the Carbon-14 has decayed by electron emission to Nitrogen-14, and infers that this artifact is approximately 10,000 years old, as the half-life of Carbon-14 appears to be 5,730 years. But what our scientist does not realize is that every time he makes a measurement, the Flying Spaghetti Monster is there changing the results with His Noodly Appendage. We have numerous texts that describe in detail how this can be possible and the reasons why He does this. He is of course invisible and can pass through normal matter with ease.

I'm sure you now realize how important it is that your students are taught this alternate theory. It is absolutely imperative that they realize that observable evidence is at the discretion of a Flying Spaghetti Monster. Furthermore, it is disrespectful to teach our beliefs without wearing His chosen outfit, which of course is full pirate regalia. I cannot stress the importance of this enough, and unfortunately cannot describe in detail why this must be done as I fear this letter is already becoming too long. The concise explanation is that He becomes angry if we don't.

You may be interested to know that global warming, earthquakes, hurricanes, and other natural disasters are a direct effect of the shrinking numbers of Pirates since the 1800s. For your interest, I have included a graph of the approximate number of pirates versus the average global temperature over the last 200 years. As you can see, there is a statistically significant inverse relationship between pirates and global temperature.

In conclusion, thank you for taking the time to hear our views and beliefs. I hope I was able to convey the importance of teaching this theory to your students. We will of course be able to train the teachers in this alternate theory.

I am eagerly awaiting your response, and hope dearly that no legal action will need to be taken. I think we can all look forward to the time when these three theories are given equal time in our science classrooms across the country, and eventually the world; One third time for Intelligent Design, one third time for Flying Spaghetti Monsterism (Pastafarianism), and one third time for logical conjecture based on overwhelming observable evidence.

Sincerely Yours,
Bobby Henderson, concerned citizen

Source: Henderson, Bobby. *The Gospel of the Flying Spaghetti Monster*. New York: Villard Books, 2006.

AFTERWARD

In 2006, four of the six religious conservatives on the board who had approved the change in the science curriculum lost their seats in a primary election. On February 13, 2007, the newly constituted board voted 6–4 to reject the amended science standards enacted in 2005.

Since the dissemination of Henderson's letter in 2005, "The Church of the Flying Spaghetti Monster," a parody religion, has grown and developed rapidly around the world, particularly on college campuses. The satire itself has been praised by the Associated Press as "a clever and effective argument" and the *Daily Telegraph* as "a masterstroke, which underlined the absurdity of Intelligent Design." Countless elaborations on the supposed beliefs and practices of the religion have been created and disseminated by its erstwhile followers. Henderson himself maintains the Church's Web site at http://www.venganza.org, and published *The Gospel of the Flying Spaghetti Monster* through Villard in 2006.

ASK YOURSELF

1. Was Henderson's original (satirical) argument an effective foil against the reasoning of the Kansas Board of Education? Was its central thesis (that there is no more reason to reject Pastafarianism than Judeo-Christian-derived creationism) valid?
2. Why do you think the Church of the Flying Spaghetti Monster has grown so quickly? Why has it found a particular following on college campuses?

TOPICS AND ACTIVITIES TO CONSIDER

- Imagine you were a Kansas state board member in 2005 who took Henderson's letter seriously. Write a reply giving your reasons that Flying Spaghetti Monsterism does not deserve the same consideration and equal classroom time as intelligent design.
- Investigate the phenomena of parody religions and fictional religions. How do they differ?

෨ Select a mainstream religion. How would you go about proving that it was not originally created as a parody? Conversely, how might you argue that Pastafarianism, Bokononism, and other parody religions were created with serious intentions?

Further Information

Henderson, Bobby. *The Gospel of the Flying Spaghetti Monster*. New York: Villard Books, 2006.

Web Site

Official Web site of the Church of the Flying Spaghetti Monster: http://www.venganza.org.

CONTEMPORARY VOICES

39. The Passions of Richard Dawkins— "To Live at All Is Miracle Enough" (1998) and "Religion's Misguided Missiles" (2001)

INTRODUCTION

British evolutionary biologist and Oxford professor emeritus Richard Dawkins (b. 1941) made his first major contributions in the 1970s and 1980s advocating a gene-centered view of evolution. The first excerpt below is from *Unweaving the Rainbow*, a book written to dispel the common misconception that understanding and explanation spoils our appreciation and wonder regarding the world around us. In doing so, Dawkins makes a case for an entirely naturalistic, nontheistic engagement with wonder and meaning.

The terrorist attacks of September 11, 2001, had a profound effect on Dawkins, who turned the bulk of his attention from the popular understanding of science to the direct critique of religion and its effects, as well as the promotion and articulation of atheism as a self-sufficient worldview.

KEEP IN MIND AS YOU READ

Unweaving the Rainbow takes its title from the poem "Lamia" by John Keats, which suggests that knowing the true nature of something beloved causes its "charms [to] fly." Among the implications of the poem is that Isaac Newton's discovery that the rainbow is a refraction of white light robbed the "awful rainbow" (i.e., awe-full) of its splendor:

> Do not all charms fly
> At the mere touch of cold philosophy?
> There was an awful rainbow once in heaven:
> We know her woof, her texture; she is given
> In the dull catalogue of common things.
> Philosophy will clip an Angel's wings,
> Conquer all mysteries by rule and line,
> Empty the haunted air, and gnomed mine
> Unweave a rainbow

Dawkins wrote his book, including the following passage, in refutation.

Document: Richard Dawkins, "To Live at All Is Miracle Enough," from Unweaving the Rainbow (1998)

We are going to die, and that makes us the lucky ones. Most people are never going to die because they are never going to be born. The potential people who could have been here in my place but who will in fact never see the light of day outnumber the sand grains of Arabia. Certainly those unborn ghosts include greater poets than Keats, scientists greater than Newton. We know this because the set of possible people allowed by our DNA so massively exceeds the set of actual people. In the teeth of these stupefying odds it is you and I, in our ordinariness, that are here. . . .

After sleeping through a hundred million centuries we have finally opened our eyes on a sumptuous planet, sparkling with colour, bountiful with life. Within decades we must close our eyes again. Isn't it a noble, an enlightened way of spending our brief time in the sun, to work at understanding the universe and how we have come to wake up in it? This is how I answer when I am asked— as I am surprisingly often—why I bother to get up in the mornings. To put it the other way round, isn't it sad to go to your grave without ever wondering why you were born? Who, with such a thought, would not spring from bed, eager to resume discovering the world and rejoicing to be a part of it?

Source: Dawkins, Richard. *Unweaving the Rainbow: Science, Delusion, and the Appetite for Wonder.* Boston: Houghton Mifflin, 1998.

The second excerpt represents the above-mentioned turning point in Dawkins's career. Written just three days after the attacks of September 11, it sounds the first note of what came to be called the New Atheism. "My last vestige of 'hands off religion' respect disappeared in the smoke and choking dust of September 11th 2001," he said three years later, "followed by the 'National Day of Prayer,' when prelates and pastors did their tremulous Martin Luther King impersonations and urged people of mutually incompatible faiths to hold hands, united in homage to the very force that caused the problem in the first place."

Document: Richard Dawkins, "Religion's Misguided Missiles," September 15, 2001

A guided missile corrects its trajectory as it flies, homing in, say, on the heat of a jet plane's exhaust. A great improvement on a simple ballistic shell, it still cannot discriminate particular targets. It could not zero in on a designated New York skyscraper if launched from as far away as Boston.

That is precisely what a modern "smart missile" can do. Computer miniaturisation has advanced to the point where one of today's smart missiles could be programmed with an image of the Manhattan skyline together with instructions to home in on the north tower of the World Trade Centre. Smart missiles of this sophistication are possessed by the United States, as we learned in the Gulf war, but they are economically beyond ordinary terrorists and scientifically beyond theocratic governments. Might there be a cheaper and easier alternative?

In the second world war, before electronics became cheap and miniature, the psychologist BF Skinner did some research on pigeon-guided missiles. The pigeon was to sit in a tiny cockpit, having previously been trained to peck keys in such a way as to keep a designated target in the centre of a screen. In the missile, the target would be for real.

The principle worked, although it was never put into practice by the US authorities. Even factoring in the costs of training them, pigeons are cheaper and lighter than computers of comparable effectiveness. Their feats in Skinner's boxes suggest that a pigeon, after a regimen of training with colour slides, really could guide a missile to a distinctive landmark at the southern end of Manhattan island. The pigeon has no idea that it is guiding a missile. It just keeps on pecking at those two tall rectangles on the screen, from time to time a food reward drops out of the dispenser, and this goes on until . . . oblivion.

Pigeons may be cheap and disposable as on-board guidance systems, but there's no escaping the cost of the missile itself. And no such missile large enough to do much damage could penetrate US air space without being intercepted. What is needed is a missile that is not recognised for what it is until too late. Something like a large civilian airliner, carrying the innocuous markings of a well-known carrier and a great deal of fuel. That's the easy part. But how do you smuggle on board the necessary guidance system? You can hardly expect the pilots to surrender the left-hand seat to a pigeon or a computer.

How about using humans as on-board guidance systems, instead of pigeons? Humans are at least as numerous as pigeons, their brains are not significantly costlier than pigeon brains, and for many tasks they are actually superior. Humans have a proven track record in taking over planes by the use of threats, which work because the legitimate pilots value their own lives and those of their passengers.

The natural assumption that the hijacker ultimately values his own life too, and will act rationally to preserve it, leads air crews and ground staff to make calculated decisions that would not work with guidance modules lacking a sense of self-preservation. If your plane is being hijacked by an armed man who, though prepared to take risks, presumably wants to go on living, there is room for bargaining. A rational pilot complies with the hijacker's wishes, gets the plane down on the ground, has hot food sent in for the passengers and leaves the negotiations to people trained to negotiate.

The problem with the human guidance system is precisely this. Unlike the pigeon version, it knows that a successful mission culminates in its own destruction. Could we develop a biological guidance system with the compliance and dispensability of a pigeon but with a man's resourcefulness and ability to infiltrate plausibly? What we need, in a nutshell, is a human who doesn't mind being blown up. He'd make the perfect on-board guidance system. But suicide enthusiasts are hard to find. Even terminal cancer patients might lose their nerve when the crash was actually looming.

Could we get some otherwise normal humans and somehow persuade them that they are not going to die as a consequence of flying a plane smack into a skyscraper? If only! Nobody is that stupid, but how about this—it's a long shot, but it just might work. Given that they are certainly going to die, couldn't we sucker them into believing that they are going to come to life again afterwards? Don't be daft! No, listen, it might work. Offer them a fast track to a Great Oasis in the Sky, cooled by everlasting fountains. Harps and wings wouldn't appeal to the sort of young men we need, so tell them there's a special martyr's reward of 72 virgin brides, guaranteed eager and exclusive.

Would they fall for it? Yes, testosterone-sodden young men too unattractive to get a woman in this world might be desperate enough to go for 72 private virgins in the next.

It's a tall story, but worth a try. You'd have to get them young, though. Feed them a complete and self-consistent background mythology to make the big lie sound plausible when it comes. Give them a holy book and make them learn it by heart. Do you know, I really think it might work. As luck would have it, we have just the thing to hand: a ready-made system of mind-control which has been honed over centuries, handed down through generations. Millions of people have been brought up in it. It is called religion and, for reasons which one day we may understand, most people fall for it (nowhere more so than America itself, though the irony passes unnoticed). Now all we need is to round up a few of these faith-heads and give them flying lessons.

Facetious? Trivialising an unspeakable evil? That is the exact opposite of my intention, which is deadly serious and prompted by deep grief and fierce anger. I am trying to call attention to the elephant in the room that everybody is too polite—or too devout—to notice: religion, and specifically the devaluing effect that religion has on human life. I don't mean devaluing the life of others (though it can do that too), but devaluing one's own life. Religion teaches the dangerous nonsense that death is not the end.

If death is final, a rational agent can be expected to value his life highly and be reluctant to risk it. This makes the world a safer place, just as a plane is safer if its hijacker wants to survive. At the other extreme, if a significant number of people convince themselves, or are convinced by their priests, that a martyr's death is equivalent to pressing the hyperspace button and zooming through a wormhole to another universe, it can make the world a very dangerous place. Especially if they also believe that that other universe is a paradisical escape from the tribulations of the real world. Top it off with sincerely believed, if ludicrous and degrading to women, sexual promises, and is it any wonder that naive and frustrated young men are clamouring to be selected for suicide missions?

There is no doubt that the afterlife-obsessed suicidal brain really is a weapon of immense power and danger. It is comparable to a smart missile, and its guidance system is in many respects superior to the most sophisticated electronic brain that money can buy. Yet to a cynical government, organisation, or priesthood, it is very very cheap.

Our leaders have described the recent atrocity with the customary cliché: mindless cowardice. "Mindless" may be a suitable word for the vandalising of a telephone box. It is not helpful for understanding what hit New York on September 11. Those people were not mindless and they were certainly not cowards. On the contrary, they had sufficiently effective minds braced with an insane courage, and it would pay us mightily to understand where that courage came from.

It came from religion. Religion is also, of course, the underlying source of the divisiveness in the Middle East which motivated the use of this deadly weapon in the first place. But that is another story and not my concern here. My concern here is with the weapon itself. To fill a world with religion, or religions of the Abrahamic kind, is like littering the streets with loaded guns. Do not be surprised if they are used.

Source: *The Guardian* (UK), September 15, 2001. Reproduced by permission of the author.

AFTERWARD

Dawkins's most significant contribution in the area of religious critique has been *The God Delusion* (2006), a book that has sold over 2 million copies in English and been translated into 31 other languages. It is primarily this book that has earned his inclusion, along with Sam Harris, Daniel Dennett, and Christopher Hitchens, among the "Four Horsemen" of the New Atheism.

Dawkins returned to his earlier emphasis on the wonder of the natural world as revealed by science in his 2011 book *The Magic of Reality*.

ASK YOURSELF

1. At the end of the first essay, Dawkins offers the suggestion that working to understand the universe and our place in it is a "noble [and] enlightened" way to spend our brief time on Earth. Is this sufficient to give meaning and purpose to life? What, if anything, would you add as a necessary part of a meaningful life?
2. The second essay attempts to make the case that without the religious ideology of the hijackers, the attacks of September 11 would not have been possible. Do you agree? Why or why not?

TOPICS AND ACTIVITIES TO CONSIDER

- Name three events in your own family history without which you would not have been born.
- Take part in a formal debate about whether religious beliefs have been a primarily positive or negative societal influence in human history.

Further Information

Dawkins, Richard. *The God Delusion*. Boston: Houghton Mifflin, 2006.
Dawkins, Richard. *Unweaving the Rainbow: Science, Delusion, and the Appetite for Wonder*. Boston: Houghton Mifflin, 1998.

Web Site

The Richard Dawkins Foundation for Reason and Science: http://richarddawkins.net/.

40. Doubt as Catalyst—Jennifer Michael Hecht's *Doubt: A History* (2003)

INTRODUCTION

Though credit is usually given to "The Four Horsemen" (Harris, Hitchens, Dawkins, and Dennett) for ushering in an era of stronger challenges to religious ideas in the first decade of the 21st century, a case can be made that historian, poet, and humanist Jennifer Michael Hecht (b. 1965) was among the first to break the ice with her 2003 book *Doubt: A History*. The book works from the provocative thesis that doubt—of religious claims, of authoritative sources, of received tradition and wisdom—has been an important catalyst of progress throughout human history.

In the book's introduction, Hecht explores what she calls the "great schism" between what humans are and what we wish we were. In the process, she creates a frame in which great doubt and great belief share much more in common than either does with the mass of disinterested humanity.

KEEP IN MIND AS YOU READ

Hecht's original idea was to write a history of atheism specifically, not of doubt more generally. "When my book came out in 2003, my publishers were the ones who thought it shouldn't be called 'A History of Atheism,'" Hecht said in a 2008 interview with Point of Inquiry podcast. But the broader title encouraged her to follow the thread of philosophical doubt—the questioning of certainty in all areas of inquiry.

Though Hecht's book is historical, this introduction is geared more to a change of perspective—a new way to view that history and to place one's self in it—than to the description and interpretation of events.

Document: Jennifer Michael Hecht, from
Doubt: A History: The Great Doubters and Their Legacy of Innovation from Socrates to Jesus to Thomas Jefferson and Emily Dickinson *(2003)*

A Great Schism

Great believers and great doubters seem like opposites, but they are more similar to each other than to the mass of relatively disinterested or acquiescent men and women. This is because they are both awake to the fact that we live between two divergent realities: On one side, there is a world in our heads—and in our lives, so long as we are not contradicted by death and disaster—and that is a world of reason and plans, love, and purpose. On the other side, there is the world beyond our human life—an equally real world in which there is no sign of caring or value, planning or judgment, love, or joy. We live in a meaning-rupture because we are human and the universe is not.

Great doubters, like great believers, have been people occupied with this problem, trying to figure out whether the universe actually has a hidden version of humanness, or whether humanness is the error and people would be better off weaning themselves from their sense of narrative, justice, and love, thereby solving the schism by becoming more like the universe in which they are stuck. Cosmology can be stunning in this context. It is meaningful to get to your wedding on time, to do well in the marathon for which you have been training, to not spill coffee on your favorite shirt. But if we take a few steps back from the planet Earth and from our tiny moment in history, we see a very different picture: the Earth is a ball of water and dirt swarming with creatures, living and dying, passing in and out of existence, shifting around the continents. A few steps further back and we see planets coming into being, stars being born and dying, galaxies swarming in clusters across billions of years. The Earth blips into existence, life appears and swarms, and the Earth blips out of existence. From this perspective, the importance of a favorite shirt, a finish in the next marathon, and even whether you show up at your wedding —all of this begins to seem inconsequential. Concentrating on the macro-picture of reality is enough to make you sit down on a park bench and never get up again. When you face this schism in meaning, the idea that the universe has an agenda can get you off the park bench and back to your life. . . .

The great doubters and believers have been preoccupied with another great schism: the one between what human beings are and what we wish we were, what we do and what we understand. That we love, and that love, among other possibilities, brings forth life, is very strange. We cannot say it is inexplicable, and yet, when it happens (either true love, or conception, or both) we stand amazed.

Source: Hecht, Jennifer Michael. *Doubt: A History: The Great Doubters and Their Legacy of Innovation from Socrates and Jesus to Thomas Jefferson and Emily Dickinson.* New York: HarperCollins, 2003, xii–xiii, xv.

AFTERWARD

In addition to taking her place as one of the foremost expositors of the history of freethought, Hecht is an award-winning poet. She teaches in the graduate writing programs of Columbia University and The New School in New York City.

ASK YOURSELF

1. Hecht's assertion that "great believers and great doubters seem like opposites, but they are more similar to each other" than to the disinterested masses echoes the final passage in Dan Barker's 1984 letter announcing his atheism to religious friends: "I am not your enemy. Our enemy is the one who doesn't care about these subjects—who thinks that you and I are silly to be concerned with life and values . . . It is the non-thinker who bothers me and with whom meaningful interaction is impossible." Do you agree with this idea that the real difference is between the engaged and the disengaged, not between believers and nonbelievers?

2. What does Hecht mean when she says, "We live in a meaning-rupture because we are human and the universe is not"? What is the result of that rupture?

TOPICS AND ACTIVITIES TO CONSIDER

Hecht's book is organized into chapters by historical period. Choose one chapter as the jumping-off point for a research paper or presentation of your own on doubt in ancient Greece, ancient Judea, medieval Islam, or another period of interest to you.

Further Information

Hecht, Jennifer Michael. *Doubt: A History: The Great Doubters and Their Legacy of Innovation from Socrates and Jesus to Thomas Jefferson and Emily Dickinson.* New York: HarperCollins, 2003.

Web Sites

Interview with the author on National Public Radio: http://being.publicradio.org/programs/doubt.

Official Web site of Jennifer Michael Hecht: http://www.jennifermichaelhecht.com.

41. Voices of Unbelief in 21st-Century Africa— Leo Igwe (Nigeria) and Alan Tacca (Uganda)

INTRODUCTION

The political colonization of the continent by European powers in the 19th and 20th centuries was accompanied by "spiritual colonization" as the state religions of the home nations lay claim to the populations of the colonies. By the mid-20th century, Christianity was the dominant religious identity throughout the continent.

Many of the nations of Africa discarded the mainstream religions of Europe as they achieved their independence in the last half of the 20th century. But as Nigerian humanist Leo Igwe writes below, American Pentecostalism has rushed to fill the religious vacuum in many countries.

Alan Tacca has been called "the Sam Harris of Uganda" for his articulate writing from an atheist perspective. He is a regular columnist for the Uganda *Daily Monitor*—a position unusual even for atheists in the West—in which he frequently offers criticism of religious belief and practice such as those below.

KEEP IN MIND AS YOU READ

Both Igwe and Tacca write and live in overwhelmingly religious countries with minuscule nonreligious populations. Nigeria's population (2009) is 50.4 percent Islamic and 48.2 Christian, leaving 1.4 percent for all others combined; as of 2002, Uganda is 85 percent Christian and 12 percent Islamic, with less than 1 percent of the population identifying as nontheistic.

Religiously based violence is frequent in both countries. A guerilla group known as the Lord's Resistance Army has engaged in armed rebellion against the government of Uganda since 1987 with the stated goal of establishing a theocratic state based on the Ten Commandments, while Nigeria has been the location of repeated violent clashes between Muslim and Christian populations.

Document: Leo Igwe, "Africa and Evangelical Christianity"

Born-Again Africa

Pentecostalism: a movement within Christianity that emphasizes the direct, individual experience of God, salvation, and preparation for the Rapture over more traditional doctrinal elements

The BBC article[1] poignantly captures the ongoing religious devastation, exploitation, wanton destruction, and cultural rape of Africa by Evangelical Christianity, also known as **Pentecostalism**. Throughout sub-Saharan Africa, Pentecostalism is spreading like a wild fire leaving death, rot, darkness and destruction in its wake.

Thousands of Pentecostal churches are mushrooming in cities and rural areas across the continent. In fact, in Africa, there are more churches and mosques than schools, industries and research centres. According to the *Focus on Africa* magazine, Evangelical Christianity has more than 125 million devotees in Africa—19 percent of the continent's population—up from 17 million people who described themselves as "born-again Christians" in 1970.

Several factors are responsible for the rapid spread and proliferation of Pentecostal infamy in Africa. First is the growing disenchantment with the mainstream (orthodox) Christian sects—Roman Catholic, Anglican, Methodist, Lutheran, etc. These churches place a lot of emphasis on rules, hierarchy, and doctrines, while the Evangelical groups are said to be more 'liberal' and personal.

The Pentecostal churches emphasize the infallibility of the Bible as a literal historical record that should be accepted hook line and sinker. They insist on salvation for everybody through faith in Jesus and the Holy Spirit. They look forward to the second coming of Jesus and the Rapture. Evangelical groups have a mode of worship that is characterized by spiritual abandonment as expressed in speaking in tongues, dancing, singing and clapping of hands and other unorthodox forms of devotion.

Primitive Business

The second reason why Pentecostal churches are making waves in Africa is their emphasis on miracles and faith healing. Africans are suckers for magic, miracles and paranormal claims. Evangelical churches now capitalize on that. They promise divine healing and instant solutions to all problems—poverty, hunger, failure, diseases, accidents, etc. Pentecostal pastors claim they can make the deaf hear, the blind see, the lame walk and the barren give birth to children. They tell us they can raise the dead, make the poor rich and the unemployed to get jobs. Africans are therefore trooping to Pentecostal churches in their millions in search of their miracles.

Another reason for the apparent boom in Pentecostal Christianity in the black continent is American support and influence. The Pentecostal movement originated in America. It arose in the early part of the 20th century in reaction to modernism. And with the growing decline in religious belief in America and

---

[1]BBC *Focus on Africa*, July–September 2005.

the entire western world, evangelists are looking to Africa for converts, for followers and disciples. . . .

Pentecostalism has therefore become a thriving business in Africa. In fact it has become the shortest route to wealth and affluence for the continent's teeming population of unemployed youths. Local pastors employ all sorts of means, tricks and techniques to extort money from gullible folks (as well as foreign friends). They use this money to build magnificent churches, erect costly apartments, and buy luxurious cars and aircrafts. They live ostentatiously while their church members live and languish in poverty, misery and squalor.

Source: Igwe, Leo. "Africa and Evangelical Christianity." *International Humanist News*, August 3, 2005.

Document: Alan Tacca, "The West Should Abolish God" (2006)

After September 11 and several bombs, two recent events have brought into focus the contrasting environments in which Western man and Middle Eastern man meet each other. In Denmark, most people could not understand why newspaper cartoons making fun of a prophet should cause such uproar. The second event was the indictment of Abdul Rahman for converting from Islam to Christianity 16 years ago.

Under Western pressure, a possible execution seems to have been averted by Afghan authorities only at the price of passing off Rahman as mad. For his part, Rahman said he believed in The Trinity and would rather die than renounce his new faith. St. Peter must be green with envy.

About our times, British Premier Tony Blair has decried the benign inactivity of mankind versus Islamic extremism. Groping for profundity, he has said that the confrontation is not a clash of (different) civilisations but a clash about (one) civilisation. I do not know how much of this is semantics and how much is Western-styled political correctness, but it has not stopped US President George W. Bush from advocating an interventionist stance. Not to be left out, Prince Charles of the United Kingdom has been campaigning for more understanding between different cultures.

In the Middle East, the west is perceived as the Christian world. Similarly, the West regards the Middle East as the central ground of Islam. These two worlds are in effect playing out their cultural rivalry. Oil, ancient Jewish religious claims and the dictates of modern Israel's power game keep the heat up. But in the psyche of these competing cultures is the question of God and his prophets. Most believers in the West think that Jesus is the number two chief in heaven, while most Muslims believe that Prophet Mohammed is the ultimate guiding light.

However, what I have called "most believers" in the West are a shrinking minority. When Mr Bush and Mr Blair harp on their Christian credentials, they do not only irritate Muslim fundamentalists, but also speak a language that a lot of Westerners now find alien.

For to them, the concept of God is clearly a cultural construct, the spread and ceremonial order of Christianity—the result of imperial, poetic and artistic enterprise. Indeed, we may soon get a bishop who says openly that God is a wonderful symbol, but a figment all the same. Unfortunately, instead of allowing this trend to run its course, and closing one parish church after another, the West is importing clerics from former colonies to fill the gaps.

My view is that the West should work towards the abolition of God. Western powers did this in their colonial dominions. They reasoned that the gods and spirits in these societies were products of the primitive cultures they found there. So they actively undermined those gods until they were stripped of all dignity. It is now time to declare their God also primitive.

Poor Rahman, the Afghan Christian convert, does not know that his pet anchor, The Trinity, had nothing to do with the "persons" of the Godhead, but has its origins in the complex ranking system of the dynastic priests in early Christianity. It is of course outrageous that the trial, let alone the execution, of Rahman should even be contemplated, but the West should be showing its own children the misconceptions in Christianity, and that virtue and beauty come from the human realm.

The human mind is creative and strong enough to shape its advance in a godless universe. The decline of faith in the West could be an opportunity for reducing tension rather than a vacuum for Bush and Blair to fill with their sermons.

For a start, Western nations could remove the idea of God from all their national emblems, anthems and State functions. The ubiquitous cross should give room to secular symbols in public cemeteries—not to mention the black books by which one swears oaths in the courts. In short, leave God and His prophets to those societies where many people still need Him. A devaluation of God could in the long term pull the rag from under the feet of many fanatics.

Source: Tacca, Alan. "The West should abolish God," *Uganda Daily Monitor*, April 1, 2006.

Document: Alan Tacca, "Can God Survive an Independent Investigation?" (2010)

During the last six months, hundreds of people have been killed in Nigeria across the Muslim-Christian divide. Over the same period, hundreds more have been killed in different parts of the world by various groups loosely identified as Jihadists.

Also, a mass of testimonies and confessions has been assembled, connecting senior clerics in the Catholic and Pentecostal churches to gross and persistent sexual violations against members of their flock, especially minors, including a horrifying case of the serial abuse of deaf children by a Catholic priest in the USA.

Following these revelations, one of the arguments is that the men who do God's work are human; like us, they are vulnerable.

However, I am not really bothered by the hypocrisy of these gentlemen. I am instead going for **Abraham's God** himself. Where is he? Where are his corrective actions? Why is he silent?

In the days when the Holy books about Abraham's God were being written, the territory of the prophets was not under much scrutiny. The poetic and the divine overlapped; the logical got lost in layers of magical con artistry.

> **Abraham's God:** a reference to the God of Christianity, Judaism, and Islam, the three monotheistic religions. Abraham is credited scripturally as patriarch of all three traditions

Long tradition put a seal of "truth" and slapped a taboo on questioning the validity of it all. In some parts of the world, you can still be executed for questioning the sacred texts related to Abraham's God.

Today, only Abraham's God enjoys this privilege. From the islands of the Pacific, through Africa's shrines, to the temples of India, there is no tradition that confers as much impunity as the traditions associated with Abraham's God.

When Pacific islanders sacrifice a member of their tribe to restore the kindness of the gods, we (the outsiders) quickly recognise the action as a ritual killing rooted in primitive religion.

But we still demand that it be treated as premeditated murder. We do not say that the killing had to do with the failed rains, the poor harvest and the threat to the survival of the islanders.

Furthermore, the self-righteous among us often feel a need to turn the islanders from their belief system to . . . yes . . . to one of the Abrahamic faiths.

However, when Jewish, Christian and Muslim 'extremists' kill each other across their religious lines, we stretch ourselves to find economic and political explanations behind the conflict; explanations that help us to absolve religion.

So you hear the expression, that the violence, or hatred, or revenge, had nothing to do with religion. Yet they are everywhere in the Holy books.

From Abraham to Moses, to Elijah, the slaughter of priests and followers of rival faiths was fairly normal practice. The visions of divine vengeful retribution through several generations to the genocide of non-believers are laid out in the Mosaic books and John's Apocalyptic Revelation. Today's extremists are speaking the language of God undiluted.

Are these visions valid? If they are not, where is God to clarify the true position? If he spoke regularly and tirelessly 4,000 years ago, why is he silent now? Has the expanding universe outstretched his reach? If all today's self-proclaimed prophets can be exposed as frauds, how do we know that the ancient ones were completely authentic?

However limited, man has the power of reason. It is in his nature to investigate and analyse. It is a con artist's device to condemn or strike with guilt those who desire to investigate. Like a Chogm thief, he fears the power of evidence. It is a liar who glorifies those who, like children, believe without supporting evidence. In a primitive fearful society, it works.

Why should it be so in our times? Because they have studied religion more deeply than the average believer, do some senior clerics sin freely because they know there is no God out there looking at them? Can God survive an independent investigation commissioned by an organisation like the UN?

Source: Tacca, Alan. "Can God Survive an Independent Investigation?" *Uganda Daily Monitor*, April 4, 2010.

AFTERWARD

Leo Igwe served as International Humanist and Ethical Union (IHEU) Representative for Western and Southern Africa until October 2011 when he began a three-year doctoral studies program investigating witchcraft accusations in Africa.

Alan Tacca continues in his position as "On the Mark" columnist for the Uganda *Daily Monitor*.

ASK YOURSELF

1. In your view, does knowing that Igwe and Tacca are nonreligious increase or decrease their effectiveness and believability as critics of religious belief and practice?
2. What might a Pentecostal leader say in response to Igwe's accusations?
3. What might a Christian believer say in response to Tacca when he asks, "Where is [God]? Where are his corrective actions? Why is he silent" in the face of violent or unethical behavior by his followers?

TOPICS AND ACTIVITIES TO CONSIDER

Prepare a research paper on the history of religious "importation" in a given African country. Whenever possible, include sources from that country.

Further Information

"The Story of Africa," including the continent's history of religious belief and practice: http://www.bbc.co.uk/worldservice/africa/features/storyofafrica/.

Web Sites

Alan Tacca's columns at the Uganda *Daily Monitor*: http://www.monitor.co.ug. In the top menu, select OpEd > OpEd Columnists > ON THE MARK: Alan Tacca.

Nigerian Humanist Movement: http://www.nigerianhumanists.com.

Uganda Humanist Association: http://uganda.humanists.net.

42. "Religion Poisons Everything"—Christopher Hitchens's *God Is Not Great* (2007)

INTRODUCTION

Journalist and polemicist Christopher Hitchens (1949–2011) is often considered the most unrelenting and direct of the "Four Horsemen" of the New Atheism. He was born and spent the first part of his journalistic career in the United Kingdom before emigrating to the United States in 1981. His published work has included excoriating critiques of public figures including President Bill Clinton, Henry Kissinger, and Mother Teresa.

In *God Is Not Great*, Hitchens contends that religion is "the main source of hatred in the world," and that it "poisons everything" with which it is associated.

KEEP IN MIND AS YOU READ

A practical note for the lay reader: Hitchens has often been noted for his command of language, rhetoric, and critical thinking, as well as a deep and wide embrace of history and literature. As a result, his writing includes many names, terms, and phrases that may be unfamiliar to the lay reader. Because the inclusion of definitions for scores of unfamiliar terms in the margins of the excerpt below is likely to add complexity rather than diminish it, margin notes are provided for only one phrase.

Document: Christopher Hitchens, God Is Not Great (2007)

There are four irreducible objections to religious faith: that it wholly misrepresents the origins of man and the cosmos, that because of this original error it manages to combine the maximum of servility with the maximum of solipsism, that it is both the result and the cause of dangerous sexual repression, and that it is ultimately grounded on wish-thinking.

I do not think it is arrogant of me to claim that I had already discovered these four objections (as well as noticed the more vulgar and obvious fact that religion is used by those in temporal charge to invest themselves with authority) before my boyish voice had broken. I am morally certain that millions of other people

Saul of Tarsus on the Damascene road: reference to the biblical story in which Saul (later Paul) converts to Christianity after seeing a vision of Jesus

came to very similar conclusions in very much the same way, and I have since met such people in hundreds of places, and in dozens of different countries. Many of them never believed, and many of them abandoned faith after a difficult struggle. Some of them had blinding moments of un-conviction that were every bit as instantaneous, though perhaps less epileptic and apocalyptic (and later more rationally and more morally justified) than **Saul of Tarsus on the Damascene road**.

And here is the point, about myself and my co-thinkers. Our belief is not a belief. Our principles are not a faith. We do not rely solely upon science and reason, because these are necessary rather than sufficient factors, but we distrust anything that contradicts science or outrages reason. We may differ on many things, but what we respect is free inquiry, openmindedness, and the pursuit of ideas for their own sake. We do not hold our convictions dogmatically: the disagreement between Professor Stephen Jay Gould and Professor Richard Dawkins, concerning "punctuated evolution" and the unfilled gaps in post-Darwinian theory, is quite wide as well as quite deep, but we shall resolve it by evidence and reasoning and not by mutual excommunication. (My own annoyance at Professor Dawkins and Daniel Dennett, for their cringe-making proposal that atheists should conceitedly nominate themselves to be called "brights," is a part of a continuous argument.) We are not immune to the lure of wonder and mystery and awe: we have music and art and literature, and find that the serious ethical dilemmas are better handled by Shakespeare and Tolstoy and Schiller and Dostoyevsky and George Eliot than in the mythical morality tales of the holy books. Literature, not scripture, sustains the mind and—since there is no other metaphor—also the soul. We do not believe in heaven or hell, yet no statistic will ever find that without these blandishments and threats we commit more crimes of greed or violence than the faithful. (In fact, if a proper statistical inquiry could ever be made, I am sure the evidence would be the other way.) We are reconciled to living only once, except through our children, for whom we are perfectly happy to notice that we must make way, and room. We speculate that it is at least possible that, once people accepted the fact of their short and struggling lives, they might behave better toward each other and not worse. We believe with certainty that an ethical life can be lived without religion. And we know for a fact that the corollary holds true—that religion has caused innumerable people not just to conduct themselves no better than others, but to award themselves permission to behave in ways that would make a brothel-keeper or an ethnic cleanser raise an eyebrow.

Most important of all, perhaps, we infidels do not need any machinery of reinforcement. We are those who Blaise Pascal took into account when he wrote to the one who says, "I am so made that I cannot believe."

There is no need for us to gather every day, or every seven days, or on any high and auspicious day, to proclaim our rectitude or to grovel and wallow in our unworthiness. We atheists do not require any priests, or any hierarchy above them, to police our doctrine. Sacrifices and ceremonies are abhorrent to us, as are relics and the worship of any images or objects (even including objects in the form of one of man's most useful innovations: the bound book). To us no spot on earth is or could be "holier" than another: to the ostentatious absurdity of the pilgrimage, or the plain horror of killing civilians in the name of some sacred wall or cave or shrine or rock, we can counterpose a leisurely or urgent walk from one side of the library or the gallery to another, or to lunch with an agreeable friend, in pursuit of truth or beauty. Some of these excursions to the bookshelf or the lunch or the gallery will obviously, if they are serious, bring us into contact with belief and believers, from the great devotional painters and composers to the works of Augustine, Aquinas, Maimonides, and Newman. These mighty scholars may have written many evil things or many foolish things, and been laughably ignorant of the germ theory of disease or the place of the terrestrial globe in the solar system, let alone the universe, and this is the plain reason why there are no more of them today, and why there will be no more of them tomorrow. Religion spoke its last intelligible or noble or inspiring words a long time ago: either that or it mutated into an admirable but nebulous humanism, as did, say, Dietrich Bonhoeffer, a brave Lutheran pastor hanged by the Nazis for his refusal to collude with them. We shall have no more prophets or sages from the ancient quarter, which is why the devotions of today are only the echoing repetitions of yesterday, sometimes ratcheted up to screaming point so as to ward off the terrible emptiness.

While some religious apology is magnificent in its limited way—one might cite Pascal—and some of it is dreary and absurd—here one cannot avoid naming C. S. Lewis—both styles have something in common, namely the appalling load of strain that they have to bear. How much effort it takes to affirm the incredible! The Aztecs had to tear open a human chest cavity *every day* just to make sure that the sun would rise. Monotheists are supposed to pester their deity more times than that, perhaps, lest he be deaf. How much vanity must be concealed—not too effectively at that—in order to pretend that one is the personal object of a divine plan? How much self-respect must be sacrificed in order that one may squirm continually in an awareness of one's own sin? How many needless assumptions must be made, and how much contortion is required, to receive every new insight of science and manipulate it so as to "fit" with the revealed words of ancient man-made deities? How many saints and miracles and councils and conclaves are required in order first to be able to establish a dogma and then—after infinite pain and loss and absurdity and cruelty—to be forced to rescind one of those dogmas? God did not create man in his own image. Evidently, it was the other way about, which is the painless explanation for the profusion of gods and religions, and the fratricide both between and among faiths, that we see all about us and that has so retarded the development of civilization.

The mildest criticism of religion is also the most radical and the most devastating one. Religion is man-made. Even the men who made it cannot agree on what their prophets or redeemers or gurus actually said or did. Still less can they hope to tell us the "meaning" of later discoveries and developments which were, when they began, either obstructed by their religions or denounced by them. And yet—the believers still claim to know! Not just to know, but to know everything. Not just to know that god exists, and that he created and supervised the whole enterprise, but also to know what "he" demands of us—from our diet to our observances to our sexual morality. In other words, in a vast and complicated discussion where we know more and more about less and less, yet can still hope for some enlightenment as we proceed, one faction—itself composed of mutually warring factions—has the sheer arrogance to tell us that we already have all the essential information we need. Such stupidity, combined with such pride, should be enough on its own to exclude "belief" from the debate. The person who is certain, and who claims divine warrant for his certainty, belongs now to the infancy of our species. It may be a long farewell, but it has begun and, like all farewells, should not be protracted.

The argument with faith is the foundation and origin of all arguments, because it is the beginning—but not the end—of all arguments about philosophy, science, history, and human nature. It is also the beginning—but by no means the end—of all disputes about the good life and the just city. Religious faith is, precisely *because* we are still-evolving creatures, ineradicable. It will never die out, or at least not until we get over our fear of death, and of the dark, and of the unknown, and of each other. For this reason, I would not prohibit it even if I thought I could. Very generous of me, you may say. But will the religious grant me the same indulgence? I ask because there is a real and serious difference between me and my religious friends, and the real and serious friends are sufficiently honest to admit it. I would be quite content to go to their children's bar mitzvahs, to marvel at their Gothic cathedrals, to "respect" their belief that the Koran was dictated, though exclusively in Arabic, to an illiterate merchant, or to interest myself in Wicca and Hindu and Jain consolations. And as it happens, I will continue to do this without insisting on the polite reciprocal condition—which is *that they in turn leave me alone*. But this, religion is ultimately incapable of doing. As I write these words, and as you read them, people of faith are in their different ways planning your and my destruction, and the destruction of all the hard-won human attainments that I have touched upon. *Religion poisons everything*.

Source: From *God Is Not Great* by Christopher Hitchens. Copyright © 2007 by Christopher Hitchens. By permission of Grand Central Publishing. All rights reserved. New York: Twelve Books/Hachette Book Group, 4–8, 10–11.

AFTERWARD

Though Hitchens's position as one of the great articulators of the atheist perspective was already secure, it was *God Is Not Great* that decisively fixed his name in the media and the popular mind (along with Richard Dawkins, Sam Harris, and Daniel Dennett) as one of the "Four Horsemen" of the New Atheism.

"THE NEW ATHEISTS"

Though strong, direct atheist voices had been heard for centuries, a new urgency and higher profile came into being in the first decade of the 21st century with the publication of books strongly critical of religion by atheist authors Richard Dawkins, Daniel Dennett, Sam Harris, and Christopher Hitchens—known informally as "The Four Horsemen of the New Atheism."

These writers and other advocates of a more confrontational form of atheism have cited the terrorist attacks on the United States on September 11, 2001—in which they argue religion played a crucial role in both motivation and execution—as the "wake-up call" compelling them to more directly challenge the privileged cultural position of religious belief and ideology.

Shortly after the release of his memoir *Hitch-22* in 2010, Hitchens was diagnosed with esophageal cancer. While undergoing treatment, he continued writing and speaking when possible, including a series of articles in *Vanity Fair* about his confrontation with the disease and his contemplation of mortality from a secular perspective. He died on December 15, 2011.

ASK YOURSELF

Hitchens's tone has been characterized as "brutal," "uncompromising," and "incendiary." His supporters claim that this approach is well justified both by the seriousness of the problem and by the fact that it is so little recognized. His detractors insist that his clear contempt for all things religious alienates any potential readers beyond those who already agree with him. What do you think? If you do not already share Hitchens's perspective, was any part of the excerpt effective or convincing to you?

TOPICS AND ACTIVITIES TO CONSIDER

Select one of the claims made by Hitchens to support his thesis that "religion poisons everything." Craft a counterpoint in response. Have Hitchens's point and your counterpoint read aloud to your class. Use the exchange as the basis for a class discussion.

Further Information

"The Four Horsemen," a two-hour discussion of the "New Atheism" by Richard Dawkins, Daniel Dennett, Sam Harris, and Christopher Hitchens. Available on YouTube: http://www.youtube.com/watch?v=9DKhc1pcDFM.

Hitchens, Christopher. *God Is Not Great: How Religion Poisons Everything*. New York: Twelve Books/Hachette Book Group, 2007.

Web Site

Unofficial Christopher Hitchens site: http://www.dailyhitchens.com.

43. Setting One's Own Place at the Table—a Secular "Thought for the Day" (2007)

INTRODUCTION

"Thought for the Day" is a brief daily reading on BBC Radio 4 that offers "reflections from a faith perspective on issues and people in the news." In 2002, the British Humanist Association and National Secular Society, the two primary nontheistic organizations in the UK, petitioned the news service to allow contributions from a nontheistic perspective as well. When the request was denied, the Humanist Society of Scotland created "Thought for the World," a Web site with its own "Thought for the Day"—not a radio program, but a daily secular podcast. The secular "Thought for the Day" invited prominent British humanists to offer reflections on daily life and events from a humanist perspective.

Nigel Warburton is a professor of philosophy at the Open University, a distance-learning institution in the United Kingdom. Kate Hudson is a leading antinuclear and antiwar campaigner and general secretary of the Campaign for Nuclear Disarmament in the UK.

KEEP IN MIND AS YOU READ

Though polls differ depending on wording and methodology, there is widespread consensus that the United Kingdom continued its rapid secularization during this period. In a 2006 poll by the *Guardian* newspaper, only 33 percent of UK respondents described themselves as religious. In response to the question "Do you believe in God?" in a YouGov poll two years earlier, just 44 percent of respondents said yes. A series of Gallup polls between 2006 and 2011 put the nonreligious population as high as 76 percent in the UK.

Like many atheists in the early 21st century, especially in countries where secularism occupies a less tenuous social position than in the United States, Warburton and Hudson turn their attention away from critiques of religion and defense of their own belief positions, reflecting instead on how best to live and behave in a world without gods. In their brief addresses, Warburton relates his thoughts and feelings after his close encounter with a suicide, while Hudson explores the motivations and importance of the international peace movement.

Document: Nigel Warburton,
Thought for the Day (2007)

I was on the train to London a few days ago when, as we were passing through a station at high speed, there was a disconcerting jolt . . . we went over something on the rails. The train carried on for a few hundred yards, and then stopped . . . and we waited. There had been an obstruction on the track, we were told, and we had to get clearance. An 'incident' had occurred. Nothing more specific. After an hour and a half of waiting, and learning that the driver had had to be replaced, most of us realised what had happened: someone had thrown themselves under the train.

At this point selfish concerns about being late for appointments evaporated considerably. Most people's thoughts, I suspect, were with the train driver and with the friends and family of whoever had taken this desperate step. But not for too long. We had to get back to our lives despite having been unwilling accomplices in someone else's suicide.

When we eventually pulled into Paddington, we bustled into the underground and got on with whatever we had to do. That's what being alive is like. It's a cliché, but still true, that death is all around us, often painful death, but we are shielded from it most of the time. We rarely encounter death or even give it much thought. But perhaps we should.

As a philosopher I think it is something worth thinking about quite hard. I like the classical idea that philosophy should teach us how to accept death. But it can take a real death to focus the mind.

If, like me, you believe that death is the end of all experience, then there is great consolation in thinking that when it has happened there won't be anything else. That's it. Epicurus was surely right when he said: 'when I am there death is not, and when death is there, I am not.' As he pointed out, we don't worry about the eternity before we existed, why be concerned about the eternity during which we won't exist in the future?

Atheists often describe believers as indulging in wishful thinking when they claim that there is a wonderful afterlife to come. But from my perspective, never-ending life would be a kind of hell that would remove meaning from everything I did, like an interminable piece of music that never reached its final chord. If wishful thinking is believing something that would be pleasanter than the truth, then this is a misnomer. I don't want what the philosopher Bernard Williams called the sheer tedium of immortality—even if it were an option.

What is bad about death is what it does to other people: the ones left behind to grieve, and experience absence. Slow death, and pain in dying are terrible facts of the human condition. But death itself is nothing to fear. Paradoxically, death, like love, makes life worth living.

Document: Kate Hudson,
Thought for the Day (2007)

One day, when I was a child, my father put a poster up at home. It was a quotation from **Che Guevara**, and it said, 'Let me say, at the risk of seeming ridiculous, that the true revolutionary is guided by great feelings of love.' It somehow seemed compelling but I wasn't quite sure what it meant. My father was happy to explain: 'It means he will act to try and change the world and make it better for everybody, because he loves all people, not just a few.' The all-embracing nature of that love seemed remarkable to me, and the active nature of it too. That one sentence has inspired me probably more than anything else.

> **Che Guevara (1928–1967):** a Marxist revolutionary and atheist who played a significant role in the Cuban Revolution

In recent years that sentence has come to my mind again, as I have become more involved with the peace movement. As a CND [Campaign for Nuclear Disarmament] activist, I've had the privilege to meet a great number of people who've worked tirelessly, often over many decades, to try and prevent the suffering and sorrow of war, and to ensure that the great tragedies of Hiroshima and Nagasaki will never be repeated. Indeed, the story of CND is the story of ordinary people's struggles: to shape a world without nuclear weapons and war, based on legality and morality; to make our governments responsive and accountable over our right to stay alive, our right to breathe air free of radioactive pollution, our right to say no to the indiscriminate killing of other peoples. Whether or not the individuals involved would think of it in this way or not, I don't know, but I would say they are motivated by a love for humanity.

And I certainly don't think this is a minority sentiment in society. I was very struck by the selfless motivation of those who protested against war on Iraq on February 15th, 2003. Before the big anti-war demos of recent years, the largest demonstrations since the Second World War had been the CND marches of the early 1980s. People demonstrated in their hundreds of thousands against siting cruise missiles in Britain, because they feared that a nuclear war would be fought in Europe. This was a matter of life and death to us, and we protested for our own survival. But when 2 million people demonstrated on February 15th 2003, they were not marching to protect themselves. They were protesting against a war on a country they will never see, for a people they will never know. For me, that demonstration was a true expression of love for humanity, in action. For me, that love for humanity is the true heart of the peace movement, and it is something that we can all share and demonstrate.

Source: Nigel Warburton and Kate Hudson. *Thought for the Day*. BBC Radio 4, 2007.

AFTERWARD

The secular Thought for the Day recorded 35 readings by humanists including philosophers A. C. Grayling and Stephen Law, Scottish political commentator Iain McWhirter, advice columnist Claire Rayner, political columnist Polly Toynbee, human rights activist Maryam Namazie, and comedian Ariane Sherine. The podcast was active from 2007 to 2009 and remains available online.

ASK YOURSELF

"It's a genuinely difficult question," said BBC controller Mark Damazer of whether to allow a nontheistic presence on Radio 4's Thought for the Day. "Thought for the Day is a unique slot in which speakers from a wide range of religious faiths reflect on an issue of the day from their faith perspective." He continued to note that the rest of the program was devoted to "secular concerns."

Do you agree with Damazer that a secular news program is the equivalent of commentary from a nontheistic perspective? If you were among the BBC decision makers, what would you have done, and how would you have defended your choice to the public?

TOPICS AND ACTIVITIES TO CONSIDER

Write and deliver a three-minute Thought for the Day—"reflections from a faith perspective on issues and people in the news"—from the perspective of your own worldview, whether religious or secular.

Web Sites

Campaign by the British Humanist Association to challenge exclusion of nonreligious voices from the BBC's Thought for the Day program: http://www.humanism.org.uk/campaigns/broadcasting/thought-for-the-day.

Thought for the World (Humanist Society of Scotland): http://www.thoughtfortheworld.org/.

44. Leaving Islam—Ayaan Hirsi Ali's "How (and Why) I Became an Infidel" (2007)

INTRODUCTION

Born and raised in an Islamic Somali family, Ayaan Hirsi Ali (b. 1969) says she lived "by the Book [and] for the Book" (the Qur'an) as a child, and that the prospect of an arranged marriage to a distant cousin caused her to seek asylum in the Netherlands in 1992.

During her studies at Leiden University, Hirsi Ali became increasingly skeptical of Islam. She cites the terrorist attacks of September 11 as a further blow to her religious identification and finally came to consider herself an atheist in May 2002.

Shortly thereafter, she was elected to the Dutch Parliament and became an active critic of Islam, including the oppressive treatment of women in Islamic societies and families.

In 2005, Hirsi Ali was named one of *Time* magazine's 100 Most Influential People. Her 2006 memoir *Infidel* was published in English in 2007.

KEEP IN MIND AS YOU READ

As a woman speaking out against Islam, Hirsi Ali violated not only religious mandates but cultural norms regarding the place of women in Islamic society and clan loyalty. After fleeing Somalia and speaking out against Islam, a *fatwa* was issued calling for her execution. In 2004, after she wrote the screenplay for a short film called *Submission*, which criticizes Muslim treatment of women, the film's director, Theo van Gogh, was brutally murdered on the streets of Amsterdam, and a five-page note addressed to Hirsi Ali was pinned to his chest with a butcher knife.

Document: Ayaan Hirsi Ali, "How (and Why) I Became an Infidel," from The Portable Atheist (2007)

Leaving Allah was a long and painful process for me, and I tried to resist it for as long as I could. All my life I had wanted to be a good daughter of my clan, and that meant above all that I should be a good Muslim. . . . I struggled to conform. I voluntarily robed in a black hijab that covered my body from head to toe.

I tried to pray five times a day and to obey the countless strictures of the Koran and the Hidith. I did so mostly because I was afraid of Hell. . . .

Ultimately, I think, it was books, and boys, that saved me. No matter how hard I tried to submit to Allah's will, I still felt desire—sexual desire, urgent and real, which even hellfire could not suppress. It made me ashamed to feel that way, but when my father told me he was marrying me off to a stranger, I realized that I could not accept being locked forever into the bed of a man who left me cold.

I escaped. I ended up in Holland. With the help of many benevolent Dutch people, I began to gain confidence. . . . I decided to study political science, to discover why Muslim societies—Allah's societies—were poor and violent, while the countries of the despised infidels were wealthy and peaceful. I was still a Muslim in those days. I had no intention of criticizing Allah's will, only to discover what had gone so very wrong.

It was at university that I gradually lost my faith. The ideas and facts that I encountered were thrilling and powerful, but they also clashed horribly with the vision of the world with which I had grown up. . . .

Then the Twin Towers were toppled in the name of Allah and his prophet, and I felt that I must choose sides. Osama bin Laden's justification of the attacks was more consistent with the content of the Koran and the Sunna than the chorus of Muslim officials and Western wishful thinkers who denied every link between the bloodshed and Islam. . . .

Interviewers often asked if I had considered adopting the message of Jesus Christ. The idea seemed to be that I should shop for a better, more humane religion than Islam, rather than taking refuge in unbelief. . . .

The only position that leaves me with no cognitive dissonance is atheism. It is not a creed. Death is certain, replacing both the siren-song of Paradise and the dread of Hell. Life on this earth, with all its mystery and beauty and pain, is then to be lived far more intensely; we stumble and get up, we are sad, confident, insecure, feel loneliness and joy and love. There is nothing more; but I want nothing more.

Source: Hirsi Ali, Ayaan. "How (and Why) I Became an Infidel." In *The Portable Atheist: Essential Readings for the Nonbeliever.* Edited by Christopher Hitchens. Cambridge, MA: Da Capo Press, 2007, 477–480.

AFTERWARD

Hirsi Ali relocated to the United States in 2006 and founded the AHA Foundation in 2007, a nonprofit devoted to the defense of Muslim women's rights. Currently a Resident Fellow with the American Enterprise Institute, she continues to maintain a security detail as the fatwa against her has not been lifted.

ASK YOURSELF

1. Which of Hirsi Ali's reasons for doubting Islam echo the doubts described by Christian doubters elsewhere in this book? Which seem more specific to Islam?

2. Reread the chapter on Ibn al-Rawāndī. How do Hirsi Ali's criticisms of Islam mirror those of Ibn al-Rawāndī in the ninth century?

TOPICS AND ACTIVITIES TO CONSIDER

View Theo van Gogh's film *Submission* on YouTube and discuss: http://www.youtube.com/watch?v=G6bFR4_Ppk8.

Further Information

Hirsi Ali, Ayaan. *Infidel*. New York: Free Press, 2007.
Hirsi Ali, Ayaan. *Nomad*. New York: Free Press, 2010.

Web Site

The AHA Foundation: http://www.theahafoundation.org.

45. *Letter to a Christian Nation—* Sam Harris (2006)

INTRODUCTION

The first of the "Four Horsemen" to publish a book-length critique of religion in the period following the September 11th terrorist attacks was Sam Harris (b. 1967). *The End of Faith: Religion, Terror, and the Future of Reason* (2004) argues that humanity can no longer afford to take a neutral, coexistent attitude toward fundamentalist religious ideologies, which he argues constitute a threat to civilization itself.

Harris offers a separate but equally impassioned critique of religious moderates, claiming that their general defense of faith provides cover for abuses perpetrated in the name of fundamentalism by protecting it from forceful critique. The book remained on the *New York Times* best-seller list for eight months.

Two years after the release of *The End of Faith*, Harris published *Letter to a Christian Nation* in response to criticism, largely from U.S. Christians, of the previous book.

KEEP IN MIND AS YOU READ

After *The End of Faith*, Harris's critics claimed that he does not differentiate sufficiently between religious moderates and fundamentalists and that the beliefs he criticizes are no longer widely held. Harris uses *Letter to a Christian Nation* primarily to answer such charges, using statistics, argumentation, and the published statements of major denominational leaders to make his case, often with wit and clarity lacking from many similarly focused books. "The president of the United States [George W. Bush] has claimed, on more than one occasion, to be in dialogue with God," he wrote. "If he said that he was talking to God through his hairdryer, this would precipitate a national emergency. I fail to see how the addition of a hairdryer makes the claim more ridiculous or offensive."

Document: Sam Harris, excerpt from Letter to a Christian Nation (2006)

You believe that the Bible is the word of God, that Jesus is the Son of God, and that only those who place their faith in Jesus will find salvation after death. As a

Christian, you believe these propositions not because they make you feel good, but because you think they are true. Before I point out some of the problems with these beliefs, I would like to acknowledge that there are many points on which you and I agree. We agree, for instance, that if one of us is right, the other is wrong. The Bible is either the word of God, or it isn't. Either Jesus offers humanity the one, true path to salvation (John 14:6), or he does not. We agree that to be a true Christian is to believe that all other faiths are mistaken, and profoundly so. If Christianity is correct, and I persist in my unbelief, I should expect to suffer the torments of hell. Worse still, I have persuaded others, and many close to me, to reject the very idea of God. They too will languish in "eternal fire" (Matthew 25:41). If the basic doctrine of Christianity is correct, I have misused my life in the worst conceivable way. I admit this without a single caveat. The fact that my continuous and public rejection of Christianity does not worry me in the least should suggest to you just how inadequate I think your reasons for being a Christian are. . . .

CONSIDER: every devout Muslim has the same reasons for being a Muslim that you have for being a Christian. And yet you do not find their reasons compelling. . . . Why don't you lose any sleep over whether to convert to Islam? Can you prove that Allah is not the one, true God? Can you prove that the archangel Gabriel did not visit Muhammad in his cave? Of course not. But you need not prove any of these things to reject the beliefs of Muslims as absurd. The burden is upon them to prove that their beliefs about God and Muhammad are valid. They have not done this. They cannot do this. Muslims are simply not making claims about reality that can be corroborated. This is perfectly apparent to anyone who has not anesthetized himself with the dogma of Islam.

The truth is, you know exactly what it is like to be an atheist with respect to the beliefs of Muslims. . . . Understand that the way you view Islam is precisely the way devout Muslims view Christianity. And it is the way I view all religions.

Source: Harris, Sam. *Letter to a Christian Nation*. New York: Knopf, 2006, 3–7.

UNBELIEF BY THE NUMBERS

Because of ongoing cultural stigma, self-censorship, and the variety of ways in which the question is asked, the presence and prevalence of unbelief is among the most difficult population features on which to obtain reliable statistical information.

A strong trend toward a higher presence of secularism has been evident in the developed world since the Second World War. The American Religious Identification Survey put nonreligious self-identification in the United States at 8 percent in 1990 and 15 percent in 2008. The number is between 39 and 65 percent in the UK, depending on the survey and question, while Sweden, Denmark, and Norway are as high as 80 to 85 percent nonreligious.

By contrast, Uganda, Tanzania, Iran, and Nigeria have nonreligious self-identities below 2 percent, while surveys in Bangladesh show fewer than one-tenth of 1 percent as nonreligious.

A generational trend is also evident in the United States. A 2010 Pew study found that 25 percent of respondents age 18–29 identified as nonreligious (specifically "atheist," "agnostic," or "nothing in particular") —more than any previous U.S. generation at the same ages.

AFTERWARD

In 2007, Harris and his wife, Annaka, founded Project Reason, a 501(c)(3) organization promoting science and secular values. In 2009 he completed a PhD in neuroscience at UCLA and the following year published *The Moral Landscape: How Science Can Determine Human Values*, asserting that morality and critical thinking need not, in fact should not, be separated.

ASK YOURSELF

1. Harris begins by asserting to his hypothetical Christian reader that "we agree . . . that if one of us is right, the other is wrong." Do you agree with this?

2. "I contend that we are all atheists," said Stephen F. Roberts. "I just believe in one fewer god than you. When you understand why you dismiss all the other possible gods, you will understand why I dismiss yours." Harris uses a form of this argument, claiming that a Christian can gain insight into atheism by considering his or her own disbelief in the tenets of Islam. Do you consider this an effective exercise for religious believers?

TOPICS AND ACTIVITIES TO CONSIDER

- Harris speaks of a "conversational taboo" around religious belief. Break this taboo by engaging in conversation about beliefs with others whose beliefs differ from yours.

- Harris also advocates going beyond conversation to challenge each other's beliefs. Are you comfortable doing this? Does your relationship with the codiscussant determine your comfort level? Are you more or less willing to engage critically with someone you know and like?

Further information

Harris, Sam. *The End of Faith*. New York: Norton, 2004.
Harris, Sam. *Letter to a Christian Nation*. New York: Knopf, 2006.

Web Sites

Official Web site: http://www.samharris.org.
Project Reason: http://www.project-reason.org.

46. Turning Attention to Race and Gender—Sikivu Hutchinson's "This Far by Faith?" (2009)

INTRODUCTION

After the success of several best-selling atheist books, high-profile advocates, and a rising percentage of the population, many atheist writers have increasingly turned their attention to broader social issues, including gender and race. Dr. Sikivu Hutchinson is one of an increasing number of women and people of color adding their voices to what has been a predominantly white and male atheist movement. In the process, Hutchinson reignites the critiques of patriarchal religion sounded by Wright, Rose, and Goldman, adding and combining the complex dimension of race to gender. "While black male non-believers are given more leeway to be heretics or just MIA from church," she said in a 2011 interview, "black women who openly profess non-theist views are deemed especially traitorous, having 'abandoned' their primary role as purveyors of cultural and religious tradition."

KEEP IN MIND AS YOU READ

Christian identity, belief, and practice have been prominent touchstones for the African American community from the earliest days of the slave trade to the present. Prominent African Americans as early as Frederick Douglass criticized the role of Christianity in perpetuating first slavery, then racial inequality in the United States. Douglass offered his critique from within Christianity, while later black activists including Malcolm X adopted Islam, citing its greater affinity with African identity and history. Hutchinson is one of a small but growing number of African Americans adopting atheism as a worldview and offering an unblinking critique of what they see as the ongoing role of religion in black oppression and marginalization.

Document: Sikivu Hutchinson, "This Far by Faith? Race Traitors, Gender Apostates & the Atheism Question" (2011)

Martin Luther King Jr. once dubbed Sunday at 11:00 a.m. the most segregated hour in America, a microcosm of the titanic divide that specifically separates black and white America. Yet racial divisions are not the only prominent schism in the Sunday churchgoing ritual that encompasses much of the social and cultural life experience of one of the most God-obsessed nations on the planet. Despite all the "liberal" revisions to biblical language and claims to progressivism among some Christian denominations, mainstream Protestantism is still, of course, a Jim Crow throwback and a man's man's world. As Mark Galli, editor of the Evangelical magazine *Christianity Today* once remarked, "It's a cliché now to call institutional religion 'oppressive, patriarchal, out of date and out of touch.' So what else is new? I feel sorry for those people who don't think there's anything greater than themselves . . . It leaves out the communal dimension of faith."

From the Deep South to South Los Angeles, this "communal dimension of faith" is one of the most compelling and problematic aspects of women's investment in organized religion. When it comes to accounting for the disproportionate male to female ratio for self-identified atheists, there has been much wrongheaded conjecture about the supposed emotionalism of women versus the rationality of men. Bloggers muse about women's intuitive sensitivity to the warm and fuzzy "verities" of religious dogma.

Women are portrayed as naturally timorous and thus less inclined to question or suspend belief about the inconsistencies of organized religion. For the most part, there has been no serious evaluation of the perceived gendered social benefits of religious observance versus the social costs of espousing such a gender non-conforming "individualist" ideology as atheism, particularly with respect to American born women of color. Indeed, in many communities of color the very structure of organized religion offers a foundation for the articulation of female gendered identity that has been a source of agency and an antidote to marginalization. On the other hand, patriarchy entitles men to reject organized religion with few implications for their gender-defined roles as family breadwinners or purveyors of cultural values to children. Men simply have greater cultural license to come out as atheists or agnostics because of the gender hierarchies that ascribe rationalism, individualism, intellectualism and secular or scientific inquiry to masculinity. So women in traditionally religious communities who come out in real time (as opposed to online) risk greater ostracism because women don't have the cultural and authorial privilege to publicly express their opposition to organized religion as men.

African American women provide an illustrative case in point. Imagery such as filmmaker Tyler Perry's bible-thumping, malapropism-spewing Madea, stereotypically heavyset black women in brightly-colored choir robes belting out gospel music and sweat-drenched revelers cataleptic from getting the holy ghost are some of the most common mainstream representations of black femininity. These caricatures are buttressed by the unwavering financial and social support of the black church, which is predominantly Christian-based, by African American communities of all income brackets. According to blackdemographics.com, African Americans remain the most solidly religious racial group in the United States, outstripping whites in their churchgoing fervor by a nearly 20 percent margin. Sunday in and Sunday out, between the hours of 8 a.m. to 4 p.m., a familiar scene emerges in both working and middle class black communities across the nation. Black women shuttle dutifully to church in their sartorial best, backbone of a dubious institution that still accords them only second-class citizen standing. The gender dynamics in the breakdown of regular churchgoers reflect an utterly predictable disparity in power and access. While more black women have been allowed to assume leadership roles in black churches in recent years, they remain a minority among deacons, pastors and senior pastors of most black congregations. So although black women are far more likely than men to attend church more than once a week, the officialdom of black religious establishments, and certainly the political face of the black church, is steadfastly male.

What is the relationship between these gendered religious hierarchies and cultural politics in African American communities? Christian religiosity pervades the slang of misogynist black hip hop artists and sports figures and worms its way into their Jesus touting boilerplate award acceptance speeches. Christian religiosity engorges multi-million dollar faith-based empires in poor urban black communities where "prime" real estate is often a triad of storefront churches, liquor stores and checking cashing places. Sex scandals and financial improprieties fester amongst the leadership of black churches yet sexist and homophobic rhetoric remain a mainstay. Blind faith speaks through bulging collection plates and special tithes to the latest charity, pastor's pet cause or capital campaign, "blessing" donors with another chit to heaven and certitude that black apostates are also race traitors. If mainstream African American notions of black identity are defined by a certain degree of essentialism, then religious identity is certainly a key element. Alternative belief systems are viewed with suspicion because they are deemed to be inconsistent with authentic black identity.

Given this context it is unsurprising that comedian and self-appointed dating guru Steve Harvey's diatribe against atheism this past spring went largely unchallenged by African American cultural critics. Doling out sage dating advice, Harvey warned black women to avoid atheist gentlemen callers at all costs because they simply have no morals. Harvey's swaggeringly ignorant declaration was not only a repudiation of atheism but a thinly veiled warning to black women that they should tow the religious line with their personal choices. Failure to do so would have serious consequences for racial solidarity and their ability to be good (black) women, compromising their heterosexual marketability and legitimacy as marriage partners and mothers. It is this brand of essentialism that makes stereotypes associating black identity politics with an anti-secularist stance and religious superstition so irritatingly persistent.

While the greater religiosity of women of color in comparison to men is no mystery, why is it that this peculiarly gendered regime has gone relatively unquestioned? The gravity of the social and economic issues confronting black communities—and the tremendous cultural capital and social authority that organized religion exercises within them—compels further analysis. Just as women are socialized to identify with and internalize misogynistic and sexist paradigms, religious paradigms that emphasize domestication and obeisance to men are integral to mainstream American notions of femininity. For many observant women questioning or rejecting religion outright would be just as counterintuitive as rejecting their connection to their lived experiences. In this regard religious observance is as much a performance and reproduction of gender identity as it is an exercise of personal "morality." Many of the rituals of black churchgoing forge this sense of gendered identity as community. Whether it be maintaining ties with peers within the context of a church meeting, ensuring impressionable children have some "moral" mooring by sending them to Sunday School or even invoking sage bits of scripture to chasten malcontents, enlighten casual acquaintances or infuse one's quotidian doings with purpose—all carefully delineate enactments of kin and community that have been compulsorily drilled into women as the proper fulfillment of a gendered social contract. And if this gendered social contract were violated en masse, patriarchy and heterosexism would have less of a firmament.

What, then, are the lessons for promoting secular humanist, agnostic or atheist belief systems? First, that there must be more clearly defined alternatives to supernaturalism which speak to the cultural context of diverse populations of women and people of color. Second, that moral secular values should provide the basis for robust critique of the serious cultural and socioeconomic problems that have been allowed to thrive in communities of color under the regime of organized religion. Finally, in an intellectual universe where rock star white men with publishing contracts are the most prominent atheists and atheism is perceived in some quarters as a "white" thing, it is also critical that acceptance and embrace of non-supernatural belief systems be modeled in communities of color "on the ground." Only then can secularism defang the seductions of the communal dimension of faith that defines our most segregated hour.

Source: Hutchinson, Sikivu. *Moral Combat: Black Atheists, Gender Politics, and the Values Wars.* Los Angeles: Infidel Books, 2011. Reprinted with permission.

AFTERWARD

Sikivu Hutchinson has become one of the most influential and highly regarded voices in contemporary atheism, African American social commentary, and the intersection of the two.

ASK YOURSELF

If critiques by feminist and black atheist commentators are correct, the Christian church has been one of the primary causes and perpetuators of oppression and denial of equal rights for women and African Americans. Given this, why do you think women and African Americans are among the most reliably loyal populations in Christian belief and practice?

TOPICS AND ACTIVITIES TO CONSIDER

Visit the Sunday morning services of a few churches in different denominations. Does Martin Luther King Jr.'s description of "the most segregated hour in America" still hold true? If so, what do you think accounts for this phenomenon? Does any denomination appear to be more racially integrated than the others?

Further Information

Allen, Norm R., Jr., ed. *The Black Humanist Experience.* Amherst, NY: Prometheus Books, 2002.

Hutchinson, Sikivu. *Moral Combat: Black Atheists, Gender Politics, and the Values Wars*. Los Angeles: Infidel Books, 2011.

Pinn, Anthony, ed. *By These Hands: A Documentary History of African American Humanism*. New York: New York University Press, 2011.

Pinn, Anthony. *The End of God-Talk: An African American Humanist Theology*. New York: Oxford University Press, 2012.

Web Sites

Black Agenda Report: http://www.blackagendareport.com/.

BlackFemLens: http://blackfemlens.blogspot.com/.

47. "The Defining Statement of World Humanism"—The Amsterdam Declarations of 1952 and 2002

INTRODUCTION

As atheist and humanist self-identification grew rapidly in developed countries following the Second World War, the need emerged for an international umbrella organization to connect and represent the many local and national freethought organizations that had emerged worldwide. The London-based International Humanist and Ethical Union (IHEU) was formed for this purpose at the first World Humanist Congress in Amsterdam in 1952.

Representatives to the World Humanist Congress ratified a statement of the fundamental principles of modern humanism. Called "The Amsterdam Declaration," this statement quickly became the defining document of modern humanism.

In 2002, as representatives convened again in Amsterdam for the 50th-anniversary World Humanist Congress, an updated declaration called "The Amsterdam Declaration 2002" was unanimously approved.

KEEP IN MIND AS YOU READ

Each of the two Amsterdam Declarations is a product of its time. The first reflects the concerns of a world recently emerged from the fight against fascism and newly immersed in the shadow of potential nuclear destruction. The second reflects a world in which both threats and opportunities have changed while the basic tenets of humanism remain essentially intact.

Document: Amsterdam Declaration 1952

This congress is a response to the wide spread demand for an alternative to the religions which claim to be based on revelation on the one hand, and totalitarian systems on the other. The alternative offered as a third way out of the present crisis of civilisation is humanism, which is not a new sect, but the outcome of a long tradition that has inspired many of the world's thinkers and creative artists and given rise to science itself.

Ethical humanism unites all those who cannot any longer believe the various creeds and are willing to base their conviction on respect for man as a spiritual and moral being. The fundamentals of modern, ethical humanism are as follows:

1. **It is democratic.** It aims at the fullest possible development of every human being. It holds that this is a matter of right. The democratic principle can be applied to all human relationships and is not restricted to methods of government.

2. **It seeks to use science creatively, not destructively.** It advocates a world-wide application of scientific method to problems of human welfare. Humanists believe that the tremendous problems with which mankind is faced in this age of transition can be solved. Science gives the means, but science itself does not propose the ends.

3. **Humanism is ethical.** It affirms the dignity of man and the right of the individual to the greatest possible freedom of development compatible with the right of others. There is a danger that in seeking to utilise scientific knowledge in a complex society, individual freedom may be threatened by the very impersonal machine that has been created to save it. Ethical humanism, therefore, rejects totalitarian attempts to perfect the machine in order to obtain immediate gains at the cost of human values.

4. **It insists that personal liberty is an end that must be combined with social responsibility in order that it shall not be sacrificed to the improvement of material conditions.** Without intellectual liberty, fundamental research, on which progress must in the long run depend, would not be possible. Humanism ventures to build a world on the free person responsible to society. On behalf of individual freedom humanism is un-dogmatic, imposing no creed upon its adherents. It is thus committed to education free from indoctrination.

5. **It is a way of life, aiming at the maximum possible fulfillment, through the cultivation of ethical and creative living.** It can be a way of life for everyone everywhere if the individual is capable of the responses required by the changing social order. The primary task of humanism today it to make men aware in the simplest terms of what it can mean to them and what it commits them to. By utilising in this context and for purposes of peace the new power which science has given us, humanists have confidence that the present crisis can be surmounted. Liberated from fear, the energies of man will be available for a self-realisation to which it is impossible to foresee the limit.

Ethical humanism is thus a faith that answers the challenge of our times. We call upon all men who share this conviction to associate themselves with us in this cause.

IHEU Congress 1952

Document: Amsterdam Declaration 2002

Humanism is the outcome of a long tradition of free thought that has inspired many of the world's great thinkers and creative artists and gave rise to science itself.

The fundamentals of modern Humanism are as follows:

1. **Humanism is ethical.** It affirms the worth, dignity and autonomy of the individual and the right of every human being to the greatest possible freedom compatible with the rights of others. Humanists have a duty of care to all of humanity including future generations. Humanists believe that morality is an intrinsic part of human nature based on understanding and a concern for others, needing no external sanction.

2. **Humanism is rational.** It seeks to use science creatively, not destructively. Humanists believe that the solutions to the world's problems lie in human thought and action rather than divine intervention. Humanism advocates the application of the methods of science and free inquiry to the problems of human welfare. But Humanists also believe that the application of science and technology must be tempered by human values. Science gives us the means but human values must propose the ends.

3. **Humanism supports democracy and human rights.** Humanism aims at the fullest possible development of every human being. It holds that democracy and human development are matters of right. The principles of democracy and human rights can be applied to many human relationships and are not restricted to methods of government.

4. **Humanism insists that personal liberty must be combined with social responsibility.** Humanism ventures to build a world on the idea of the free person responsible to society, and recognises our dependence on and responsibility for the natural world. Humanism is undogmatic, imposing no creed upon its adherents. It is thus committed to education free from indoctrination.

5. **Humanism is a response to the widespread demand for an alternative to dogmatic religion.** The world's major religions claim to be based on revelations fixed for all time, and many seek to impose their world-views on all of humanity. Humanism recognises that reliable knowledge of the world and ourselves arises through a continuing process of observation, evaluation and revision.

6. **Humanism values artistic creativity and imagination** and recognises the transforming power of art. Humanism affirms the importance of literature, music, and the visual and performing arts for personal development and fulfilment.

7. **Humanism is a lifestance aiming at the maximum possible fulfilment through the cultivation of ethical and creative living** and offers an ethical and rational means of addressing the challenges of our times. Humanism can be a way of life for everyone everywhere.

THE EMERGENCE OF NONCREEDAL RELIGION

The presence of increasingly progressive religious expressions in the 20th century reached perhaps its ultimate expression in 1961 when two of the most liberal and nondogmatic denominations, the American Unitarian Association and the Universalist Church of America, merged to create Unitarian Universalism (or "UUism"). UUism is a creedless denomination, meaning membership is not defined by the acceptance of a shared corpus of beliefs. Instead, the denomination is built on shared principles and purposes, including "the inherent worth and dignity of every person" and "justice, equity and compassion in human relations."

Another example of a noncreedal religion is Ethical Culture, an association of local "Ethical Societies" who build community and find meaning and fulfillment by living in accordance with ethical principles. Both UUism and Ethical Culture embrace the term "religious" because they serve similar human purposes with religion—the search for meaning, building community, mutual support, the celebration of rites of passage—but do not require a declaration of shared metaphysical beliefs.

Our primary task is to make human beings aware in the simplest terms of what Humanism can mean to them and what it commits them to. By utilising free inquiry, the power of science and creative imagination for the furtherance of peace and in the service of compassion, we have confidence that we have the means to solve the problems that confront us all. We call upon all who share this conviction to associate themselves with us in this endeavour.

IHEU Congress 2002

Source: International Humanist and Ethical Union (IHEU) Web site: http://www.iheu.org.

AFTERWARD

Since its formation, IHEU has become the official representative of humanism in international political and social organizations. As of 2011 it is an international nongovernmental organization with Special Consultative Status with the United Nations and has General Consultative Status with the Council of Europe as well as Observer Status with the African Commission on Human and People's Rights.

ASK YOURSELF

1. Like Corliss Lamont and some other authors in this book, the authors of the 2002 Declaration chose to capitalize the words "Humanist" and "Humanism," while the authors of the 1952 original chose (like Kurt Vonnegut and others) to use the lower case. How does this choice change the effect of the word and concept on you as a reader?

2. One change in language between the two documents reflects an important shift in societal awareness between the 1950s and the early 21st century. Can you identify that change?

3. What are the advantages and disadvantages of international declarations of this kind?

4. Which of the principles in the Declarations do you agree with, and to what degree?

TOPICS AND ACTIVITIES TO CONSIDER

Create a declaration of principles for a group to which you belong. What process will you follow? How easy is it to gain consensus?

Further Information

Herrick, Jim. *Humanism: An Introduction.* Amherst, NY: Prometheus Books, 2005.

Web Site

International Humanist and Ethical Union: http://www.iheu.org.

Selected Bibliography

GENERAL INTRODUCTIONS TO ATHEISM/AGNOSTICISM

Baggini, Julian. *Atheism: A Very Short Introduction*. New York: Oxford University Press, 2003.

Krueger, Douglas E. *What Is Atheism? A Short Introduction*. Amherst, NY: Prometheus Books, 1998.

Le Poidevin, Robin. *Arguing for Atheism: An Introduction to the Philosophy of Religion*. London: Routledge, 1996.

REFERENCE/ANTHOLOGIES

Flynn, Tom, ed. *The New Encyclopedia of Unbelief*. Amherst, NY: Prometheus Books, 2007.

Hitchens, Christopher. *The Portable Atheist*. New York: Da Capo, 2007.

Ingersoll, Robert. *What's God Got to Do with It? Robert Ingersoll on Free Thought, Honest Talk and the Separation of Church and State*. Edited by Tim Page. Hanover, NH: Steerforth Press, 2005.

Joshi, S. T. *Atheism: A Reader*. Amherst, NY: Prometheus Books, 2000.

Knight, Margaret, ed. *The Humanist Anthology: From Confucius to Attenborough*. Revised by James Herrick. London: Barrie & Rockliff, 1995.

Web Sites

Historical documents at the Secular Web: http://www.infidels.org/library/historical/.

Historical documents at Positive Atheism: http://positiveatheism.org/tochist.htm.

Modern documents at the Secular Web: http://www.infidels.org/library/modern/.

HISTORICAL OVERVIEWS

Berman, David. *A History of Atheism in Britain: From Hobbes to Russell*. London: Croom Helm, 1988.

Hecht, Jennifer Michael. *Doubt: A History: The Great Doubters and Their Legacy of Innovation from Socrates and Jesus to Thomas Jefferson and Emily Dickinson*. New York: HarperCollins, 2003.

Hunter, Michael, and David Wootton, eds. *Atheism from the Reformation to the Enlightenment*. Oxford: Clarendon Press, 1992.

Jacoby, Susan. *Freethinkers: A History of American Secularism*. New York: Henry Holt, 2004.

Robertson, J. M. *A History of Freethought in the Nineteenth Century*. London: Dawsons, 1969.

Thrower, James. *A Short History of Western Atheism*. London: Pemberton Books, 1971.

ATHEISM/AGNOSTICISM BY COUNTRY OR PERIOD

In China

Kasoff, Ira. *The Thoughts of Chang Tsai (1020–1077)*. Cambridge: Cambridge University Press, 1984.

Xun Zi. *Xunzi: Basic Writings*. Edited by Burton Watson. New York: Columbia University Press, 2003.

In India

Embree, Ainslie, ed. *Sources of Indian Tradition*. Vol. 1, *From the Beginning to 1800*. 2nd ed. New York: Columbia University Press, 1988.

Hiorth, Finngeir. *Atheism in India*. Mumbai: Indian Secular Society, 1998.

Luce, Edward. *In Spite of the Gods: The Rise of Modern India*. New York: Anchor Books, 2007.

Nehru, Jawaharlal. *The Discovery of India*. London: Oxford University Press, 1946.

Rao, Goparaju Ramachandra. *An Atheist with Gandhi*. Ahmedabad, India: Navijan Trust, 1951.

Web Sites

The Atheist Centre: http://www.atheistcentre.in/.

BBC Religions—a Guide to Jainism: http://www.bbc.co.uk/religion/religions/jainism.

In Ancient Greece and Rome

Bett, Richard, ed. *The Cambridge Companion to Ancient Scepticism (Cambridge Companions to Philosophy)*. London: Cambridge University Press, 2010.

In Islamic Culture

Stroumsa, Sarah. *Freethinkers of Medieval Islam: Ibn al-Rawāndī, Abū Bakr al-Rāzī and Their Impact on Islamic Thought*. Boston: Brill, 1999.

In Medieval Europe

Arnold, John H. *Belief and Unbelief in Medieval Europe*. London: Hodder Education, 2005.

In the Enlightenment

Blom, Philipp. *A Wicked Company: The Forgotten Radicalism of the European Enlightenment*. New York: Basic Books, 2005.

Edelstein, Dan. *The Enlightenment: A Genealogy*. Chicago: University of Chicago Press, 2010.

Meslier, Jean. *Testament: Memoir of the Thoughts and Sentiments of Jean Meslier*. Edited and translated by Michael Shreve. Amherst, NY: Prometheus Books, 2009.

In 19th-Century England

Blinderman, Charles S. "Huxley and Kingsley." *Victorian Newsletter* 20 (1961): 25–28.

Darwin, Charles. *The Autobiography of Charles Darwin, with Original Omissions Restored*. Edited by Nora Barlow. New York: Harcourt, Brace, 1958.

Irvine, William. *Apes, Angels, and Victorians: A Joint Biography of Darwin and Huxley*. London: Weidenfeld and Nicolson, 1955.

Shelley, Percy Bysshe. *The Necessity of Atheism and Other Essays*. Albany, NY: Prometheus Books, 1993.

Wilson, A. N. *God's Funeral: The Decline of Faith in Western Civilization*. New York: Norton, 1999.

In 20th-Century England

Web Site

Margaret Knight page of the British Humanist Association: http://www.humanism.org.uk/humanism/humanist-tradition/20century/margaret-knight.

In the United States (19th–Early 20th Century)

Goldman, Emma. *Living My Life*. New York: Knopf, 1931.

Greeley, Roger, ed. *The Best of Robert Ingersoll, Immortal Infidel: Selections from His Writings and Speeches*. Amherst, NY: Prometheus Books, 1993.

Page, Tim. *What's God Got to Do with It?: Robert Ingersoll on Free Thought, Honest Talk and the Separation of Church and State*. Hanover, NH: Steerforth Press, 2005.

Twain, Mark. *Autobiography of Mark Twain: The Complete and Authoritative Edition*. Vol. 1. Berkeley: University of California Press, 2010.

Twain, Mark. *Letters from the Earth: Uncensored Writings*. Edited by Bernard DeVoto. New York: HarperCollins, 1962.

Twain, Mark. *Mark Twain's Fables of Man*. Edited by John S. Tuckey, Kenneth Sanderson, Bernard Stein, and Frederick Anderson. Berkeley: University of California Press, 1972.

Web Sites

Center for (John) Dewey Studies at Southern Illinois University–Carbondale: http://www.siuc.edu/~deweyctr/.

Emma Goldman at Project Gutenberg: http://www.gutenberg.org/browse/authors/g#a840.

Twain on religion: http://www.positiveatheism.org/hist/quotes/twain.htm.

OTHER SELECTED BIOGRAPHICAL/AUTOBIOGRAPHICAL SOURCES

Barker, Dan. *Godless: How an Evangelical Preacher Became One of America's Leading Atheists*. Berkeley, CA: Ulysses Press, 2008.

Braden, Bruce. *"Ye Will Say I Am No Christian": The Thomas Jefferson/John Adams Correspondence on Religion, Morals, and Values*. Amherst, NY: Prometheus Books, 2005.

Jammer, Max. *Einstein and Religion*. Princeton, NJ: Princeton University Press, 2002.

Web Sites

The Carl Sagan Portal: http://www.carlsagan.com.
The Primo Levi Center: http://www.primolevicenter.org/Home.html.

ATHEISM/AGNOSTICISM AMONG EARLY ADVOCATES OF WOMEN'S RIGHTS

Doress-Walters, Paula. *Mistress of Herself: Speeches and Letters of Ernestine Rose, Early Women's Rights Leader.* New York: Feminist Press at CUNY, 2008.
Gaylor, Annie Laurie, ed. *Women Without Superstition: No Gods, No Masters.* Madison, WI: Freedom From Religion Foundation, 1997.
Morris, Celia. *Fanny Wright: Rebel in America.* Cambridge, MA: Harvard University Press, 1984.

AFRICAN AMERICAN ATHEISM AND HUMANISM

Allen, Norm R., Jr., ed. *African American Humanism.* Albany, NY: Prometheus Books, 1991.
Allen, Norm R., Jr., ed. *The Black Humanist Experience.* Albany, NY: Prometheus Books, 2002.
Hutchinson, Sikivu. *Moral Combat: Black Atheists, Gender Politics, and the Values Wars.* Los Angeles: Infidel Books, 2011.
Pinn, Anthony, ed. *By These Hands: A Documentary History of African American Humanism.* New York: New York University Press, 2001.

HUMANISTIC JUDAISM

Web Site

Society for Humanistic Judaism: http://www.shj.org.

SCIENCE AND WONDER FROM THE ATHEIST/AGNOSTIC PERSPECTIVE

Adams, Douglas. *The Salmon of Doubt: Hitchhiking the Galaxy One Last Time.* New York: Random House, 2002.
Dawkins, Richard. *Unweaving the Rainbow: Science, Delusion, and the Appetite for Wonder.* Boston: Houghton Mifflin, 1998.
Sagan, Carl. *The Demon-Haunted World: Science as a Candle in the Dark.* New York: Random House, 1995.
Sagan, Carl. *The Varieties of Scientific Experience.* Edited by Ann Druyan. New York: Penguin Press, 2006.

NONTHEISTIC ETHICS

Epstein, Greg. *Good Without God: What a Billion Nonreligious People Do Believe.* New York: HarperCollins, 2009.

Grayling, A. C. *Meditations for the Humanist: Ethics for a Secular Age*. London: Oxford University Press, 2003.

Knight, Margaret. *Morals Without Religion*. London: Dobson Books, 1955.

SELECTED RELIGIOUS CRITICISM/ANALYSIS

Dawkins, Richard. *The God Delusion*. Boston: Houghton Mifflin, 2006.

Dennett, Daniel. *Breaking the Spell: Religion as a Natural Phenomenon*. New York: Penguin Books, 2007.

Harris, Sam. *The End of Faith: Religion, Terror, and the Future of Reason*. New York: Norton, 2005.

Hitchens, Christopher. *God Is Not Great: How Religion Poisons Everything*. New York: Twelve Books/Hachette Book Group, 2007.

Loftus, John. *The Christian Delusion: Why Faith Fails*. Amherst, NY: Prometheus Books, 2010.

Thomson, J. Anderson. *Why We Believe in God(s): A Concise Guide to the Science of Faith*. Charlottesville, VA: Pitchstone, 2011.

NONTHEISTIC SPIRITUALITY

Batchelor, Stephen. *Buddhism Without Beliefs*. New York: Riverhead Trade, 1997.

Batchelor, Stephen. *Confession of a Buddhist Atheist*. New York: Spiegel & Grau, 2011.

Comte-Sponville, Andre. *The Little Book of Atheist Spirituality*. New York: Penguin Books, 2008.

INDEX

Boldface page references indicate that the index entry is the source or subject of a document excerpt.

About the Author

Dale McGowan, PhD, is editor and coauthor of *Parenting Beyond Belief* and *Raising Freethinkers*, the first comprehensive resources for nonreligious parents. He teaches nonreligious parenting seminars across the United States and is founding executive director of Foundation Beyond Belief, a humanist charitable foundation. In September 2008 he was named Harvard Humanist of the Year. Dale lives in Atlanta with his wife and three children.